THESE
HONORED
DEAD

SHAPED ALIKE

THESE HONORED DEAD

HOW THE STORY OF GETTYSBURG
SHAPED AMERICAN MEMORY

THOMAS A. DESJARDIN

DA CAPO PRESS
A MEMBER OF THE PERSEUS BOOKS GROUP

Designed and typeset by C. Cairl Design
Set in 12.5-point Perpetua

The Library of Congress has cataloged the hardcover edition as follows:

Desjardin, Thomas A., 1964–
  These honored dead : how the story of Gettysburg shaped American memory / by Thomas A. Desjardin.
      p. cm.
Includes bibliographical references (p.) and index.
  ISBN 0-306-81267-3 (hardcover)
  1. Gettysburg, Battle of, Gettysburg, Pa., 1863.   2. United States—History—Civil War, 1861–1865—Influence.   3. United States—History—Civil War, 1861–1865—Historiography.   4. National characteristics, American.   5. Memory—Social aspects—United States.
I. Title.
  E475.53.D47 2003
  973.7'349'072—dc22

                                        2003017130

First Da Capo Press hardcover edition 2003
ISBN 0-306-81382-3 (pbk.)

Published by Da Capo Press
A Member of the Perseus Books Group
http://www.dacapopress.com

Da Capo Press books are available at special discounts for bulk purchases in the U.S. by corporations, institutions, and other organizations. For more information, please contact the Special Markets Department at the Perseus Books Group, 11 Cambridge Center, Cambridge, MA 02142, or call (800) 255-1514 or (617) 252-5298, or e-mail special.markets@perseusbooks.com.

1 2 3 4 5 6 7 8 9—07 06 05 04

To John J. Pullen
A friend, mentor, and shining example
And to his loving and lovely wife, Margaret

CONTENTS

ACKNOWLEDGMENTS

I AM NOT SURE IT IS POSSIBLE to be a student of Maine and Civil War history and not be indebted to John J. Pullen for the example that he set, both as a Mainer and a gifted author. John exuded a graciousness that is seldom found in one who is as accomplished and widely lauded as he was. Having the good fortune to know John and to share many an enlightening conversation with him was an enormous privilege to me as a historian, a writer, and a person.

Through seven years of thinking my way through the ideas that eventually became this book, Marta Robertson at Gettysburg College provided support, motivation, and encouragement in ways that I will always consider invaluable. My great friend Jeff Hall at Brandeis has argued, cajoled, and encouraged my efforts on Gettysburg for more than a decade now. I am indebted to him for countless instances when his unique perspective helped me form and expand my own ideas on how people and Gettysburg get along. Jeff also took time from a busy and successful research career to line edit this manuscript.

Scott Hartwig, who probably knows more about Gettysburg than anyone alive, first lured me to the battlefield in 1995, and the years that I spent there, particularly in the park library, gave me not only a firm foundation of Gettysburg knowledge, but also a curiosity about the place, the people, and the meanings we all apply to them. Scott has never hesitated

to read whatever I might have written and to offer valuable insights. Also
at Gettysburg, my great friend Troy Harman and I spent many an hour
pondering and debating the things about the place that we thought no one
else ever thought of. His friendship and these conversations have helped
me understand the story of Gettysburg in a much better way. As with
Troy, my many conversations and correspondences with another good
friend, Glenn LaFantasie, have helped provoke thoughts and new ideas
that contributed heavily to the pages that follow. Glenn has a pragmatic
point of view regarding the battle and an enviable ability to communicate
his perspective.

Historian Rick Sauers has done some heavy lifting in Civil War
resources, providing Gettysburg researchers with easy access to the
important *National Tribune* articles on the battle, making it possible for
others to find valuable information otherwise buried out of reach. His
work on both John B. Bachelder and the Dan Sickles–George Meade controversy are also invaluable to students of the battle. In addition, he graciously agreed to read chapters in this work and offer new insights.

As a rule, a day seldom passed in Civil War Mecca that I didn't greatly
benefit from a myriad of conversations, debates, and gab sessions involv-
ing the park rangers and licensed battlefield guides at the park whose
ever-present thirst for more knowledge on their favorite subject is inspiring. In addition, the Gilder-Lehrman Institute of American History supported this work with a research fellowship for which I am grateful.

My agent Anne Hawkins never lost faith in the ideas of this book and
the author who penned them. Her contribution to this work is tremen-
dously significant and I am eternally grateful for her guidance and coun-
sel. Dana Wilson was among the first to read the bare bones beginnings of
the chapters that later made up this book and provided very valuable
advice and ideas at an important early stage. Fern Desjardin has been the
author's greatest supporter and provider of encouragement in as many
ways as a mother can for her son. Thanks, mom!

Lori-Ann Jordan, love of my life and a great lobstering partner, made much of this work possible by willingly contributing in every way she could and being always at the ready with words of encouragement and inspiration.

And finally to the millions of Gettysburg enthusiasts whose curiosity for this strange and wonderful story seems boundless. It is their interaction with the mythology of Gettysburg that inspired this book and opened a world of understanding to the author.

Pittsfield, Maine
May 2003

INTRODUCTION

No one wears big round plastic ears at Gettysburg. When you're ten years old, that's an important piece of information. Especially when your first visit to the battlefield comes during the second full summer that a place known as Walt Disney World has been open—enough time for friends and acquaintances to bring home wondrous stories of a child's idea of heaven. Nevertheless, the family vacation of my tenth summer was a visit to a place close to an adult's idea of the Magic Kingdom: the Gettysburg National Military Park. To a fan of history, and particularly a Civil War buff like my father, a battlefield tour was the adult equivalent of a trip through the haunted mansion or Cinderella's castle.

On the battlefield, my father and older brother wandered up hills in search of Maine monuments and moments of bonding, my sister got deathly ill from a chocolate overdose, and I was scolded for being restless and impatient—a far cry from having my picture taken with Donald Duck. I suppose we were there so that my father could fulfill a lifelong dream to stand on a hill known as Little Round Top and make some important connection to the men who fought there. Some of those men were from Maine, his lifelong and ancestral home, and they had done wondrous things there in defense of the nation.

My father was born five years before World War II, so he was raised in an environment full of reverence for the heroes of the Greatest Generation who saved the world in a war filled with messages of noble causes and fighting against evil. The two things he mentioned most reverently in nostalgic anecdotes were the people and times of the 1940s and the deeds of Maine men in the Civil War. On this Pennsylvania hillside, the two seemed to merge.

Though he never said so, some of what he felt at Gettysburg had to do with his own father, a decorated veteran of both World War II and Korea with whom he had little contact growing up. Perhaps my father was connecting with the simple Maine men who "saved the Union" on that hill, and this substituted in some small way for his own lack of military service, an absence of combat heroism in a world seemingly full of it. Or maybe he was trying to reconcile his boyhood image of war heroes with the damage that the war in Vietnam was doing to heroic warrior images.

Like World War II, the Civil War conjures the idea of a simpler, more noble time when people made remarkable sacrifices for a just cause that everyone back home seemed to agree with. Newsreel footage of Americans fighting on the Rhine had a decidedly different tone than the nightly news reports from Hanoi two decades later. To a child of the 1940s and 1950s, living an adult life in the 1960s and 1970s, the simplicity, nobility, and popular unanimity of days gone by may have been a fulfilling if bygone concept. To nearly every American in 1974, even in the turbulent wake of Vietnam, assassination, civil rights marches, and corruption, Gettysburg was a place where the message and lessons seemed clear, simple, and basic, even if not every American agreed on what those were. Although not everyone could walk the ground at Normandy or Iwo Jima, Gettysburg was within driving distance and spoke of similar themes, offering those who sought it a chance to reconnect with the world before the 1960s changed things forever.

At the rock near the summit of Little Round Top stands a bronze sculpture of some guy in a uniform with binoculars (as seen by a ten-year-old).

There my brother, sister, and I got a lecture, delivered in that factually questionable way in which most fathers pass on history to their children, presented as if it were a classroom lesson. We were to understand what the place meant and why it should be important to us—or else. Being good Americans seemed to require that we understand and appreciate what happened there, and Dad wanted to make sure we got with the program at an early age. As the youngest, I was the least likely to get it (the pool at the hotel was the object of my desires), but I don't think any of us except Dad wallowed in the meaning of the place on that first trip. We did, however, get a lot of life lessons for years afterward draped in the anti-1960s symbolism of Gettysburg. It was good context for my father.

Another eighteen years passed before I made my second visit to the battlefield and Little Round Top. Having learned from my father's books what Maine men had done there, I too had become smitten. Two more years and I was enrolled in graduate school studying nineteenth-century American history and reading, researching, and writing about Gettysburg and Little Round Top. When I was nearly finished with my studies, the park historian at Gettysburg invited me to come out for the summer, do some research, live on the battlefield, and give tours to visitors. Six years later, I was still living there, still reading, researching, and writing about the battle and battlefield while discovering a wealth of ideas that the place never stops teaching us, or allowing us to learn, if we make the effort.

No sooner had I arrived and melted into the community of Civil War buffs, tour guides, and National Park Service employees than I became the object of the good-natured ridicule that all new arrivals endure. Like most others, I came to Gettysburg thinking that I knew a lot about the battle, and like most others I quickly discovered that I knew a lot about what people *think* they know about the battle—and most of it was wrong. Thus my initiation into the community involved a debunking of the myths, legends, and folklore that pervade the popular history. Quite naturally, I became fascinated as much by the manner in which Americans distort and reshape the history of Gettysburg as with discovering the truth about the battle. I soon learned that the former just about extinguishes any hope of the latter. The truth about Gettysburg is buried beneath layer upon layer of flawed human memory and our attempts to fashion our past into something that makes our present a little easier to live in.

The idea that we shape the history of Gettysburg to our own purposes is not something that only happened in the past. It is happening today all over the country and indeed the world. Through this process we attach meaning to what happened roughly seven generations ago and make it a symbol of what is good and important to us. Having done this, we revere the story and the place, passing it on to the next generation with our new adornments while sending to the future an image of the past to revel in and learn from. We create mythology.

Meaning is an important part of Americans' relationship to Gettysburg. In my own experience with the place and its story, I have witnessed too many different kinds of meaning to count. For my father, it was in the connection he felt to the soldiers who fought there: regular people like him who came from where he did and had done something highly significant, unusual, and heroic. It rejuvenated his faith in the heroism of his childhood. For me, it is a vehicle through which I can learn about how people process their past, how they shape and use their history. And I can watch it happen there as if studying an experiment in a lab.

To others, it is a mystery, a puzzle, something to be untangled and figured out. People get married there, commit suicide there, even have their children there in an effort to connect with the place and its meaning to them. A 1990s visit to the battlefield inspired chief executive officer Jack Welch and his company, General Electric, to completely reorganize their business strategy. As a result, company revenues rose by 64 percent. Military personnel use it as a training ground, Boy Scouts can get a merit badge after hiking the Johnny Reb and Billy Yank trails, and school groups learn about history there. Artists, musicians, and television and film companies find inspiration, profit, even ghosts on its acreage. At Gettysburg, Native

Americans share ceremonies on the same land where descendents of the white men who drove them from it gather for family outings and reunions.

In my own experience, this happens most on Little Round Top, a hill on the south end of the battlefield that has developed a meaning and mythology all its own. This hill is not much different from a dozen other parts of the field in this respect, all of them like classrooms in the larger school building and each with different lessons to share. In the half dozen years since I became a full-time resident of the area, I have had the opportunity to observe and share meanings with hundreds of visitors and residents alike.

About once a year, I happen on a close friend and colleague who makes a pilgrimage up from Virginia with his daughter. Each year the two walk over the path that one regiment from Alabama took on its way to attack Union soldiers on the hill. It is not an easy walk. Briars, brush, boulders, even an occasional territorial bull hamper the adventurers, but they come again and again. I suspect that long ago it ceased to be a trip about the battle or the soldiers and is now more of an opportunity for father and daughter to share a common experience. Gettysburg merely provides the setting and they are not the only Gettysburg-inspired case of father-daughter connection. Sometimes it is even mother-daughter. A few years ago a friend from California had a birthday and, as a gift, her daughter offered to pay for a trip and accompany her anywhere she wanted to go. Mom chose Little Round Top at Gettysburg. Neither was disappointed and Mom has returned a number of times since.

Back in the early 1960s, the Lawrence family of Kansas City, Kansas, came to Gettysburg on occasional pilgrimages and developed a ritual of battlefield visits, always camping at the same campground, rising at the same hour, and so on. In the mid–1990s, two of the boys, who were a few steps ahead of the rest of us with Internet technology, developed a small online discussion group where people with a shared reverence for Gettysburg could chat and swap ideas. By 1996, the group had upward of a thousand members exchanging daily e-mails on an inexhaustible list of subjects. That summer a few hundred of them made the trip from far and wide to gather on the field and swap their ideas in person. In deference to the group's leaders, they gathered, weary but eager, at 6:00 A.M. on Little Round Top, the time and place set by Lawrence family tradition. They have met there—mustered as they call it—every year since (though the brothers relented one hour on the starting time). To the brothers Lawrence, Gettysburg's meaning is as much a connection to their family and the nostalgia of childhood memories as a love of the battlefield itself. Group members exhibit a real sense of community through their shared curiosity, wonder, and love of the story. For the 2001 muster, the group hosted the parents of the Lawrence clan in celebration of the tradition they started that, with a little boost from technology, brought so many people together.

From the moment the guns quieted on the fields of Gettysburg in July 1863, people of every type have been heaping one meaning after another onto the history of the battle. Along the way these meanings have effectively changed what most people see as the history of the event, at the same time drawing more people to the story and inspiring them to find meaning of their own. In its 2001 annual travel report, the staff of *USA Today* declared Gettysburg "the consensus top choice as the essential American place, Gettysburg is the symbolic heart of America."[1]

Stupefied as I was by the sudden realization of my historical ignorance on joining the Gettysburg community, I became fascinated with how the mythology of Gettysburg had duped so many people and I began paying more attention to the ongoing, living process in which it was happening. For example, there is a statue on Little Round Top at which I got my father-to-son lecture; every June the Lawrence family tradition calls hundreds of Internet friends to gather around it. It depicts in life-size bronze (a bit larger actually) the moment when General Gouverneur K. Warren discovered that the entire Union line was imperiled by a Confederate assault falling on its flank. Warren scrambled to find troops to defend the hill and, in a scene that John Wayne should have made into a movie, became the "hero of Little Round Top" for generations to come. As legend portrays it and filmmaker Ken Burns tells us, this defense saved "the Union army and quite possibly the Union itself."[2]

On its fringes, legend even claims that North America would have been Balkanized along the lines of numerous regional differences, spurred on by the example of a successful Confederate secession. From there, it is a short leap to a rerendering of world history. On what path would World War I have taken us without, first, American industrial might and, later, military involvement? How would Europe and Russia alone have stopped Hitler's blitzkrieg? What if the coal in Kentucky and West Virginia had been separated by national boundaries and tariffs from Pennsylvania steel and factories in the East? How quickly would technology have advanced without the combined drive and intellect of a whole United States? No atom bomb, no space program, slower moves toward automobiles, airplanes, computers? All of this held in place historically by what happened on this rock.

The importance of this place makes it worthy of a statue at least. Or does the statue inspire people to give the place such meaning? Chicken or egg? Are Warren's actions so important that they deserve a statue and such reverence? Or did the statue depict such a grand tale that it inspired people to attach immense meaning to his actions? Did Warren save the world on Little Round Top? Or did Americans build a legend around the statue because they need to know that a person can make a huge difference—and remind themselves that he was one of them?

The answer to these questions may lie in the original story. Gettysburg mythology generally traces its roots back to the earliest eyewitness accounts of the battle, borne out in thousands of diaries, letters, and memoirs written by veterans after the war. Before later generations could reshape the story into images that satisfied their own needs, the people who experienced the battle firsthand held the only possible link to a factual truth. All of the history, legend, and folklore grew from these original accounts. It is on this precarious foundation, then, that the story of Gettysburg was built. The strength of this foundation lies in our belief in the truthfulness of these early accounts. If we were to discover that the underpinning stones are weak, then the whole story might collapse, and with it might fall our identity as a people.

Imagine the implications. It would sever my father's link to the values of his childhood and his children's to the better simpler pre–1960s era. The Lawrence family would have based its nostalgic glue on a place not nearly as important as the parents thought when they chose it as a vacation site. The group that follows them to Little Round Top every summer would be wasting its time. A father and daughter would have deepened their affection for each other in a plain old field. General Electric would be 64 percent less profitable. Countless marriages would have begun in an inconsequential setting, babies born in just another small town. If we accept that the story of Gettysburg is not as we have made it, then we lose much that makes us feel good about ourselves, makes us who we are.

Rather than accept such unpleasant consequences, often people repair cracks in the foundation or replace whole stones in an effort to keep the story safe and available to later generations. Adding an embellishment here, a mistaken thought there, avoiding or ignoring contrary evidence when it appears, we keep the story in line with our image of it, adjusting our beliefs about the past to suit our needs in the present. When we feel that it is threatened, we may even renovate the story, rearranging our meaning to suit newly discovered facts. Or we may build an addition, heaping still more importance on the story.

The popularity of Gettysburg as a subject for veterans to write about created a huge body of literature on the battle. There are clearly more original accounts of this battle than of any other Civil War event. Frequently these accounts conflict with and contradict others. It was not even unusual for the same veteran to contradict himself from one piece of writing to the next. This is one of the most important features of its mythology. The more material there is, the more basis for varied meanings.

Just as the Bible provides enough evidence to support thousands of meanings—even contradictory ones—so does Gettysburg's original source material. The Bible is full of contradictions. The same book that instructs its readers, for example, to take an eye for an eye, also requires that they turn the other cheek. As a result, groups both for and against the death penalty find meaning in the teachings of the same Bible. Each side uses it to support their position and perhaps quiet their conscience. In this same way, Gettysburg is the most gruesome, yet most popular Civil War battle. It is the one that soldiers most wanted to forget but most often wrote about. It is the symbolic high point of Southern bravery and honor, but the Confederates lost. Their leader, Robert E. Lee, failed at Gettysburg, but the South still venerates him as a hero and military genius. His admission that the loss "was all my fault," only seems to increase his popularity.

With this vast sea of material swelling archives, libraries, and historical societies, a person can justify nearly any perspective that they may wish to put forth. Evidence and arguments abound on the genius or ineptitude of both Lee and his counterpart, George G. Meade. Union General Daniel E. Sickles either saved or nearly doomed the nation at Gettysburg, depending on which set of "facts" one chooses to emphasize. Little Round Top was the point at which democracy was nearly lost, or just an irrelevant feature of geography. Take your pick.

In the hundreds of tours I have given of the battlefield to teachers, tourists, and television folks, I often pause on Little Round Top to point out the two spots where veterans claimed Colonel Strong Vincent fell mortally wounded. They are two hundred feet apart. Given the salient fact that Vincent wasn't even six feet tall, much less two hundred, the two equally convincing markers (one an engraved rock, the other a small marble monument) must be at odds with each other.

"That's the great thing about Gettysburg," I nearly always point out. "It is a multiple choice battlefield. If you don't like a particular version of events, just read on a few pages and you're likely to come upon a different one."

The chapters that follow, then, are part exploration and part explanation of the multitude of meanings that Americans have attached to the story of Gettysburg in the first 140 years since the battle ended. They lay out some of the social, political, and cultural themes that have helped shape Gettysburg mythology, and they attempt to expose some of the myths—from the great whoppers to the minor mistakes—that have made it such an important national symbol.

THESE
HONORED
DEAD

CHAPTER 1

THE MANY MEANINGS OF GETTYSBURG

A symbol of national purpose, pride, and ideals.
GARRY WILLS[1]

Afterthe motorcade halted at the base of an observation tower in the
midst of the Gettysburg battlefield, President Dwight Eisenhower
stepped out of the car just ahead of his guest, British general Bernard
Montgomery. Thirty-eight reporters and photographers trailed close
behind. When the president of the United States travels, the White House
press corps follows. It is so ravenous for something to print that colleagues call it the "body watch," acknowledging its penchant for turning
the slightest gesture on a slow news day into a front-page story. Onlookers identified the two dignitaries' status visually: the working-class American wore a simple jacket and slacks with a flashy bright tie, the aristo-
cratic British visitor a tailor-made suit, double-breasted and pinstriped
with a bright silk handkerchief peeping out of the breast pocket. The two
didn't like each other very much. During World War II, Monty once
described Ike to Winston Churchill's chief military adviser as "completely
and utterly useless." For his part, Ike once allowed, "Montgomery's the
only man in either army I can't get along with."[2]

The heavy fog and drizzle of this Sunday morning in May 1957 obscured the view from the top of the tower, which was shrouded from the group below. Despite this, Montgomery nearly sprinted up the stairway, fully aware that his host, only eighteen months removed from a heart attack, would have to follow. As he did, Eisenhower might have wished his guest would just then meet with some calamity.

Two days before arriving at the president's home on the Pennsylvania battlefield for the visit, Montgomery had publicly stated that, had he been in charge of either Civil War army in 1863, he would have sacked both Robert E. Lee and George G. Meade, the Confederate and Union commanders respectively, for their performance at Gettysburg. Eisenhower knew the South's reverence for Lee in particular, and he was dealing with touchy political issues in Dixie, including a civil rights bill pending before Congress. Naturally prone to fits of anger, he initially wanted to cancel Monty's visit but realized that it was too late. Given their strained relationship, Monty's previsit statements, and his habit of blurting out foolish comments for the benefit of the press, the tour was already fraught with tension as they descended from their aerial view of the fog.

When pressed again by the trailing reporters about the tactics and strategy of his Civil War counterparts, Monty relented, saying, "I would not have fought the battle that way." Eisenhower, trying to add a bit of levity to the tense morning jaunt, reminded Monty who had been in charge in those days. Probably to shake the reporters off of the topic, he quipped, "If you had, I would have sacked you." His effort met with rousing laughter.[3]

Later in the tour, sensing front-page copy in the air, reporters again raised the sticky subject. Monty played along. "Both Lee and Meade should have been sacked," he repeated. "Don't you agree, Ike?" To the press, rather than Monty, the president replied pleadingly. "Look, I live here. I represent both the North and the South. He can talk."

Though he never agreed with Montgomery's comment directly and never uttered such a view himself, Ike had been drawn in by a press corps starved for a story. In no time the national media machine manufactured a controversy. Headlines blared the news across the nation and deep into the South.

EISENHOWER JOINS MONTGOMERY IN CRITICIZING MEADE AND LEE.

LEE, MEADE DESERVED "SACKING," IKE AND MONTY SAY AT GETTYSBURG.

Time magazine lamented that when the two generals agreed that Lee and Meade should have been fired, "they committed themselves irrevocably to battle."[4]

That battle raged most fiercely below the Mason-Dixon line, where citizens took the comments as a personal affront to their honor. The *Jackson (Mississippi) News* printed its banner headline SOUTHERN BLOOD BOILS in capital letters for emphasis. The widow of Robert E. Lee III joined in the chorus of contempt, calling the comments "disgusting."[5] Before long, the southern press had turned the story into an unflattering assessment of the generalship of Ike and Monty in World War II. Perhaps the most humorous and biting was a parody of the tour by the Scripps-Howard News Service that described Meade and Lee touring the scene of the Battle of the Bulge. Meade declared it "an absolutely monstrous thing," while Lee added that both Ike and Monty should have been sacked.

Stung a bit by the uproar he created, Monty lamented, "The women of the South are after me." Then he revealed his utter lack of understanding of the relationship between Americans and Gettysburg. "I suppose that battle never had so much publicity since it was fought."[6]

Within days, the little Gettysburg tour grew into a serious political problem for Eisenhower. As one Washington newspaper editorialized, "It is difficult to comprehend the strategy of a commander-in-chief who sets out to woo the South with sweet talk about the virtues of modern Republicanism and winds up on Sunday saying that General Lee bungled the battle of Gettysburg and should have been sacked."[7]

What Eisenhower understood, and Montgomery was now learning firsthand, was that Americans take the meaning of Gettysburg and its heroes very seriously, even if most cannot agree on exactly what that meaning is.

Two decades later, another president with visitors tried to make use of Gettysburg's multiplicity of meanings, though this time with a decidedly more positive result. Jimmy Carter had long been a Civil War buff, and its greatest battle was seldom far from his thoughts. One of his ancestors had fought at Gettysburg, and in 1976, while he watched the results of the Democratic primary in Pennsylvania come in, candidate Carter noticed that he had won the vote in the electoral district that included the battlefield. To his delight, he remarked, "We ought to tell the Georgians that we finally won in Gettysburg."[8]

Two years later, while sitting at the presidential retreat at Camp David just a few miles southwest of the famous battlefield, his thoughts drifted there again. He was in the fourth day of intense negotiations designed to bring peace between Egypt and Israel—a conflict that predated Moses. The leaders of both nations where there with him (Anwar Sadat of Egypt and Menachem Begin of Israel), but their views could scarcely have been farther apart. On one key negotiating point, Begin had declared, "My right eye will fall out, my right hand will fall off before I ever agree."[9]

In Carter's view the two leaders were thinking in the wrong direction. "I tried for three days to get them to talk about the future," Carter said. "But all they would talk about was the past." Faced with the standoff and searching for some way to bring the parties to a different level of thought, Carter first kept them apart for a while, then proposed an excursion. "We went to the Civil War battlefield at Gettysburg one day," he later recalled, "and I made them both agree not to talk about the Middle East or about anything that happened since 1865."

Thanks to the meaning and mythology attached to the Gettysburg story since 1863 (much of it carved in stone in more than a thousand monuments and markers), Carter's choice of destination was a fertile place for symbolic demonstration and persuasion. Two powers of the same region, grown from the same land but with differing cultural histories, once differed so greatly with each other that they engaged in the bloodiest war the continent had ever known; the worst of the fighting happened on the ground they were touring. When the war was over, the two powers became one again, healed their wounds, set aside many of their differences, and went on to form the most powerful nation on earth. If North and South could accomplish this, then Egypt and Israel had a chance too. As he admitted later in his memoirs, Carter wanted to demonstrate the high cost of war and persuade the two leaders to sign the first ever peace agreement between Israel and an Arab nation.

The Egyptian took to the field right away. As a military student, Sadat had studied Gettysburg in detail and recognized it as the turning point in the Civil War. Begin, however, was slower to the mark as he knew nothing about the battle. When the group passed the monument commemorating Lincoln's Gettysburg Address, however, Begin recited it from memory in a thick Yiddish accent, probably adding an Israeli emphasis to the line "that this nation . . . shall not perish from the earth." It took many more hours of negotiating, but less than a week later the three leaders took part in a historic signing ceremony for an agreement that brought peace between the two long warring nations. Menachem Begin even gave in on his sticking point without losing an eye or his right hand.

To be sure, many factors helped bring about the Egyptian-Israeli peace in 1978, most of them having nothing to do with Gettysburg. But years after they signed the accords, the participants expressed a belief that the trip to America's hallowed ground had meant a great deal. Carter said as much in a speech long afterward.

Sadat made one interesting observation. Since our visit to Gettysburg he had been thinking that I, as a Southerner, could understand what it meant to be involved in a terrible war, and also knew how difficult it was to rebuild both the material things and the spirit of the people after a recog-

nized defeat. He had observed how long it had taken the wounds of our
war in Vietnam to be finally healed with my election, and his hope was to
encourage all people in the Middle East to heal their hurt and hatred and
to move confidently toward an era of peace.[10]

For Carter, Gettysburg was a reminder of the high cost of war and an
example of reconciliation among adversaries. Sadat, lured by the military
aspect of the field, felt the hope and healing in the Vietnam-era ideas it
elicited. Begin was taken with the ideas embodied in Lincoln's address.
Though perhaps not in the way he intended, Carter's idea worked. Both
negotiating parties found meaning in the Gettysburg story that, though
different from the other, helped inspire their actions toward peace.

Since the guns of Gettysburg ceased their booming in early July 1863
and Lincoln stepped away from his two-minute speech on the same
ground four months later, the story of this three-day conflict has come to
mean many things to many people. Because of the multiplicity of meanings that it represents, it has become a symbol for an incalculable number
of ideas, causes, groups, and principles for Americans and for people the
world over, many of them polar opposites. Since its establishment as a
National Park in 1895, for example, Gettysburg has been the scene of
civil rights speeches and Ku Klux Klan rallies. In 1938, months before the
outbreak of World War II, President Franklin Roosevelt dedicated the
Eternal Light Peace Memorial on land that had once been the scene of
America's bloodiest nonpeaceful event.

American mythology has established Gettysburg as the greatest,
biggest, most important, most heroic, most savage, bloodiest battle the
nation ever fought. The hyperbole extends to the soldiers who fought
there, who were the best, endured the worst, fought the hardest, and
achieved for Americans a place in the pantheon of history's greatest military conflicts. It is our Waterloo, our Stalingrad, and our defining
moment. Without surviving Gettysburg, legend has it, the United States
would not have survived, and with its death would have fallen the idea of

global democracy. Nothing less than worldwide freedom was saved there. In contrast, though no less important, is the idea that because the South lost at Gettysburg, the entire Confederacy and all that it represented was lost. Today Southerners can almost pick that very moment.

From the legends, Americans can claim heroes equal to those of the Charge of the Light Brigade, the three hundred Spartans at Thermopylae, or the warriors of ancient Troy. In doing so, they establish, despite their nation's relative youth, a sense of historical importance that rivals the powers of their European brethren. In the six score and fourteen years since it took place, the Battle of Gettysburg has come to occupy a central place in American society and culture. It has, as Garry Wills points out, "become a symbol of national purpose, pride, and ideals."[11]

Those who elevate the importance of Gettysburg have a point. If a proportionate number of Americans fought the battle today, it would involve more than 1.3 million people. Nearly 100,000 of them would die. During the first three days in July 1863, one out of every two hundred Americans took part in what is now known as the bloodiest battle of the nation's most costly war. Five times as many Americans died at Gettysburg as on D day in 1944. Although the latter is now popularly known as "the Longest Day," as a percentage of the national population, Gettysburg inflicted thirty-five times as many casualties. Given these figures, it is no mystery why Gettysburg has become so prominent among American historical events and consequently has become a significant source of legend and myth. Several generations of Americans have molded the story of Gettysburg into what society views as the "what happened": a mythological construct that reveals much about Americans and their individual and collective identities. This mythology allows people from President Carter to everyday tourists to conjure a wide array of symbolic meanings that they can draw from, or attach to, the story of Gettysburg.

In addition to its superlative image, Gettysburg is full of irony and contradiction, something Americans also love in their stories. Having taken command just three days prior to the battle, General George G. Meade was the first Union commander to defeat Robert E. Lee in battle. Yet days later President Lincoln angrily chastised Meade who, in turn, offered his resignation. Lincoln declined, but within months, and despite winning this greatest of battles, Meade slipped into obscurity beneath the shadow of Ulysses S. Grant. In contrast, immediately following Gettysburg, General Lee took full blame for the failure of his army and offered his resignation to President Jefferson Davis. Yet Lee, despite losing the greatest of battles, is remembered as one of the best military commanders that America has ever produced. In history, the general who won, lost, and the general who lost, won.

Legend has it that the South lost the Civil War because of Gettysburg. But the war went on for almost two years afterward. To many Americans, Gettysburg is the place where our nation was saved. To many southerners, it is the place where a dream met its death.[12] Both regions celebrate the place with equal vigor. Four months after the battle, Abraham Lincoln gave his Gettysburg Address at the dedication of a cemetery for the Union dead. It is now considered the greatest American oration ever delivered. Yet just months after he gave it, Lincoln was convinced he could not win reelection.

If Gettysburg was such an important event, such a crucible for shaping the world that came after it, then why did the winning general fade into oblivion while the losing general became one of our greatest military heroes? If the South lost both the battle and the war, why do Southerners so revere this battlefield—a symbol of that loss—as hallowed ground? If the Civil War lasted another two years, could its decisive moment come at Gettysburg—in the middle of it?

The answer to these puzzles is at the heart of what Gettysburg has become and why Americans have made it so. Wrapped in mystery and mythology, steeped in symbolism and meaning, Gettysburg is now a catch-all of ideas, representing and demonstrating nearly any principle or cause imaginable. This status results from decades of struggle among those who held decidedly vested interests in shaping the story in one fashion or another, intent on ensuring that those who followed after would see Gettysburg in a particular way. Based on the deeply flawed memories of the participants and other eyewitnesses and then expanded through decades of social and political debates, the story of Gettysburg has become a flexible, dynamic mythology, reflecting nearly anything Americans see as positive.

This process began with the foundation blocks—the "facts" as many see them—that sprouted from the deeply flawed memories of the eyewitnesses. As Gettysburg became the most famous battle of the war, it also became the one about which veterans wrote the most. The mountain of information that they left to posterity provides more opportunity for misinterpretation than most other Civil War events. The more accounts that are published about a given aspect of the battle, the greater the opportunity for citing some part of the battle as significant in its meaning. Before long, there was an account somewhere that helped support virtually any argument, idea, or symbolization. Peeling back these layers of recollection, however, historians alert to avoid being drawn into the hyperbole and high drama will discover that these accounts cannot all be true. These historians might later come to conclude that *most* of what the veterans stated as fact cannot be true and that they were fully conscious of their inability to remember and write the truth.

If Americans can never really know which parts of the Gettysburg story are true and which are at least partly false, then the story is as malleable as clay to anyone who wants to create meaning and wrap it in Gettysburg symbolism. A myriad of accounts, whether conflicting or agreeing with one another—or both—simply provide more opportunity for attaching importance to the story while drawing it into a modern issue or idea. This is how human beings create mythology and it is how Gettysburg has become such a critical and ever-present symbol in our society.

CHAPTER 2

INFIRM FOUNDATIONS

By-and-by, out of the disjointed mass of reports, out of the traditions and tales that come down from the field, some eye that never saw the battle will select, and some pen will write what will be named the history.

LIEUTENANT FRANK HASKELL[1]

I n the dying twilight of a warm July evening a lone gray figure sat atop his horse with barely a movement. His cold stare fixed on the thin line of blue a mile across the low valley, where campfires had begun to burn along the ridge, and he began to struggle with the questions that would haunt his remaining years. Should he have moved sooner? Later? With more force or more stealth? He would have the long dark hours of night to wage his own personal war with doubt and regret. It was a war he could not win. Hoping to force the thoughts from his mind with the mental exercise of planning, he began to consider what tomorrow would require. By afternoon, he would need to have his army on the move away from this place and the enemy for which he was now no match. Before beginning the long, slow march to safety, however, he knew that in the morning he had one last task here, and his thoughts turned to what would this time be an unpalatable chore.

"Colonel Taylor," he muttered aloud but with almost no visible motion. An attentive aide stepped closer and responded.

"Yes, General Lee?"

"In the morning," instructed the general, "we must have the men ready to depart from this place. But before we order the trains back onto the roads we will have to conclude our efforts here." Turning in the saddle to look at Taylor, he was expressionless. "Have the men ready to make the final record of this battle. Then we must leave here."

Far across the fields of Gettysburg, Robert E. Lee's principal enemy sat back in a simple chair in the stark two-room home of a German widow accepting the congratulations of his subordinate generals. George Gordon Meade, in command of the Union Army for only five days, had just achieved its first victory over Lee and his army of Southerners. Through cigar smoke and the smell of woolen sweat his colleagues asked his thoughts on the situation at hand.

"Lee is beaten," he allowed. "He will have to leave us now and head back to Virginia for supplies, ammunition, and to lick his wounds. We have some work of our own to do beginning tomorrow, and we'll want to get the history written first thing. See to it, gentlemen."

Not long after dawn again lit the fields, dallying only long enough to cook their breakfast, the men of both armies gathered on their respective sides to carry out the important ritual that has followed every battle since men began to fight other men. Long lines of soldiers in blue and gray stacked their muskets, abandoned their guns, and moved toward central positions where they assembled by regiment and brigade, by division and corps. From the backs of wagons, in order to be seen and heard above the crowd, the official historians of both armies opened their ledger books and began to record the events of the previous three days, taking pains to include each soldier's account, reconciling one with another. Within a few hours these same men would gather to begin merging their individual records into what would become the single official history of the Battle of Gettysburg. For generations to come, this record would be repeated in newspapers, magazines, and textbooks, passing on the story of this great conflict as told by the men who took part in it while their memories were still fresh and undimmed by time.

———◆———

JULY 4, 1863—THE FIRST DAY *after* the battle of Gettysburg—was one of relative inactivity among the men of both armies. The idea of assembling tens of thousands of soldiers to record an official history never crossed the mind of either commanding general. The scene depicted above is ridiculous, yet most Americans seem to vaguely believe that there really is some official and factual account of the battle as told by the participants—the "what really happened" story. While people seldom ponder how this story may have come into being, they seem to believe that somewhere and somehow the truth is recorded in a place that hardworking scholars can locate and pass on to the rest of us. The fact of the matter, however, is that history does not spontaneously appear from the mists of battle and find a home on the shelves of musty old archives.

History is created. It is a construction borne of people's desire to make sense of the past. The heart of the issue is that history is not necessarily a record of the facts but rather a reckoning of the stories of past events arranged so that they make sense to those who do the reckoning. There is no "what *really* happened" of Gettysburg, only a multitude of different versions of events drawn from a myriad of sources, each with a different perspective and a different set of goals in mind when they made their record. In large part, people who were not there wrote the history of the Battle of Gettysburg. Much of what has filtered down as a historical record was assembled by eloquent and ambitious men who were not soldiers, were never in a battle, and only set foot on the field of battle weeks, years, even decades after the shooting stopped.

If the men who fought the battle had assembled on the field on July 4, 1863, to record a collective account of what happened to them in the preceding seventy-two hours, many of the pages would have been left blank. One of the most prevalent themes among soldiers who did record their thoughts in diaries and letters around that time is confusion. Men were stupefied by the experience of battle—the deafening noise, the whirlwind of pain and death, the numbness of shock and horror—and had no idea what had just happened. Even the more sober and clear-headed would only have seen and remembered what occurred within a few feet of them, as that was as far as their vision and consciousness allowed them to record.

Nevertheless, these men eventually created for posterity a written record of the battle. In many cases the men who had most adamantly denied the human ability to comprehend the experience were the very same people who wrote histories decades later. Understanding what occurred in the time that intervened between their believing that no truth could ever be recorded and writing what they had sworn could never be written, is to understand how humans create their history. In this way Gettysburg is no different from most great events in human history. Beginning in July 1863, flourishing in the 1880s, and continuing into the present, Americans have merged a host of social, cultural, and political issues with the recollections of Gettysburg veterans to create various histories of the battle so as to make some sense of it. The result is not what *really* happened, but what we have come to agree that we think or hope happened, and that "truth" changes as often as the years.

AT THE MOMENT some soldier fired the last shot of the Battle of Gettysburg it was already impossible for anyone to clearly understand what had just taken place. Realizing this, survivors immediately expressed a sense of awe and incomprehensibility in page after page of letters and diary entries. As they struggled to describe their experiences, they began to realize and then explain that such a description was virtually impossible.

In the several pages of a letter to his brother, for example, Lieutenant Frank Haskell, a survivor of the Union force that bore the brunt of Pickett's Charge on the last day of the battle, attempted to describe the great drama in which he had just participated. "A full account of *the battle as it was* will never, can never be made," he wrote. "Who could sketch the changes, the constant shifting of the bloody panorama? It is not possible."[2]

Haskell was but one eyewitness who found himself unable to effectively relate his experience in battle. Nothing outside of living it could compare, and any effort to describe the events using some common civilian reference was futile. "Many things cannot be described by pen or pencil," he wrote. "Such a fight is one. Some hints and incidents may be given, but a description or picture never. From what is told the imagination may for itself construct the scene; otherwise he who never saw can have no adequate idea of what such a battle is."[3]

Haskell's impressions of the battle in its immediate aftermath were hardly unique. In fact, an inability to describe the experiences and events of the three days of conflict seemed the norm among many veterans. In a letter to his brother from the field on July 6, Maine corporal William Livermore attempted to convey the scene of the conflict's aftermath. When he had filled a few pages, he realized the futility of his effort. "After what I have written," he confessed, "you have no idea of the scene nor I did not much til this battle. You look at it in too small a scale."[4]

This reaction by veterans was not uncommon among men who survived combat. Scholarly work on postwar memories of combat veterans is plentiful, pointing out the near impossibility of clearly seeing, remembering, and recalling things that occur at times of intense fear and emotion. The "fog of war," as many describe it, casts a dark shadow over attempts by veterans to piece together their war experiences and consequently assembling histories based on them is a precarious task.

Standing on Gettysburg's famous hill, Little Round Top, in the summer of 1996, visitors in a special tour group asked former U.S. Army Captain Lewis Millet, a Korean War veteran among them, for his thoughts. The

group listened intently, since he was standing on ground over which a
Maine Civil War officer led a famous bayonet charge and received a Medal
of Honor. The group anxiously awaited his words, knowing that in the
Korean War he, too, had been a Maine officer who led a bayonet charge
and received the Medal of Honor for it. Millet's citation reads:

> Capt. Millett ordered the 3d Platoon forward, placed himself at the head
> of the 2 platoons, and, with fixed bayonet, led the assault up the fire-
> swept hill. In the fierce charge Capt. Millett bayoneted 2 enemy soldiers
> and boldly continued on, throwing grenades, clubbing and bayoneting the
> enemy, while urging his men forward by shouting encouragement.
> Despite vicious opposing fire, the whirlwind hand-to-hand assault carried
> to the crest of the hill. His dauntless leadership and personal courage so
> inspired his men that they stormed into the hostile position and used their
> bayonets with such lethal effect that the enemy fled in wild disorder. Dur-
> ing this fierce onslaught Capt. Millett was wounded by grenade fragments
> but refused evacuation until the objective was taken and firmly secured.[5]

Being aware of his experience, everyone wanted to hear what his
words might reveal about the kind of combat that occurred on the hill
where they were standing. If he disappointed his fellow travelers, what he
had to say was still very instructive. To paraphrase his description, he
related that "I was fighting in Korea. I remember being on the bottom of
the hill, and then I remember being on the top of it, wounded. They tell
me I led a bayonet charge, and if they say so, I guess it's true, though I
don't remember any of it."[6]

Adrenaline, chaos, confusion, noise, anger, pain, blood—all capture
the mind's focus when one's life is on the line in combat. Remembering
which rock one passed, where a buddy stood when he was hit, or how
long the fight lasted are virtually impossible to record and later recollect
with so many other issues weighing on the brain. Gettysburg is no excep-
tion. George Meade, who commanded the Union Army at Gettysburg,

made it plain when he said that "in the excitement of battle no individual's memory, unsupported by corroborative evidence is to be relied on, however honest or truthful the individual may be."[7]

Beyond truthfulness is the issue of perspective. The human mind cannot recall things of which it does not take notice. Thus, anything that occurs outside of his immediate vicinity is beyond a soldier's ability to retain, as one Southern officer recalled to his commanding general five years after Gettysburg.

> My recollection of the whole movement of the morning of the first days fight at Gettysburg is so vague and indistinct, up to the time the engagement commenced, that I can tell scarcely anything. In fact, General, I was very much like the French Soldier of whom you sometimes told us, who never saw anything while the battle was going on except the rump of his fat file leader. In battle I rarely knew anything that occurred beyond the immediate vicinity of my own command. In battle when I commanded a company it engaged my whole attention, when a regiment, I knew little of any other command, and so on.[8]

In gathering the recollections of soldiers who were at Gettysburg, one soon finds enormous variations in what might seem simple facts. By various accounts, Pickett's Charge began at some time between 11:00 A.M. and 2:00 P.M., and the famous bombardment that preceded it lasted anywhere from forty-five minutes to three hours. Every veteran experienced the same event, yet as a group, they arrived at very different recollections. The pages of veterans' reminiscences are chock-full of disagreements about things as mundane as the size of rocks and as significant as where a general fell mortally wounded.

Even memories that men retained from combat often faded into uncertainty. In his book *Embattled Courage*, for example, Gerald Linderman described how the memories of many Civil War veterans often blended into events that they could hardly separate from one another. This effect only worsened among veterans who survived several engagements over two or three years of combat. For former soldiers, "their perceptions of what they had done from one day of battle to the next shifted, over-lapped, and merged, leaving them with blurred memories and blunted emotions . . . many specific actions and particular battles became sub-merged in a generalized blur."[9] One of the reasons for this blurring, says Linderman, was that the most useful time during which veterans could have established these memories more firmly in their minds were the times they were least likely to want to remember them. In the immediate aftermath of battle, soldiers found themselves suffering from psychologi-cal wounds. Dwelling on the horrific memories of war only worsened their condition, and many put these thoughts out of their minds as well as they could for years or even decades. By the time the pain healed, the events had fallen further away in time so that their power to recollect the details had greatly diminished and many of the facts were lost forever.[10]

Once the psychological wounds began to ease, soldiers began to talk and write about the war in larger numbers. When they sat down to do so, however, often at someone's request, they could hardly say, "I don't really remember anything." So they began to construct stories based loosely on the few fragments of memory they retained.

Departing the field in 1863, the survivors of both armies already shared a great lack of comprehension, and, with some exceptions, most were content to leave their memories of war alone for more than a decade. In the interim, veterans set about readjusting to civilian life, mourning departed friends and relatives, and dwelling more on the future than on their traumatic recent past. By the late 1870s, however, a natural postwar aversion to reflecting on the war, in public at least, began to melt away, and men of both sides began to find public ways to share their memories with the reunited nation. For Confederates, chief among these outlets was a monthly collection of letters and articles, the *Southern Historical Society Papers,* which first appeared in 1876. Within just a few issues, the authors of these works, mostly higher-ranking officers of the former Confederate armies, took part in sometimes heated exchanges over the events of the war. Within a few years the men who once wore gray had several periodicals in which to share their memories and gain the insights of fellow veterans. Over the next few decades they exchanged experiences in regional and more widely distributed collections, such as *Southern Bivouac*, *Our Living and Our Dead*, and later the *Confederate Veteran*.

At the same time, their Yankee counterparts found voices in publications such as the *War Papers* of the Military Order of the Loyal Legion of the United States (MOLLUS). These were the selectively published reminiscences of Union officers who presented formal speeches at meetings of each northern state's chapter of the organization. Far less formal, but often highly charged, were the articles that appeared in the *National Tribune*, a newspaper devoted almost exclusively to the Civil War exchanges of Union veterans of all rank. In time, many of these arguments became so adversarial that the editors began printing them under the heading "Fighting Them Over."

In the 1880s, probably the most important decade for Civil War literature, two multivolume works combined Blue and Gray accounts into one source. The first eventually totaled more than 125 volumes and took more than two decades to complete. When it was done, the War Department's *Official Records of the Union and Confederate Armies in the War of the Rebellion* had come close to its goal of assembling every postbattle report, major order, and official correspondence produced during the war. Within its pages, veterans had ready access to the sometimes sanitized and highly political "official" information both from the field and from Washington. In the midst of its publication, *Century* magazine nearly doubled its circulation while running the series entitled "Battles and Leaders of the Civil War." A more literary mixture of accounts and sketches, it was reprinted as a four-volume set of books in 1888.

In these periodicals and the growing number of regimental histories, autobiographies, and memoirs appearing in print to wider audiences,

veterans shared their opinions, feelings, and memories with former enemies and comrades alike. This widening sea of information gave them
what they saw as a clearer view of the war in which they had taken part.
In particular, reading the accounts of men who had been down at the bottom of the hill or out across the field opposing them helped the former
combatants form sharper images of their own experiences and of the
wider battle as it had happened around them. At least as often, and probably more, reading the accounts of their comrades misled and confused
them into formulating at least partially incorrect memories, if not full-
blown myths. Often one mistaken comment or statistic led to another,
until the memory that they settled on as fact bore little resemblance to
what they thought they knew shortly after the battle.

Even as they built these legends and misunderstandings among themselves and began to construct common themes or agreed on versions of
events, the veterans acknowledged the flaws inherent in their attempts to
describe the battle. They recognized the challenge in trying to collapse
the recollections of tens of thousands of men into one cohesive narrative.
Not that it slowed down their myth making, but as the years passed, the
early lack of explanatory power often lingered among those struggling to
describe their time at Gettysburg.

Decades after the battle, many veterans placed disclaimers in front of
or within their accounts. Colonel William C. Oates of Alabama, for
example, qualified his difference of opinion with a former Gettysburg foe
while excusing what he saw as misstatements in the Federal account. "All
of us, on both sides," he explained, "who were in such hot places as that
were made to exaggerate in favor of our respective sides, and do it honestly in most cases."[11] Hardening his view of the Yankee, he later added,
"He is like many others on both sides at this late date who are disposed to
make themselves the whole push."[12] One of Oates's comrades in arms
wrote of just one part of the battle that "some of these accounts are simply silly. Some are false in statement. Some are false in inference. All in
some respects are untrue."[13]

On the Union side a veteran refuted the claim of a fellow bluecoat in print by accusing him of choosing selective sources. "This history," he charged, "was written several years after the war, from memory and such reports and letters as best served his purpose."[14] Still other Yankee witnesses prefaced their recollections to fellow veterans in newspapers by expressing their lack of confidence in their own memory. "The foregoing account is my recollection of Gettysburg, July 2, 1863," a New Yorker explained. "It may be faulty; it was more than 22 years ago, and I was but 19 years of age then. The business cares and thoughts of an active life have come in between."[15] Perhaps the most succinct admission about remembering what happened came from a Union general when he wrote, "There is no reliance however to be made on our memories."[16]

As they engaged in their story-building discussions, veterans saw the "truth" and the story moving along ever widening paths. "Much that has been written as a history," an Ohioan declared, "and as reminiscences of this battle, purporting to be absolutely true, when studied and compared with the 'Official records of the Rebellion,' and the field visited, are found to be absolutely false."[17] Another added, "The historian of the future who assays to tell the tale of Gettysburg undertakes an onerous task."[18]

By the eyewitnesses' own admission, exaggeration in hot places, politics, selectively chosen sources, the years and decades that came in between, even simple silliness, all played a role in the earliest formulation of the story of Gettysburg. Nonetheless, the veterans forged ahead in their efforts to explain, construct, and shape the history of the battle. No matter how impossible the truth was to know and describe, someone was bound to write *some* history of the battle, and anyone who worked to see a certain version of the story told and repeated, whether mistaken, biased, or outright fraudulent, might succeed in helping shape the popular history. In the 1990s the political word for this kind of history-shaping effort was "spin," or the attempt to make people believe a certain interpretation of events. Whether conscious of their efforts to shape the story of the past or innocently trying to recall and recount what had occurred, veterans began to put something down on paper. In time, though no more certain of the truth than ever, many overcame the early general reluctance to try to describe events. In the pages of countless periodicals they developed their ideas, voiced them, and even engaged in open hostility defending them.

A relative handful of veterans worked harder than most to see their memory of events stamped more firmly on the pages of battle history. These men often had a disproportionate impact on the story, not because of any crucial role they played or even witnessed during the conflict, but because in the postwar years they pushed their version of events harder, thus greatly affecting what became the collective memory of events. Reaching a wider audience than most helped perpetuate the mistakes and exaggerations that they made. Because these people were not always the most reliable witnesses, myths and legends naturally followed.

One well-known fable, originating in Chinese, Buddhist, or Islamic tradition many centuries ago, tells the tale of a group of blind men, usually varying from three to six in number, who approach an elephant and describe what it is most like. Each resulting description of the elephant differs according to the part of the beast that each man touched. One grabbed the tail and said it was like a snake, another the tusk and said it was like a spear; a third grabbed a leg and said it was like a tree, and so on. The lesson of the fable, of course, is that all people recalling an object or event unknowingly shape their view differently from others based on their small area of perspective. As a result, history often records many widely varying accounts of the same event, often from participants relatively close together at the time it occurred. Participants who worked harder to get their version of events into the public domain often succeeded in shaping history whether or not theirs was a more accurate version. If the blind man holding the elephant's tail, for example, was the only one in the group who later described his experience with the strange beast, people might soon conclude that an elephant was really a slithering reptile that hovered about five feet off the ground. No lies, no fraud, just one perspective repeated with more enthusiasm than the other descriptions.[19]

Such is the case with the recollections of the veterans and eyewitnesses of Gettysburg. Since more than 150,000 people witnessed some part of the great battle—ironically, soldiers called this "seeing the elephant"—it comes as no surprise that they produced hundreds of different variations of the same events. Seizing on various parts was not the only way that eyewitness accounts of the battle differed. Elements such as personal agendas and strong emotions also entered into the mixture of memory, confusion, and embellishment that led to the stories they produced. To illustrate this phenomenon, one need only look at a small area of the battlefield, study the accounts of those who were present within it at the same time, and examine how similar or different there accounts became.

At the south end of the battlefield, for example, is a large hill known today as Little Round Top. The west face of this hill was not only cleared of trees in 1863 but also strewn with enormous boulders, making it a virtually impregnable position that offered a view of the countryside for miles. As the fighting progressed on the battle's second day, this hill became a key focal point of both armies. Possession of it became of paramount importance. The first substantial force to reach the hill was a Union brigade of more than one thousand men in four regiments under the command of Colonel Strong Vincent. Shortly after their arrival, portions of two Confederate brigades, one from Texas and another from Alabama, attacked the hill in an attempt to seize it. Later, a Union artillery battery of six cannons and a second brigade of infantry arrived to help defend the position. After about two hours of close fighting, the Union men still held the important position, but many of their highest-ranking leaders were dead.

The summit of this hill—at least the portion on which the key fighting occurred—is less than two hundred yards across. Yet, in this relatively small area, the number of widely held myths and legends is remarkable.

If one were to tally them up, and then multiply the number of tales in that small space by the relative size of the entire battlefield, one would begin to understand how these kinds of recollections have dramatically affected the story of Gettysburg. The reminiscences of just a small handful of individuals, ranging in rank from private to general, offer an understanding of the fight on that part of the field, as well as the process through which veterans accepted certain versions of events over others, thus forming the foundation for the history of Gettysburg. Within this process, certain key players worked harder to promote their story and often succeeded. At the same time, veterans built many of their accounts by repeating the mistaken testimony of others, making it appear as if the new account corroborated testimony when it was really only a repetition of the first.

In similar ways, Gettysburg stories originated and grew to legend or myth long after the event. In many cases, a veteran made a postwar claim in print where many other veterans could read it. These men then incorporated a portion of the fellow's memory into their own, repeating his account while weaving their own recollection. If this second story then found its way into print and a wide audience came across it, most would think that they had found two corroborating sources for the same event, when they had really found one source and one person who read and then repeated the first. The popular history of what happened on the summit of Little Round Top is a revealing example of how a few men who pushed their own stories succeeded in getting others to repeat them and thus gained significant control of the history. In this way they shaped the primary source material that later historians mined for more than a century.

A veteran who made certain that his point of view had greater voice was Oliver W. Norton. A private during the battle, Norton had something of a catbird seat as it related to an important Union brigade and its commander, for whom Norton served as bugler and flag bearer. Riding alongside his brigadier, Colonel Strong Vincent, Norton was naturally close at hand when anything important occurred. As a result of his work to find a prominent place for his memories among Gettysburg histories, Private Norton became one of the most often used sources of firsthand information. Among the narratives of the fighting on Little Round Top, his story has become a prominent feature of the battle's second day. Despite being accepted as a useful and reliable eyewitness, however, ample evidence suggests that Norton's accounts should not have achieved the prominence that they have, and his effect on the history of the battle may not be as factual as many perceive. The stories and history surrounding the granite memorials in which Norton had a hand provide part of the evidence.

In the storied history of battlefield "monumentation" at Gettysburg, no organization sought to commemorate more in a smaller area than Norton's unit, the 83d Pennsylvania Regiment. From the time they placed the first ever regimental marker on the field in 1878 until virtually all of the veterans had passed on, these men erected or assisted in placing at least six permanent markers on the field. The first was a marble slab in 1878, followed by another monument complete with a life-size statue in 1889, as well as two flank markers, a brigade tablet, and an inscription chiseled in a large rock. All of these were meant, in part or whole, to commemorate their former commander, Colonel Vincent, who received a mortal wound somewhere in the area where these stone and bronze tributes to him now rest on Little Round Top. As Vincent's former bugler and aide, Norton was naturally prominent in the organization of veterans who saw to their design and placement. He helped petition battlefield authorities, choose locations for each memorial, and attended and even gave speeches at dedication ceremonies. Despite his deep involvement with each of these memorials, Norton decided in 1910 that the memory of Vincent was not properly marked on the field. Writing as a representative of the regimental veterans group forty-seven years after the battle, Norton asked the authorities who then controlled the battlefield how he might go about placing a monument to "pay a tribute to his memory."[20] A puzzled if not frustrated chairman of the Battlefield Commission replied by asking which of the other two monuments or the engraving, all placed by or under the direction of the veterans of the regiment, he proposed to obliterate.[21]

Norton's quest for yet another Vincent monument exposes a number of significant issues that helped misshape the story of Gettysburg. First, Norton was extremely biased toward the story of his own experience and that of a man he obviously held in great esteem. Second, he and his comrades recognized that future generations would look more favorably on those whose deeds at Gettysburg were clearly evident, as in stone and bronze. Third, although it is not entirely clear, at the time he sought this last monument, some forty-seven years after the battle, Norton was so old and senile that he had completely forgotten the monuments and markers he had played a key role in erecting.

These elements, taken individually, might not seem to have a drastic effect on our collective memory of the battle. These traits, after all, are not unusual among aging veterans. But Norton's long and labored effort to see that the world remembered his beloved commander had a profound effect on the story of Gettysburg. Five years after this last request to the commission, having lost his ability to see and to write, Norton published his book, *The Attack and Defense of Little Round Top*. In it he described in heroic detail the actions of Colonel Vincent, taking great pains to attach to him much of the credit for the Union victory.[22]

By the time the book was in print, Norton had been blind for many years and was so frail that he had to have someone write cheerful inscriptions inside the front cover for friends, under which he scratched out a nearly illegible signature. Despite the evidence suggesting that it was a highly biased and inaccurate memoir of a participant in the battle, Norton's story pervades the battle literature written since his book became available. Today, one would be hard-pressed to find a serious work of any significant length on the battle that does not cite Norton as a key source.

What helped weave Norton's memories into the collective understanding of the battle more deeply than those of other veterans is the universal appeal of his story. The heroic tale of the mortally wounded Vincent fighting on his native Pennsylvania soil draws people to it, while Norton's feelings for his commander touch the reader's emotions. Norton's book became more popular than others in part because he reprinted a number of key letters and reports from the battle. Except in Norton's assemblage, historians can only find these documents in numerous and varied locations, if at all, and anyone wishing to learn more about this key aspect of the battle finds that having these documents in one volume is handy.

To prepare the book over the years, Norton needed the help of a researcher, secretary, stenographer, and typist. Thus his work passed through the hands and minds of at least four other people before it was published fifty-two years after the events occurred and five years after he seemed to have forgotten the monuments he had helped place. How many of the words in the pages of the book are Norton's and how many are the translations of his assistants we cannot know. How many of the descriptions it contains are accurate and how many fell victim to the many enemies of human memory, we will not likely discover. Nonetheless, historians continue to consider his work to be of great value and borrow from it heavily.

This borrowing seems justified to some, since Norton was present and up close, and thus his memories should be highly reliable. But at the same time, someone could just as easily characterize his work as the ramblings of a senile, blind old man. Perhaps neither description of Norton is accurate. Yet those looking back most often present his writing as reliable, almost never pointing out his flaws as a source. In one of the first copies of his book Norton scribbled his name below a nicely written note of gratitude to Ellis Spear, another veteran of the fight on Little Round Top. The inscription and signature are symbolic of the book as a whole. The old bugler needed help to get the work together and in print. Some of it may be his words, some those of an aide, some lost in the translation between the two. Regardless of which, it is clear that in the end Norton could not complete the project alone, so he had someone else do much of

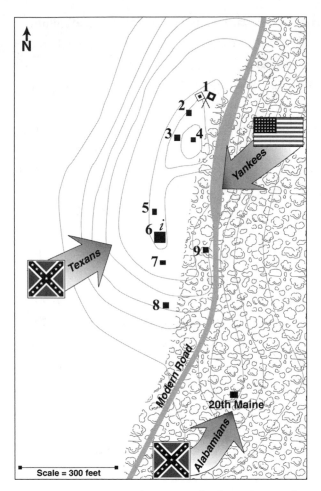

MAP 2.1

The Summit of Little Round Top

1. The Signal Station in view of Army HQ.

2. General Warren's Statue: scene of his discovery. This was the first statue placed at Gettysburg (1882).

3. Original location of 91st Pennsylvania monument marking the site of General Weed's wounding (1883).

4. The current site of this monument, relocated in 1889 atop an inscription purporting to mark the spot where Lieutenant Hazlett died.

5. 140th New York monument (1886), general location of Colonel O'Rorke's death. Hazlett's guns were roughly here on July 2.

6. The 44th New York monument (1888), a four-story high castle. *i* is the site of the Vincent inscription.

7. Vincent wounded marker—the first monument at Gettysburg (1878, replaced in 1980s).

8. The 83rd Pennsylvania monument (1889).

9. Vincent's Brigade Tablet (1898).

The distance from Warren's statue to Vincent's wounding (2 to 7) is just 600 feet. In just this tiny portion of the 6,000 acre battlefield (half of 1 percent of it), numerous myths and legends abound. By applying this ratio of myths to space, one can get a sense of the scope of Gettysburg mythology.

the work and then put his name on the final product. Despite the many reasons to question them, countless others have repeated these printed words as his ever since.[23]

What is perhaps most ironic about Norton's story is a comment that he made to his fellow veterans in 1889 while dedicating the largest of the monuments to his regiment and Vincent—one he had apparently forgotten by 1910. "The correct story of Gettysburg," he stated firmly, "has never been written, will never be written . . . Many conscientious historians have attempted to weave a symmetrical whole from such disconnected threads as they can gather, but their accounts vary as their sources of information." A quarter century after that speech, it seems that Norton fulfilled his own prophecy, becoming one of the very historians he decried decades earlier.[24]

Just a few yards from where Norton last stood beside his commander on Little Round Top, a New York officer named Porter Farley found himself in a similar position. Farley's flawed memory, coupled with his desire to get his thoughts into print, had an effect on the history of the fight for Little Round Top that may equal Norton's. Like Norton, Farley's determination to see his memories infused into the public's understanding of the battle led to the shaping of the Gettysburg story as a whole. The process through which he did this shows how some of the basic elements of the story became the foundation for what is now the popular belief.[25]

As adjutant of the 140th New York Regiment at Gettysburg, Farley served under Colonel Patrick O'Rorke who, like Norton's Colonel Vincent, was a well-educated, promising young officer. Next to his work at Gettysburg, the Irish-born O'Rorke was notable for finishing first in the same class at West Point in which George Armstrong Custer finished last. Like Vincent, O'Rorke fought his last battle on Little Round Top: a Texan's bullet killed him instantly in the heat of the fight. Like Norton, Farley wanted credit for his beloved commander, and he pushed hard for his version of events, even to the exclusion of all other units involved. His venture into story building had a specific purpose from the outset. Having read some of the earliest published histories of the battle, Farley did not like the way popular memory was treating his regiment and commander. While the hill on which they fought—which veterans had recently taken to calling "Little Round Top"—seemed to be gaining notoriety as a key point in the fight, the early histories overlooked his regiment and its commander. Out to set the record straight, he drafted a letter in 1872 to General Gouverneur K. Warren, the man who was becoming known as the "hero of Little Round Top."

Warren served as chief engineer of the Union Army in 1863, and was responsible for bringing troops to the now famous hill in classic nick-of-time fashion, saving the battle, as many claim, for the Union. In the growing public discourse on the battle, Colonel Vincent's brigade seemed to be getting the lion's share of credit for saving Little Round Top. Having served in General Stephen Weed's brigade, the second to arrive on the hill, and getting little or no popular credit at that time, Farley wrote the initial letter to determine how Vincent's brigade got there in the first place.

"Just when and at whose order did Vincent go up there . . .?" Farley inquired. "How long had he been there before we arrived . . . was he rushed up there after the enemy were seen to be making for that point?" Graciously willing to help Farley come to some clearer understanding, Warren dispatched letters to others who might be able to shed some light on the matter, including eyewitnesses such as Kenner Garrard, who took command of Weed's brigade when the general fell mortally wounded, A. S. Marvin, and Warren's brother Edgar, both on Weed's staff. The correspondence lasted for most of the 1870s and eventually drew in people who were publishing battle histories, such as John B. Bachelder, the official government historian of the battle, and Samuel P. Bates. In the process, Farley's theories on a few topics reached each of these chroniclers as well. Warren's comment in a letter to Bachelder is indicative of the frustration they faced in determining even basic points. "It is singular how difficult it is to find out the exact truth about such a simple fact."[26]

In November 1877, more than five years after the correspondence began, Farley raised the white flag on his initially firm opinion that his regiment had been last in the line of march. Despite his certainty on the matter a half decade earlier, he now conceded that the preponderance of opinions was against him and his firm certainty collapsed into complete confusion. "I thought I was perfectly clear," he wrote, "but now I feel shaken in it. The question is one upon which, from its very nature, anyone might easily be mistaken."[27] Ironically, Farley may have been correct in some of his original beliefs, but the memories of three other officers—all of whom outranked him—and one official historian forced him to bend. In deference to rank, and outnumbered by other, only mildly convincing opinions, Farley, like so many other veterans forming Gettysburg memories, altered at least this small part of his history of the battle.

On larger points, however, Farley did not yield. At Warren's suggestion, he corresponded with the heir to the throne of France, the Comte de Paris, who was then assembling—through an English translator from Poland, no less—his *History of the Civil War in America*. Farley pleaded with him "that if any reference is made to our regiment it may be a perfectly true one I take this occasion to state to you a few matters of which I was an eye witness." Among his more misguided statements, Farley claimed that when his regiment reached the summit of Little Round Top, "there was not then a single infantryman." He underlined the statement to be sure that he had clearly communicated it, before going on to further push the point. "No other regiment was there on Little Round Top at that critical moment."[28] This was not the only time he made such a statement, ruling out a onetime slip of the tongue explanation. The following year in a letter to Gettysburg historian John Bachelder he claimed that the 140th New York was "the force and the *only force* that held *Little Round Top* during the struggle of the late afternoon of the second day's fight. Such was the fact."[29]

While it is difficult to dismiss Farley's statements as an eyewitness, his account is at odds with the recollection of virtually every other soldier present on the hill at the time. These others testified in numerous accounts that the four regiments of Vincent's brigade were engaged with the enemy prior to Farley's arrival with Weed's brigade—a hardly unnoticeable situation. Either Farley simply did not notice at least 1,200 men in blue uniforms firing guns a few yards away from him or some other malady affected his memory.

Nonetheless, at least some of Farley's comments made it into the public discussion by way of the history of the Comte de Paris. As another chronicler of the battle later stated, Farley's comments "may be plainly seen in the chapter on Gettysburg in the Comte de Paris' work."[30] Despite its multinational origin, the Comte's history reached a wide audience among veterans of the war and thus crept into their conversations and formulations about Gettysburg. For Farley, this early success at reshaping the popular story toward his own desires did not mean the end of his quest. Among the other contemporary battle histories in which his writing found a place was that of his nearby comrade in arms, Oliver Norton.

It should come as no surprise that Norton and Farley found in each other a kindred soul, as both men were struggling to preserve the memory of their beloved commanders amid a flurry of battle histories that seemed to overlook them. As Norton wrote, "His grief at O'Rorke's death was like mine for Vincent's."[31] While Norton was apparently not privy to the portions of Farley's account that excluded Vincent's brigade from the hill entirely, he published numerous comments and even a complete article and letters from Farley in his 1915 book, *Attack and Defense of Little Round Top*. Norton's book preserved in print a number of memories and made readily available to generations of future historians what might otherwise have crumbled in the musty folders of archival boxes. Thus these accounts and all of their flaws had great influence on the popular history.

Perhaps the best and most lasting contribution that this Norton/Farley combination made to Gettysburg mythology is the now famous story of how General Warren saved Little Round Top. Their combined energies helped create a legend that became a focal point of a visit to, or writing about, Gettysburg. The traditional story as it has survived through the generations originated in the first letter that General Warren wrote in reply to Porter Farley's inquiries. In it, he described his arrival on Little Round Top and discovery of the Confederate line of attack in a position perilous to the Union Army.

> I saw at once that this was the key of the whole position and that our troops in the woods in front of it could not see the ground in front of them, so that the enemy would come upon them before they were aware of it . . . so, I requested the Captain of a rifle battery just in front of Little Round top to fire a shot into these woods. He did so, and as the shot went whistling through the air the sound of it reached the enemies troops and caused everyone to look in the direction of it. The motion revealed to me the glistening of gun barrels and bayonets of the enemy's line of battle already formed and far outflanking the position of any of our troops . . . I have been particular in telling this, as the discovery was intensely thrilling to my feelings and almost appalling.[32]

Warren died in 1882, before the majority of veteran reminiscences reached publication, so he did not describe his day on Little Round Top to any greater extent. However, the energetic Porter Farley was fond of the story since it was the event that led to the deployment of his regiment in this crucial area. Through his efforts, the letter made its way into print a year later, and into a number of subsequent publications, including Norton's *Attack and Defense*. In a bronze depiction of his crucial moment, Warren's friends erected the first statue ever placed on the Gettysburg battlefield in 1888. They created this memorial in large part because Warren was badly mistreated by General Philip Sheridan in the last weeks of the war, which seriously damaged Warren's reputation. Placing a statue on the site of what had become known as his greatest military moment and then helping elevate the importance of his discovery contributed to redeeming Warren's unfairly impugned honor.

This slightly larger than life-size bronze figure depicts him atop a large boulder on the summit of the hill with his field glasses in hand. His head is turned to where the Confederate assault began, posed as if caught in the legendary moment of discovery. It is this story and this permanent depiction of it that millions of visitors to Gettysburg remember, and for that, both Norton and Farley should be pleased with their efforts. Nowhere on the inscribed plaques that accompany the statue is there a hint of doubt that this mythical American moment actually occurred. Nevertheless, there is ample evidence that the story of Warren's famous discovery is embellished at best and farcical at worst.

While the only source for this tale is Warren himself, written in that 1872 letter to Farley, all other descriptions of the events stem from Warren's original mention. First Farley and Norton repeated it, then other veterans repeated their repetition, and so on until it became the established story—the myth. What these subsequent descriptions fail to record, however, is that in his very next letter to Farley, eleven days after the first, Warren himself expressed doubts about his account. "I wrote my letter to you," he allowed, "without consulting any notes, and I may not have given the strict order of occurrences in it. If you should wish to publish something from me, I wish you would let me have time to revise it first."[33] Overlooking Warren's own doubt about his memory of the events—and he eventually allowed Farley to quote the letter—there are substantial reasons to question the dramatic description he provided, not the least of which is that Warren was wounded in the neck just as these events unfolded.

Aside from the psychological effects that a dangerous wound might have on Warren's ability to remember clearly, another interesting piece of evidence lies in a book written some years after the discovery story began to circulate among veterans. In *Signal Corps, U.S.A. in the War of the Rebellion*, Willard Brown, a former member of the Corps, told a decidedly different tale of Warren's critical discovery of Confederates beyond the Union flank. By just about all historical accounts, Warren arrived on Little Round Top to find no more than a group of men from the Signal Corps sending messages via flag waving from the advantageously high summit. Within minutes he grasped the situation, discovered the Confederate force in the distance, and began acting on this critical piece of intelligence. As to how he discovered it, however, Brown's story differs from the legend.[34]

> When he reached the [signal] station the enemy were under cover, and were scarcely visible except to eyes accustomed to the use of the field glass. Capt. Hall found it very difficult to convince Gen. Warren that the enemy's infantry were there concealed. While the discussion was in progress the enemy opened on the station. The first shell burst close to the station, and the general, a moment later, was wounded in the neck. Capt. Hall then exclaimed, "Now do you see them?"[35]

While it is clear from the tone and tenor of Brown's rendition that he is likely exaggerating in favor of the Signal Corps—and perhaps against the growing acclaim that Warren, thanks to his own story, had by then received—this contrary evidence cannot easily be dismissed. Especially when there is a simple test that can lend physical evidence to the discussion of Warren's account. In Warren's letter to Farley—the account that started the whole story—he wrote that the cannon shot he claimed to have ordered caused movement among the Confederates. He wrote that "the motion revealed to me the glistening of gun barrels and bayonets of the enemy's line of battle. . . ."[36] No matter how good or bad Warren's memory, there is a key physical element to his account that cannot be satisfied. From the position where Warren stood on July 2, 1863, when he looked in the direction of the Confederates then assembling, he looked directly into the sun. The critical point is not that the sunlight may have blinded him, but that sunlight traveling from the sun over the Confeder-

ates cannot reflect, or glisten, and still continue on its direct path to Warren. Reflection means changing the direction of the sunlight, but to reach
Warren the light had to continue traveling straight. Obviously, it could
not both reflect and continue straight.

Given the alignment of the three elements—Warren, Confederates,
and sun—a simple test with mirrors can and has proven that a force no
less certain than the alignment of the planets rendered Warren's glistening impossible.[37] Over the years, historians have searched in vain for any
mention of Warren's order by the men who would have fired the shot, or
for an account by an aide who might have overheard or delivered the
order. In addition, a seldom referenced official document seems to indicate that the signal station knew of the Rebel force several hours before
Warren arrived on the scene. Just before noon on July 2, Lieutenant
Jerome, a signal officer on Little Round Top, sent a message to General
Meade's headquarters that read: "The rebels are in force, and our skir-
mishers give way. One mile west of Round Top signal station, the woods
are full of them."[38] Four hours later, another signal reached army headquarters from the station on Little Round Top. It read, in part: "Saw a
column of the enemy's infantry move into woods on ridge, 3 miles west
of the town, near the Millerstown road . . . Think the enemy occupies
the range of hills 3 miles west of town in considerable force." General
Warren reached the station at the summit of the hill nearly an hour
later.[39]

Clearly the evidence questioning the original account of Warren's discovery warrants serious scholarly examination. Nevertheless, his version
has become the universally accepted description of events. Thanks to the
efforts of Norton and Farley, Warren's romantic story became part of history, despite conflicting physical evidence. Another reason for this myth
may lie in the answer to a simple rhetorical question: Who would want to
see a monument depicting a general bending over with his hand gripping
his wounded neck? History has a way of coming out the way we hoped it
would rather than the way things really happened.

Just a few paces from where Warren or the Signal Corps—or both—discovered the Confederate assault on July 2, is yet another example of memory running amok and legend outpacing reality. As if the hill were not already littered with mythic stories of heroism, the modern visitor must stop to hear the touching story of the death of General Stephen Weed and Lieutenant Charles Hazlett. Weed commanded the second brigade that arrived on the hill (which included Farley), while Hazlett commanded the only artillery battery. Not surprisingly, this legendary tale involves a substantial group of veterans' accounts, including those of Norton, Farley, and Warren.

It is difficult to trace the story back to its original source and mention—the one that others then repeated under the guise of corroboration—but the touching narrative of the end of these two patriotic lives first appeared in wide circulation as the same article in which Porter Farley first repeated Warren's discovery story. In the most popular veteran periodical of the time, the *National Tribune*, Farley described the version of events that had been privately circulating for some time.

> Weed received a mortal wound. Believing that he was about to die, he was in the very act of committing his last messages to his friend Hazlett, who stooped over him, when there came the whiz and thud of another bullet as it sunk into Hazlett's brain, and that brave artilleryman fell a corpse across the body of his dying friend.[40]

Stooping to catch the dying words of his dear friend, Hazlett met the same fate on the same spot—an amazing story and a touching scene, to be sure. Four years later, Benjamin Rittenhouse, the man who replaced Hazlett as commander of the battery—and who was probably the original source for the story—delivered a paper to a Washington, D.C., veterans group. In it, he relayed a tale similar to Farley's. Like Norton and Farley before him, he advanced the cause of the legend closest to him, and the credit to his own martyred commander, still further.[41]

Most of another decade passed before an entirely different version of events appeared in the *National Tribune*. This one was from a member of Lieutenant Hazlett's battery who recorded that he was a few feet from his commander at the fateful moment. Responding to another veteran who had repeated the popular account in the *Tribune*, Thomas Scott wrote:

> Some one in an account of Gettysburg says . . . "And Lieut. Hazlett, in the act of stooping to receive his last commands, was instantly killed." Wrong again. Lieut. Hazlett was sitting on his horse to the left rear of our piece. Word came that Gen. Weed was killed. He was facing to the front. He raised his left foot out of the stirrup, turning the left side of his head to the front. He was shot in the left side of his head, over and back of the left ear. We jumped for him. I dropped the sponge-staff and took hold of him and lifted his head, but he never spoke, and died that night about 1 o'clock, and we felt as though we had lost a dear brother.[42]

Scott's story is so vivid and full of relatively insignificant detail that it appears credible on its face. It seems unlikely that an eyewitness would relate trivial elements such as which foot came out of the stirrup unless he was relating this story from his memory, almost visualizing the moment, even three decades after the fact. Further questioning the popular account of Hazlett's death is a diary entry recorded that evening on the scene. In it, a member of Hazlett's battery wrote simply that "Lieut. Hazlett was immediately killed by Rebel sharpshooters." There is no mention of Weed or his dying words, or the dramatic moment.[43]

Whether or not the romantic version of a heroic death is the factual one, two key pieces of firsthand eyewitness evidence call into question what has become the popular story. Numerous books and articles on the battle, and many more that focus solely on Little Round Top, relate the story of Hazlett without questioning its authenticity. Not one of them deals with, nor even mentions, Scott's account, despite the fact that his vivid description appears in a source no more difficult for historians to locate than any other account of the same event. While the compelling nature of the popular version has gained dominance, historians have ignored Scott's account and the seemingly corroborative diary entry. Today, thanks to some unusual monument shuffling, tourists on the battlefield fare little better.

Some years before the popular account took hold, veterans of the 91st Pennsylvania erected a monument marking their positions on the hill. Some years after the popular story took hold, they moved the monument back a few yards from its original location to a spot where someone had chiseled an inscription on a rock noting that Hazlett had died there. There they had it inscribed as depicting the spot where Weed was mortally wounded. Thus the site of Weed's and Hazlett's deaths were physically brought together to correspond with the popular legend. In 1889 the men of the 91st Pennsylvania dedicated a new and larger monument on the site where the older monument had previously stood, marking the regimental position. As with the stories of Warren and Vincent, Weed and Hazlett's dramatic tale has found a permanent home etched in the rock of Little Round Top. Most visitors to the field see and hear of the touching story that may or may not be true. As with Warren's discovery tale, the general public, along with countless historians and journalists over the decades, has chosen the dramatic death scene story because of its romantic and compelling nature. It is a story we *want* to believe, so it wins out over the more mundane version of Hazlett's instant death, when either—or neither—could be true.

It is through this complicated process of story building, and the choices that humans are prone to make toward romanticized, more heroic stories, that allowed men like Warren, Farley, and Norton to have such a significant effect on the story of the Battle of Gettysburg. Oliver Norton and Porter Farley sought to memorialize their beloved commanders by emphasizing a version of events that created sympathy for Vincent and O'Rorke and then worked hard to have it published and repeated. At the same time, General Warren's friends sought to restore his reputation after his premature death. Their work was simply indicative of personal struggles with memory and human nature.

To be sure, theirs is hardly a unique circumstance. Indeed, veterans throughout the country assembled similarly constructed stories about places all across the battlefield. The heroic events recorded by these three men took place in an area little more than one hundred yards wide. From the evidence contained within such a small piece of the battle we can begin to see how little we really know on a battlefield of thousands of acres on which more than 150,000 men struggled with each other and with their frail human memories. Eventually these collections of misassembled facts formed the ammunition chests from which larger battles were waged. The veterans were only just beginning to explore questions such as, To whose credit was the Union victory? and, Who was responsible for the Confederate loss? Based on these smaller collections of understood "facts" the debates over the larger questions has only begun to flower.

CHAPTER 3

THE STRUGGLE
OVER MEMORY

These people who were fighting this war of words . . . created a litera-
ture in the 1870s, 1880s . . . that has sat there and has been mined by
historians for decades. They knew that this would happen. They very
self-consciously created this record and knew that later historians
would use it.

GARY GALLAGHER[1]

While the story of Gettysburg is largely the result of embellishment by hundreds of veterans such as Farley and Norton, these men probably leaned just a little from the less interesting factual record. With what they probably believed was complete honesty, many of these veterans skewed their accounts one way or another as human beings often do. Their divergence from fact demonstrates more about how human nature affects memory than any intentional deception on their part. A close examination of the sources on which the history of Gettysburg stands, however, uncovers a deeper level of deception. Almost as soon as the battle ended, the history of this great event became embroiled in debates over a host of regional and national issues. Political and cultural leaders continued to debate these issues for decades. In trying to slant the meaning of Gettysburg in the direction of their cultural views, a number of leading veterans (particularly vanquished postwar Confederates) contrived, invented, and flat out lied, knowing that they were building a record on which future generations would judge the past.

Gary Gallagher, a professor at the University of Virginia, has studied the battle of Gettysburg in great depth, collaborating with virtually all of the leading Gettysburg historians. In a panel discussion some years ago, he explained how the numerous controversies that veterans argued in postwar writings were designed to reshape the story to reflect more positively on the writers and their views.

> There's an enormous controversial literature that was created by former Confederates who fought here, endlessly replaying what happened at Gettysburg in search of villains and scapegoats, and trying to explain why [General] R.E. Lee lost here when R.E. Lee was a peerless soldier. . . . These people who were fighting this war of words . . . created a literature in the 1870s, 1880s, and it dribbles on into the nineties and even the twentieth century, that has sat there and has been mined then by historians for decades. They knew that this would happen. They very self-consciously created this record and knew that later historians would use it.[2]

In deflecting blame for Lee's apparent failure at Gettysburg onto his subordinates, veteran groups collaborated to establish a mythology for future generations to absorb. And absorb it they have, leading to endless debates and discussions of who was to blame and who should have done what differently. Two of Lee's subordinates, Richard Ewell and James Longstreet, fare poorly in the controversy. On one end of the battlefield, General Ewell failed to take the heights south of Gettysburg on the battle's first day when the Union Army was weakest. His failure gave the Federals time to reinforce and entrench on ground to their advantage. Gallagher explains some of the origins of that myth.

Look at somebody like [General] John Gordon, who after the war went on and on and on about how Richard Ewell should have just taken the heights on July 1st, but when you see the letter he wrote to his wife right at the time, there's no mention of that. I think that his decision that Ewell should have done something was shaped by the controversies that came later rather than what people were thinking at the time.[3]

At the opposite end of the Confederate line, veteran mythological literature finds a scapegoat in General James Longstreet. He is accused of being stubbornly slow because he disagreed with Lee on tactics and strategy. To demonstrate that his delays, not the failure of Lee's generalship, lost the battle, prominent Confederates like Gordon, Jubal Early, and Fitzhugh Lee invented the story of a "dawn attack order" on the battle's second day, supposedly issued by Lee. Since Longstreet's attack did not get under way until late afternoon, after the Federals had time to arrange and strengthen their lines, the blame for the loss, it is argued, was his alone. Surviving members of Lee's wartime staff discredited the story as untrue but it has had a profound effect just the same. Armed with "facts" such as these (even if they had to invent them), veterans were trying to explain away the failure of the Confederate army at Gettysburg. By elevating Gettysburg to mythical status, they explained the loss of the war as a whole in a more palatable way. In this line of logic, the outcome of the entire war came down to one battle, and the battle to one day, and the day to one slow or reluctant general. Thus countless other less comfortable reasons for the loss of the war can be clouded over and explained away.

Another element of memory greatly affected the stories told by Gettysburg veterans, based largely in their need for self-esteem and identity on an individual, regional, and national level. There is an old joke that if every person who says that he or she was at Woodstock in 1969 actually was, the fields of Max Yasgur's farm would have been teeming with 10 million onlookers. In reality, less than a half million attended the music festival during that summer. In certain social circles, however, having attended is a badge of honor, if not a boost to one's self-esteem. Fabrications like this stem from people's desire to place themselves at great events—to be an eyewitness to history. At the same time, having that historical event attached to one's hometown, state, region, or nation helps validate one's identity. Humans crave connections to places and events with an interesting past. Whether we had anything to do with shaping that past is not a necessary part of our attachment to it. To be sure, being a participant or witness enhances one's social standing considerably, but just being loosely connected, as in coming from a certain famous or historical place, can also provide a sense of self-satisfaction. Attaining this "historical superiority" over others, individually or as a group, can improve one's sense of self-worth.

Understanding the pieces of history left behind by the eyewitnesses, then, is not just about how they may have misunderstood or misinterpreted the historical record, but also the psychological and sociological motivations and themes lurking just below the surface. Consider the attachment of sports fans to their local team. The logic applies as follows: I am attached to them. They are my hometown team. They have been successful; therefore I am better than people who root for an unsuccessful team. Even if I never played in a single game or even attended a single contest to cheer them on, they are mine and I am better because of it. This is the same feeling of pride that is expressed when people boast to friends that "Superjock Joe is from my hometown." While the braggart may never have met the famous sports star—or even met anyone who ever met him—just the remote connection of being from the same rough geographical area is a source of pride and self-esteem.

If this sense of connection to an important person, group, or event is strong in regard to something as trivial as the outcome of a football game, it must certainly be a stronger feeling when the fate of a nation hangs on the death struggle between two great armies. To that end, elevating the importance of the event elevates the importance of those attached to it. Saying, "I was in the bleachers when the Mets won the 1969 pennant," then arguing that it was the greatest game ever played, gives one slightly higher social standing for five minutes in a sports bar. Imagine, then, what it must feel like to be able to say, "I was a participant at one of the greatest battles in the history of the world." The glory associated with being the most important player in the victory—or avoiding the label of having been the primary cause of defeat—would certainly be worth fighting for in the postwar literature, and this is just what veterans did. This explains, at least in part, why the participants at Gettysburg began elevating their experience almost immediately. As one veteran predicted shortly after the battle, "our men made a charge that will be the theme of the poet, painter and historian of all ages."[4] In the years that followed, many of these men made sure that art and literature remembered them, and that there would be a large pool of selectively presented historical data from which to draw.

To be fair, the men of both sides who placed the events of early July 1863 on a par with the great historical events of the world did so for many reasons. Perhaps chief among them was their feeling that the great moments of world history provided the only context to which they could compare such an enormous event in their own life experience. But their sense of place in the larger world, and their sense of America's place in the world, was an ever present issue. The Gettysburg story helped bolster their own sense of worth as well. Given this tendency in people, it would be difficult to overrate the importance of the context in which the veterans of Gettysburg wrote.

Americans in the mid-nineteenth century saw their country as a shining new experiment in democracy, superior to the absolutist monarchies of Europe. This form of government was the one clear distinction that set the United States apart from its major European rivals. Seeking to prove their young nation as the equal of the world's powers, Americans found themselves lacking a heroic past and suffering from a collective case of historical inferiority. These were the most literate armies the world had ever known—and many more became educated between the war years and their postwar writing—and literature brought to many of them stories of the greatness of leaders such as Napoleon, Julius Caesar, and Alexander the Great. The more educated veterans of the battle, those most likely to write histories, found in Gettysburg an event—a past—that seemed to fill the void experienced by a nation too young to have accumulated a history. Men of both armies read about world-changing events and longed to be part of something legendary and important. As a result, they elevated their experience at Gettysburg and cluttered their reminiscences with references and comparisons of Gettysburg to great events such as Waterloo, Balaclava, and Canae in an effort to compare their nation and its experiences with older nations. "There never was better fighting since Thermopylae than was done yesterday," one veteran wrote. And another stated, "It will rank with the most celebrated battles of the world." A Philadelphian who fought there later said, "Neither Alexander nor Caesar, Charlemagne nor Frederick, Wellington nor Napoleon ever ordered so hazardous a charge." One war correspondent predicted that the field at Gettysburg would draw travelers as they "now visit Austerlitz, Wagram, Marengo, or Waterloo." Still another, "the celebrated 'charge of the 600' at Balaclava was not more daring than that of the five thousand Virginians who stormed the heights at Gettysburg." In so many words, they were saying, "We are as good as they are." Whether "we" meant the individual, the unit, or the nation as a whole, the intent was the same. To the extent that soldiers and writers could depict Gettysburg as equally important as these famous battles, they could raise their own sense of individual and national identity. As a result, in retelling the story as the years passed, they created a more heroic and legendary context.

In later memoirs, veterans further elevated their personal adventures when remembering the ultimate experience of their lives in the context of the great literary works of history, quoting Victor Hugo, Lord Tennyson, Henry Wadsworth Longfellow, or the Bible when their own words failed to fully explain their feelings. Sometimes openly, but often in more covert ways, these men placed their Gettysburg memories on par with the grandeur of the French Revolution or the Charge of the Light Brigade, rather than the confused and blurry visions they had described in the battle's immediate aftermath. Unwilling to disappoint their audience with the truth—"No one will ever really know what happened here"— they fashioned detailed and appropriately heroic tales for family, friends, and each other in memoirs, magazines, and local newspapers.

These elements of memory, confusion, embellishment, deception, and identity formed the basis of the American mythology of Gettysburg. As a result, a canon of established stories entertains and misinforms readers and visitors alike. Perhaps nowhere is the level of hyperbole and legend building more focused than on the climactic event of the battle, the epic tale that has become known as "Pickett's Charge." In 1997, Professor Carol Reardon of Penn State University began to chip away at this prominent element of Gettysburg mythology with her book, *Pickett's Charge in History and Memory.* Reardon's book points out the "construction" of the story of Pickett's Charge and how, but for a few circumstances here and there, the memory or story could have been dramatically different.[5]

Take, for example, the name itself. General George Pickett commanded only about half of the troops who made the assault. His superior, General Longstreet, designed it and technically served as its overall commander. Fully one half of the troops involved were from other states, but the charge is usually described as an exclusively Virginian affair. The reason for Pickett's fame, Reardon points out, is that both he and his men were from the area of Virginia around Richmond, the media capital of the South. Since much of the news about the war printed in newspapers in all of the Southern states came as "clippings" from the Richmond papers, the interests of Richmond readers naturally dominated. This is a matter that sits sorely with many North Carolinians even today.

Another of Gettysburg's great legends is the story of Wesley Culp. As a young man, Culp was an apprentice carriage maker in Gettysburg who made a relatively short migration down to Virginia before the war. Having joined the local militia there, Culp became a member of the 2nd Virginia Infantry Regiment. Two years later, he and his unit were posted along the Confederate line in Gettysburg at a place called Culp's Hill. It was named for Henry Culp, the farmer who owned it, and it was there that Wesley was presumed killed in battle. With that information as its source, a legend was born. In 1985 the Gettysburg volume of the Time-Life series *The Civil War* demonstrated the power of Gettysburg mythology when it told what had become the popular story of Wesley: "Culp was killed on his father's farm, fighting for the Confederacy."[6] In other variations of the tale, Wesley is said to have died on his uncle's farm. Like so many other Gettysburg myths, this is a truly compelling story—that is simply not true. Wesley's father died years before the war, and he had lived a block from the town square, not on a farm. Wesley was probably killed nearer to Wolf's Hill, and the farmer who owned Culp's Hill was a distant cousin he may scarcely have known. The tale of a young man dying on his father's farm while fighting for the enemy is too good a story to be true, but also too good for many to leave out of the larger battle narrative.

Another of the more dramatic and persistent myths of the Gettysburg story has to do with an encounter between Confederate General John B. Gordon and Union General Francis Barlow on the battle's first day, known as the "Barlow-Gordon incident."

In the 1890s, Gordon published an article entitled "An Incident of Gettysburg" in the *Southern Historical Society Papers*.[7] Then he included the story in his popular circuit lecture that he called "The Last Days of the Confederacy." The incident that Gordon described in the article goes something like this: Gordon came upon the wounded Barlow on the field as his Federal division retreated. Barlow asked Gordon to get word to Barlow's wife that his dying thoughts had been of her. Gordon complied, sending a message via flag of truce to the Federal lines, then had Barlow taken to the shade of a tree. He then returned to the battle believing Barlow would soon be dead. Barlow survived, however, and a year later learned of the death of General J. B. Gordon. Not knowing that this was a relative of the General Gordon he had met at Gettysburg, Barlow assumed his savior, Gordon, was dead. Thirteen years later, while serving as a U.S. senator, he was invited to have dinner with a General Barlow who had served in the Union Army. Each man believed the other was a different person from the one at Gettysburg, and over dinner they learned the truth to their great surprise. Gordon then recited the conversation as if it were verbatim:

> I asked Barlow: "General, are you related to the Barlow who was killed at Gettysburg?" He replied, "Why, I am the man, sir. Are you related to the Gordon who killed me?" "I am the man, sir," I responded. No words of mine can convey any conception of the emotions awakened by those startling announcements. Nothing short of an actual resurrection from the dead could have amazed either of us more. Thenceforward, until his untimely death in 1896, the friendship between us which was born amidst the thunders of Gettysburg was greatly cherished by both."[8]

That story, as related by one of the participants, stood as fact for nearly a century before a historian named William Hannah published his research in an article in 1983. His conclusions appeared in the popular magazine *Civil War Times Illustrated* under the title, "The Barlow-Gordon Incident? The Yank Never Met the Reb: A Gettysburg Myth Exploded." In it Hannah explains, "no accounts of the incident, other than those relying on General Gordon as their primary source, are known to exist."[9] Hannah also points out a number of flaws in Gordon's story, stressing that no corroborating evidence of the event exists.

Following the publication of Hannah's article, most Civil War historians accepted that the Barlow-Gordon incident was a myth—and with good reason. While the only original source of the story is General Gordon, closer examination of the facts reveals that General Barlow never mentioned it at all. In fact, in a letter written to his mother on July 7, 1863, Barlow described the same battlefield moments quite differently and made no mention of Gordon or any Confederate general. "Finally the enemy came up and were very kind, Major Pitzera, Staff officer of Gen. Early had me carried into the woods and placed on a bed of leaves. They put some water by me and then went on to the front again."[10] Surely, if the story rose to the level of "an actual resurrection from the dead," Barlow would have found it worth repeating on any number of occasions. In addition, General Gordon had been carrying on a regular correspondence with his wife around the time of the battle but failed to mention this story in any of his letters. A lengthy examination of these and other sources has convinced most scholars today that the Barlow-Gordon incident is a myth, based in the mind of Gordon rather than on an incident in the field at Gettysburg.

A search for Gordon's motive in concocting the incident must consider that Gordon wrote during a period of national reunion. By the turn of the century, a complex mix of political, social, and economic factors had spurred great reconciliation between the North and South, and this was clearly exhibited in the literature of Civil War veterans. Gordon was a leader in the literary movement that accompanied the reconciliation. Considering his own ambitions and inclinations, as well as the times in which he wrote, it is not surprising that he would offer a touching story of two old foes reunited in a cherished friendship. In addition, or perhaps as a result, Gordon does not enjoy a reputation for veracity. Professor Gallagher said of Gordon, "He sometimes only brushed up against the truth, and then would back away from it instantly."[11]

Despite the dubious basis of the story, many still celebrate the Barlow-Gordon incident at Gettysburg today. In one of the two buildings that the National Park Service uses to greet visitors and interpret the battle there is still a display that uses small figurines to depict and describe the event, even while park rangers and licensed battlefield guides outside the building decry it as myth. Remarkably, the 127th anniversary reenactment of the battle held at Gettysburg in July 2000 included a large-scale recreation—actually the initial creation—of the scene.

Barlow-Gordon is but one of many battle story issues that involve the juxtaposition of two names to label a controversy. Another that tainted the literature was the disagreement between General Winfield S. Hancock, commander of the Union Army Second Corps, and General Henry Hunt, commander of Union artillery at Gettysburg. During the immense Confederate cannonade that preceded Pickett's Charge smoke filled the air and blocked the vision of artillerymen of both sides. As a result, neither side knew whether their fire was having any effect on the enemy. Realizing this, Hunt ordered the Union batteries to cease their return fire and save their ammunition for the infantry charge that always followed such a bombardment. As he rode along the line, General Hancock, with only limited success, tried to order the batteries to open fire again. This confusion in command created a troublesome exchange among the two generals years later.[12]

In the late 1870s, Hunt wrote a letter to a U.S. Senate committee on army reorganization. In it, he described the battle of Gettysburg, including a few instances where the command structure of the artillery was misunderstood by other generals. Specifically, Hancock, who commanded an infantry corps, tried to order the Union artillery to keep firing in the moments leading up to Pickett's Charge, even after Hunt, the army's chief of artillery, had ordered them to cease firing.[13]

Hancock was made aware of Hunt's letter by friends of his in the Senate and took it as a personal assault. In reply, he wrote to William T. Sherman, then General of the Army, who sent it to Secretary of War Robert Todd Lincoln. Lincoln forwarded it to Senator and former General Ambrose Burnside, who had it published as "Senate Miscellaneous Document no. 14, 46th Congress, 1st Session, pages 40–41."[14]

Hunt then penned a lengthy and detailed rebuttal to Hancock's reply and sent it to Sherman. This time, however, the army's commander refused to send it on through channels and instead buried it in the military archives. While this perturbed Hunt greatly, he had two good reasons for not publishing the letter privately. First, the

Democratic Party had just made Hancock its presidential nominee for the coming election, leaving Hunt reticent to raise any thorny issues in a politically charged atmosphere. His second was more forceful, however. At that time, Sherman and Hancock were immediately above Hunt in the army chain of command, a fact that Hunt decided was "a sufficient reason for withholding it."[15]

Nevertheless this is one of many controversies that formed an undercurrent beneath the writings and debates of Union veterans after the war. Whether explicitly stated or not, controversies such as these were ever present in the minds of veterans, and their writings were shaped by them. Whether taking sides in attacking or defending one party or the other, or in carefully avoiding these issues, postwar writers clearly had them in mind when they put pen to paper where Gettysburg was the subject. They have greatly affected the work of historians since then and have helped shape the battle history in significant, though often unnoticed, ways.

At times, the controversies over Gettysburg centered on issues that had no bearing on the outcome but proved to be as contentious as any others. A good example of this is the death of General John F. Reynolds, the first Union corps commander to reach the battlefield on July 1, 1863. While many veterans agreed that Reynolds was knocked dead from his horse by a bullet to the back of his head or neck while he was ordering his men forward, the question of who fired the fatal shot was something that almost no one agreed on.

Perhaps the best insight on the subject came from a Pennsylvanian who was as close as anyone to Confederate General Lewis Armistead when he was mortally wounded at the apex of Pickett's Charge. When asked if he was the man who shot Armistead, Anthony McDermott replied, "That would be impossible for anybody to tell. I fired at him as well as anybody else, but it would be ridiculous for any one person to say who shot him, there were too many shooting at him."[16] Despite this honest assessment from a soldier in a similar situation, the fact that thousands of men were simultaneously firing weapons in Reynolds's immediate and chaotic vicinity did not prevent many from claiming, with certainty, that their bullet was the one that did him in.

Since human nature can hardly credit the death of a general to an act of war as mundane as some random bullet hitting him, the idea that the man who shot Reynolds must have been an expert sharpshooter came quickly to the fore, despite the fact that the soldiers closest to Reynolds when he was hit made no such claim. Little more than twenty-four hours after the incident, correspondent Lorenzo Crouse sent a dispatch to his paper in New York that included the term "sharpshooter." The *New York Times* published the story on July 4. These two factors—the idea that generals must be killed by special shooters and the widespread reporting of the same—created a legend in the literature that lasted for decades.[17]

Referring to his commander as a "shining mark to the enemy's sharp-shooters," Reynolds's aide Captain Joseph G. Rosengarten declared that the general was "struck by a Minnie ball, fired by a sharpshooter hidden in the branches of a tree almost overhead, and killed at once." A letter written by the general's sister four days after his death added some credibility to the overhead theory when she wrote that the bullet struck behind the right ear, traveling downward until it lodged in his chest. Since no autopsy of the general was likely performed, however, this claim presupposes that she had either an amazing knowledge of human anatomy and gunshot wounds, or X-ray vision.[18]

In 1902 a group from Lancaster County, Pennsylvania, happened upon a farmer in Satterwhite, North Carolina, named Benjamin Thorpe with whom they had a friendly and entertaining chat. The Pennsylvanians noticed that Thorpe's demeanor changed considerably when they mentioned their home county. When queried, Thorpe allowed that he had killed General Reynolds at Gettysburg, and had since heard that he was from Lancaster County. Thorpe had ever since felt remorse, especially after he "heard and read of what a great and good man and splendid soldier I had brought to death, I was genuinely sorry. I have been sorry ever since. . . ." According to a story printed in the local newspaper after the visitors returned home, Thorpe was but sixteen years old at Gettysburg and had climbed a cherry tree near a stone house when his captain shouted to him. "Look to your right, at the battery on the hill, there. There's a general, take him!" After taking two shots to find the range, Thorpe fired again at eight hundred yards. "Well done, Thorpe," the captain shouted. "You got him!" Shortly thereafter, Thorpe overheard a Union prisoner describing the death of Reynolds and stating that a sharpshooter must have gotten him at extreme range. The paper failed to report that, at that range, Thorpe's bullet would have had to penetrate a thickly wooded forest lot with a full coat of leaves.[19]

Not long after this article appeared, a story came out of Mt. Airy, North Carolina, that one of the quarry workers producing parts for the Pennsylvania State Monument claimed to be the man who killed Reynolds. According to Frank Wood, a North Carolina private at Gettysburg, he had been separated from his unit in the Railroad Cut and fell in behind a rail fence for protection. Just then he saw a mounted Union officer whose uniform indicated a high rank. Woods aimed, fired, and saw the man fall from his horse. He assumed the man was Reynolds when he began reading stories of the general's death. The story went on to point out that the man was working on the statue of General Reynolds to be placed on that monument, even though it described Wood as a stonecutter whereas the Reynolds statue was cast in bronze.[20]

John Hendrix was an Alabama private who remembered taking a shot that dismounted a Union officer on July 1, sometime before he was taken prisoner by the Yankees with others in his unit. While being marched to the rear, the prisoners heard the story of Reynolds's death to which Hendrix exclaimed: "That was the man I shot!"

Private E. T. Boland was at Hendrix's side during these events and returned to the battlefield years afterward. "I inspected the ground," he recalled, "and I can truthfully say at that spot John Hendrix shot a man off his horse." A third member of the same regiment later lent more credence to the story of Hendrix and Boland. During the fiftieth anniversary of the battle in 1913, W. H. Moon visited the monument that marks the spot where Reynolds fell. "I had been under the impression," he recalled, "that General Reynolds was shot by a Tennessean until I met Captain Simpson of Company F, 13th Alabama, at Gettysburg in 1913, and we went to the Reynolds monument, where he pointed to the place where he and his men were standing when he ordered them to 'shoot the man on the horse' (only about 30 yards distant), which was promptly done . . . I have no doubt of his statement being true."[21]

William J. Robbins, an Alabama veteran and the Confederate member of the Battlefield Commission in the late 1890s, lived in Gettysburg and kept a daily journal of his experiences. In March 1900, he made this entry: "Letters from Maj. Harris and others say the man who killed Gen. Reynolds at G'bg was Saml. J Duke, Co. B, 7th Tenn. Of Archer's Brig. And still lives near Chestnut Mound, Tenn., on the Cumberland river, owns a good farm, and is a quiet and good man and now about sixty-three years old."[22]

Or was it artillery fire? In his official report of the battle, Confederate General Henry Heth claimed that a cannon shot from Pegram's Artillery Battalion did Reynolds in. The commander of the battery concurred, as did the commander of a nearby artillery unit, while a third commander claimed his battery had done the work. Hearing of this last claim, two different cannoneers claimed the credit of having actually fired the shot. One officer of the 1st Tennessee Infantry claimed that the major of his regiment led an "impetuous dash" toward the regiment nearest Reynolds and rifle fire from this action killed the general.[23]

A quiet Tennessee farmer, an Alabama private, a quarry worker or farm owner from North Carolina, a sharpshooter directly above, a piece of shrapnel from a cannon ball or the entire 1st Tennessee Regiment, all killed General Reynolds—or none of them did. They fired from a tree, in line of battle, from an old stone barn or house, or behind a fence in a railroad cut—or all of them. Each of the stories appealed to veterans at one time, though each contains easily deduced reasons for dismissing them.

The death of Reynolds—regardless of who killed him—had little or no effect on the outcome of the battle. But he was the highest ranking Union officer killed in battle during the Civil War, and that made the theoretical soldier who killed him significant in an important way. There is so much literature that struggles over the death of the general that the story, like so many others related to Gettysburg, leaves readers to choose whichever version suits their notions.

The same kinds of circumstances combined to create a mythical explanation of the battle's origin. In fact, the Battle of Gettysburg started where it did because of basic tenets of military behavior. When a Civil War army traveled across the countryside, tens of thousands of men had to find adequate supplies of food and water. This required the various units to spread out, taking slightly different routes in the same general direction. On the march, the head of an army was often twenty or thirty miles—a full day's march—away from its tail, making its separated parts highly vulnerable to attack by a concentrated enemy force. Traveling in this fashion, armies and their commanders often were not completely aware of the enemy's strength or positions. Since the army that concentrated the most men sooner at the area of the fight won most battles, it was imperative that the army always be poised to unify itself at the first sign of contact with the enemy. On the morning of July 1, 1863, a small group of Union cavalrymen fired a few shots at an unsuspecting group of Confederate infantrymen, and both armies began racing to the scene, which happened to be a town called Gettysburg, Pennsylvania. If the experience of Gettysburg is elevated to legendary proportions, however, the spark that ignited the fight cannot be as mundane as happenstance and simple military behavior. Accordingly, a more interesting, if mythological, story arose to explain why Gettysburg became the scene of the conflict.

The various commanders of Confederate forces on the march in Pennsylvania during late June 1863 had a clear order from Robert E. Lee not to bring on a general engagement. This would be too risky because he did not know the whereabouts of the entire Union force. On July 1, General Henry Heth did what he was ordered not to do and triggered the largest battle ever fought in North America. Ten weeks after the battle, in the course of explaining why he had violated Lee's order, Heth wrote: "On the morning of June 30, I ordered Brigadier-General Pettigrew to take his brigade to Gettysburg, search the town for army supplies (shoes especially), and return the same day."[24]

Although this statement refers to the day *before* the battle began, not the day the shooting started, it has become the foundation of a myth about why the fighting opened on July 1. As time passed and legends flourished, others distorted Heth's comment until the understood reason for the collision of the two great armies was the search for a well-known shoe factory in Gettysburg.

This myth building persists despite its having no basis in fact. A cursory look at readily available census records reveals that Gettysburg had but a handful of cobblers; the town was known for making carriages, not shoes. Perpetuators of this myth also ignore the fact that Confederate troops had raided the town four days earlier, held it for a ransom that included 1,500 pairs of shoes, and left without any. From General Heth's solitary statement that he was low on supplies ("shoes especially") Gettysburg became, in legend at least, a shoe-making hamlet with a large factory, warehouse, or just a big pile of shoes, depending on the account. Few Civil War myths have been more persistently repeated than the Gettysburg shoe myth.

In 1997, for example, in the pages of the *American Podiatric Medical Association News,* a president emeritus of the group advised a regular columnist who made this statement.

Did you know that the greatest and bloodiest battle of the Civil War was fought over shoes? It is well documented that the Battle of Gettysburg developed because the Southern forces of General Robert E. Lee badly needed shoes. There was a warehouse full of boots and shoes in the town.[25]

The very next edition of the newsletter of Chicago's Scholl College of Podiatric Medicine included an article titled "Battle for Boots." The author advised that "according to Civil War historian Shelby Foote, the greatest battle ever fought on the North American continent began as a clash over shoes."[26]

As a result of these minor articles, an army of foot doctors, their spouses, children, nurses, and associates may be perpetuating a myth at cocktail parties, coffee breaks, and conventions around the country. They repeat the story because it makes them feel just a little bit better about the importance of their profession, through its *perceived* connection to the past.

Newer Gettysburg myths seem to have no basis in the veterans' stories at all. For example, millions of Americans believe that 50,000 men died at Gettysburg, a larger loss of American life than in the Vietnam War. In fact, approximately 10,000 men died at Gettysburg, less than one-fifth the number killed in Vietnam.[27] This misapprehension is attributable in part to Ted Turner. In 1994, as part of the television debut of the movie *Gettysburg* (which Turner financed), he broadcast his own commentary on the film and the story. He stated that more men died at Gettysburg than in the entire Vietnam War. A television audience of approximately 40 million viewers heard this statement. Turner's company perpetuated the misstatement on the packaging for the home video of the film, proclaiming to all who bought or rented the video that "when it was all over, 50,000 men had paid the ultimate price."[28]

Given the flawed memories of thousands of veterans and their complex web of communicating ideas and forming various versions of the battle story, mistaken tales, myths, and legends were virtually inevitable. Blended with the cultural issues of the time in which many of the veterans wrote their more eloquent accounts—national reunion, Lost Cause mythology, and the like—the Gettysburg veterans established a huge body of literature from which future historians could mine and draw conclusions. Failing to adequately seek these underlying themes and processes, many historians perpetuated the legends and myths until they became a permanent part of the American cultural fabric. Society can and does call on them whenever a particular theme or idea needs some historical background to shore up a modern message.

When a Yankee politician seeks support from southern voters, he can call on the theme of national reunion to those for whom the war seems ever present. When a southerner seeks to explain the loss of the Civil War, she can summon the mythical shoe factory and the image of barefoot Confederate soldiers, struggling on despite their utter lack of supplies and equipment at Gettysburg. When a television network wants higher ratings for its Gettysburg-based movie, it can summon the myth that five times more men died in the battle than actually did die. All of these are supported by decades of misunderstanding as to what really happened at Gettysburg. Those who use these myths may not even be aware of their complicity—so deeply have these tales become ingrained in our national heritage. They are accepted as part of our collective past, part of what made us who we are as a nation, part of what we need to believe about ourselves at various times in our present. Yet it is from this mass of misunderstood data, backed by a need to see ourselves in a certain way, that we as a nation have arrived at what most people think of as the story of Gettysburg.

CHAPTER 4

RASCALITY AND STUPIDITY

A pretty team!—Rascality and Stupidity. I wonder which hatches the most monstrous chicken.
CHARLES WAINWRIGHT[1]

Among the many struggles over the memory of Gettysburg, one of the most aggressively perpetrated was the concerted effort of General Daniel E. Sickles to save his own reputation at the expense of his commanding general, George G. Meade. His work to shape the history of Gettysburg began less than forty-eight hours after the battle when he expressed his opinion into the ear of Abraham Lincoln.

This struggle began on July 2, the day Sickles "lost" his leg during the battle. Although his limb was largely torn from his body below the knee by a Rebel shell and amputated shortly thereafter, to say it was lost is not accurate. Sickles kept track of the shattered appendage and later had it boiled down to the bone, placed in a small coffin, and shipped to the U.S. Army Medical Museum in Washington where he paid an occasional visit to his lost leg in the years afterward. That alone reveals something about the kind of person that was Dan Sickles.

A product of the rough-and-tumble world of New York's Tammany Hall, Sickles was once a shining star in the Democratic Party. Considered brilliant and despicable in equal measure, he was elected to Congress in

1856 despite the feeling of many, as summed up in George Templeton Strong's diary, that he was "one of the bigger bubbles in the scum of the [legal] profession, swollen and windy, and puffed out with fetid gas."[2] He had yet to complete a first term in Washington when his star-shot career crashed abruptly. He murdered, in cold blood, the son of Francis Scott Key in a park across from the White House. Philip Barton Key was the long-rumored paramour of Sickles's young wife, Teresa. Although the Congressman's chronic infidelity to her was well-known, he could not tolerate the same behavior in return. Finding his ego too traumatized to ignore the affair and his courage insufficient to settle the matter in the proper manner of the day—a duel—Sickles simply walked up to Key and fired three times, the third shot hitting him as he lay prostrate on the sidewalk. Within months, however, Sickles was back at his post in Congress, having become the first legal defendant in the United States to offer the plea of temporary insanity and the first to be acquitted.[3]

Despite the shame normally attributed to such scandalous behavior, Sickles seemed to prosper. With the help of friends, a little skullduggery, and his inexhaustible energy, he managed to raise an entire brigade and then persuaded the government to place him in charge of it as a brigadier general. By the time the army reached Gettysburg two years later, he had risen to command of the entire Third Army Corps, some 12,000 men.[4]

Sickles and his men arrived on the field during the chaotic evening of July 1 while Union forces attempted to rally on Cemetery Hill, having sustained a severe blow from the enemy during the day. By morning General Meade ordered him to place his Corps so as to extend the line of the Second Corps south along Cemetery Ridge, and this is where the trouble began. As the morning progressed, Sickles was having a sobering case of déjà vu.

At the Battle of Chancellorsville two months prior, his corps had been ordered from higher ground to lower in a place called Hazel Grove. The move to a poorer military position had cost them deeply and as Sickles surveyed his portion of the line along the ridge at Gettysburg, he recognized the same peril. Complying with Meade's order meant he would occupy the lowest portion of the ridge. Worse, several hundred yards in front of him lay a higher ridge from which the Confederates could make him suffer in an all too familiar manner. For the rest of the day messengers traveled back and forth from Meade's headquarters without, at least as Sickles saw it, clarifying the situation. So, by midafternoon, the impulsive New Yorker, without so much as notifying Meade in advance, took it upon himself to move his entire corps forward to the higher ridgeline. Despite the increased height, this was an atrocious military position, his corps bent back in a salient and covering far more ground than there were men to do it with. By the time Meade could ride out there, aghast at the implications, Confederate shells were raining down and it was too late to do anything but throw men and cannons into the area to save the army from Sickles's blunder. One of those shells eventually struck Sickles just below the knee and he was carried from the field, but not until he had lit a cigar and affected a look of defiance for his men.

Responding to the emergency, General Meade sent the entire Fifth Army Corps and parts of the Second and Sixth along with the reserve artillery to fill the many breaches in Sickles's new line. These areas became so well known to veterans that they needed only capitalize a "The" before their names for immediate recognition. The Peach Orchard crowned the summit of the higher ridge, while fighting raged back and forth across The Wheat Field toward The Valley of Death and The Devil's Den. By nightfall, the Union line had fallen back to Sickles's original position with grievous losses, but not before halting the Confederate assault.

As his ambulance party carried the now one-legged general to Washington, he had ample opportunity to ponder the long-term consequences of his actions. Meade had been furious at him when he reached the adjusted line under Rebel cannon fire. In light of the 4,000 casualties in the Third Corps alone, Meade would surely take Sickles to task in his report, if not a formal court martial. Understanding that the best way to counter Meade's impending attack was to strike first, he plotted while he convalesced.

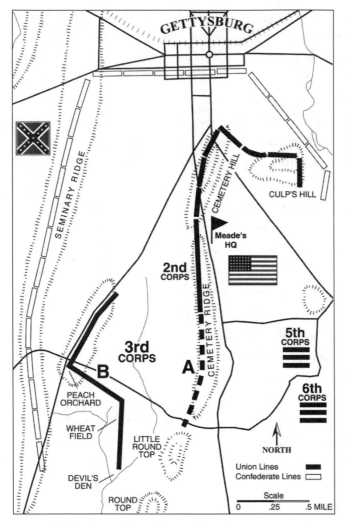

GETTYSBURG

SEMINARY RIDGE

CEMETERY HILL

CULP'S HILL

Meade's HQ

2nd CORPS

CEMETERY RIDGE

5th CORPS

3rd CORPS

A

6th CORPS

B

PEACH ORCHARD

WHEAT FIELD

LITTLE ROUND TOP

NORTH

DEVIL'S DEN

Union Lines
Confederate Lines

ROUND TOP

Scale

0   .25   .5 MILE

MAP 4.1

General Sickles'
Movement Forward

Without notifying General Meade, Sickles moved the Third Corps from its lower position along Cemetery Ridge (A) to a bent line (salient) as much as three-quarters of a mile closer to the enemy (B). Though one of his stated reasons for the move was that he could not hold the original position with the number of men he had, the new position made his line substantially longer. Before Meade could bring Sickles's men back to the line intended, the Confederate assault on the Union had begun. To compensate, Meade sent portions of the Second, Fifth, and Sixth Army Corps to support Sickles's line as it crumbled. Eventually, the Union forces held off the assault back at the original Third Corps line (A) that now extended to cover the Round Tops. As a result, the heaviest fighting of the battle took place in the area between the two Third Corps positions.

Though his leg had escaped him, neither Sickles's energy nor his cunning had, and he quickly put both of them to work in defense of his reputation.

No sooner had he arrived in Washington than the famous battle casualty began to tell his side of the story to everyone who would listen. Fortunately for Sickles, this was the nation's capital and he was a well-connected and politically talented fellow. The opportunity to get an eyewitness account of the great battle to the north—news of which had only begun to dribble in, and most of that was rumor—brought many a powerful visitor to Sickles's bed. Most prominently, a mere seventy-two hours after stretcher bearers had carried him from the field, the wounded general received a visit from his commander in chief.

Outside of hastily written dispatches from the field, this was the first account of the battle that a very anxious President Lincoln heard, and he undoubtedly hung on Sickles's every word. How well had the Federals fought? How badly was Lee's army hurt? And what of his newest army commander? Had he handled the army well? Would he pursue and crush the Rebels? All of these questions must have weighed heavily on the president's troubled mind.

As this was an informal visit between friends, there is no written record of the conversation. However, the Third Corps quartermaster was present and recalled that Sickles "certainly got his side of the Gettysburg story well into the President's mind."[5] It was not the last time that the two met in the days following the battle, and Sickles adeptly crafted his attack on General Meade in subtle but effective ways. As he grew stronger in the months that followed, Sickles continued to preach his gospel and preemptively defend his actions at Gettysburg at the expense of his commanding general. While Meade was still off fighting the war—and with apparently no intention of laying blame at the foot of the wounded corps commander—Sickles was in Washington spreading "his side" of events to anyone who would listen, particularly Abraham Lincoln.

In October, Meade submitted his official report on the battle and later admitted that he truly believed Sickles's move had resulted from a misunderstanding of his orders, something for which either general could accept some blame. It certainly did not warrant the destruction of anyone's reputation or military career. His report concluded that the Third Corps commander, "not fully apprehending the instructions in regard to the position to be occupied, had advanced, or rather was in the act of advancing, his corps some half a mile or three-quarters of a mile in front of the line of the Second Corps."[6]

On October 18, Sickles visited Meade in Virginia to ask for his old position back at the head of the Third Corps and was angered when Meade refused, citing the long convalescence of a Confederate general with a similar wound.[7] Rebuffed, Sickles went straight to the president.

Navy Secretary Gideon Welles paid a call on Lincoln at the White House two days later and recorded in his diary, "I met General Sickles at the President's today." Lincoln's anger and public reprimand of General Meade for failing to pursue and crush Lee's army after Gettysburg was well-known to everyone in Washington including Sickles, who used the president's ire to his advantage. As Welles recalled, Sickles painted Meade as a man reluctant to fight at all. Describing the events of the confused evening of July 1 at Gettysburg, Sickles told Lincoln that "General Meade arrived on the ground soon after and was for abandoning the position and falling back. A council was called. Meade was in earnest; Sickles left, but wrote Meade his decided opinion in favor of maintaining the position, which was finally agreed to against Meade's judgment."[8]

The day after Lincoln spoke at the dedication of the Soldiers National Cemetery at Gettysburg, General Henry Halleck, general in chief of all Union armies, issued his official report of the Battle of Gettysburg. Though basing his own report on that of General Meade, Halleck was far more harsh in his criticism, writing that "General Sickles, misunderstanding his orders, instead of placing the Third Corps on the prolongation of the Second, had moved it nearly three-quarters of a mile in advance—an error which nearly proved fatal in battle."[9]

At this, Sickles was wild, and echoes of his anger reverberated all the way down to the warfront. Back in the army, word of the shenanigans in Washington began to circulate through camp. A week before Christmas, General Marsena R. Patrick, the provost marshal general for the Army of the Potomac, confided to his diary that "Col. Sharpe came down [from D.C.] yesterday . . . He tells me that Sickles openly announces his intention to fight the battle with Halleck, who has made more serious and damaging charges against him than Meade did."[10]

Through all his entanglements and difficulties, fortune had always offered a ready smile for Dan Sickles and it did not fail him now. In order to wage a war to save his own reputation, and by necessity attack Meade as at least a collateral casualty, he needed the right battleground, one that would loudly record his version of events, one with great authority and controlled by willing accomplices. In his search he needed only look as far as Capitol Hill. There he found the Joint Congressional Committee on the Conduct of the War, a panel of three senators and four congressmen, dominated by Senators Benjamin Wade and Zachariah Chandler, both Republicans of a decidedly radical slant.

The Radicals of the Civil War Congress were a fierce and vengeful lot, being as antislavery, anti-South, and anti-Democrat as they could be. Eventually they called for the head of President Andrew Johnson and very nearly got it, but for now they occupied their time attacking any politician or general who did not subscribe to their vehement anti-Confederate stance. The chairman of this joint committee was Ohio Senator Benjamin Franklin Wade, whom James Garfield once called "a man of violent passions, extreme opinions, and narrow views . . . [with] a grossly profane coarse nature who is surrounded by the worst and most violent elements in the Republican Party."[11] Though Sickles was a Democrat, he was more than willing to use the committee as a platform for his campaign against Meade. Likewise, Wade and his committee saw their new strange bedfellow as a useful tool for their own work. To them Meade's ascension to army command was an abomination. The new commander was a friend

of General George B. McClellan, a Democrat and previous army commander who had failed to conquer the South, perhaps out of sympathy.
Meade had replaced Fighting Joe Hooker, whom the committee favored
highly, and any opportunity to damage Meade was a plus for their radical
desires. In late February, Sickles had an opportunity to publicly state his
case for the record and, playing on President Lincoln's well-known anger
at Meade's refusal to pursue Lee after Gettysburg, he painted Meade as a
general who shirked from a fight.

Prior to the outbreak of fighting at Gettysburg, General Meade had
prepared plans for a battle line along Pipe Creek several miles south of
Gettysburg in northern Maryland. Along this defensive line, Meade
hoped to tempt the Confederates into attacking him in a situation much
more favorable to the Union. He saw the army's movement into Maryland as a means to defend Washington and Baltimore from the invading
Rebels. Since his army was well between Lee and these important cities,
he had accomplished this purpose and would wait to fight Lee until he
could gain every advantage. To this end he sent a circular to his corps
commanders explaining the move and informing each of their part in it.
Sickles presented the circular to the committee while slanting Meade's
cautious steps as a desire to avoid a battle, frequently using a less flattering word to describe Meade's proposed movement to Pipe Creek. "The
circular," he said, "indicated a line of retreat."

Having painted Meade with a yellow stroke, Sickles then took credit
for choosing the battlefield at Gettysburg. Arriving on the field during
the evening of July 1 and surveying it, he said, "I addressed a written
communication to general Meade begging him by all means to concentrate his army there and fight a battle." To hear Sickles describe it,
Meade reluctantly acquiesced and ordered the army to come together at
Gettysburg. Despite this, Sickles continued, Meade was still in no fighting mood on July 2. "I have reason to know that his plan of operations
was changed again on Thursday [July 2] and that he resumed, in sub-
stance, the plan that he had on Wednesday morning, which was to fall

back. . . ."[12] Finally, offering a summary of the situation at army head-quarters just prior to his move forward on July 2, he testified, "I was sat-isfied, from the information which I received, that it was intended to retreat from Gettysburg."[13]

There it was. Not only should the country not look poorly on Sickles's decision to move his corps forward without the knowledge or orders of his commander, but it owed him a debt of gratitude for dissuading Meade against retreating and forcing him to fight at the favorable position at Gettysburg. Having given his testimony before the committee, Sickles now needed to find ways to support it, and he soon found a willing aide inside the army.

Abner Doubleday replaced John F. Reynolds at the head of the First Army Corps at Gettysburg when a bullet ended Reynolds's life. Shortly after Gettysburg, however, he became a general without a command when Meade removed him as commander of the First Corps in favor of a less senior officer. This, along with an errant belief that Meade was part of a plot in the army, made him a willing participant in Sickles's theater.

While Doubleday testified that he did not know of a retreat order, he attacked Meade personally, feeding into the committee's distrust. First, he attacked Meade's right to appoint officers as he saw fit. "General Meade is in the habit of violating the organic law of the army to place his personal friends in power. There has always been a great deal of favoritism in the Army of the Potomac." Then he made a statement that must have brought the committee Radicals out of their chairs with excitement. "No man who is an anti-slavery man or an anti-McClellan man can expect decent treatment in that army as at present constituted." Tainted though it was, this kind of testimony was just the ammunition the committee needed against Meade.[14]

Doubleday later regretted his statements before the committee citing a plot he perceived within the army to promote those sympathetic to Gen-eral McClellan. He admitted that "believing Gen. Meade to be a party to this arrangement, I thought he intended to carry out this policy, and testified accordingly. I afterward ascertained that I was mistaken in this respect."[15] In addition to the plot, Doubleday's testimony was driven by what he saw as a personal affront. Meade had replaced him after Gettysburg, not on personal grounds but rather in response to reports from both General Howard and General Hancock on the evening of the first day of battle that "Doubleday's command gave way."[16] Doubleday discovered this information nearly two decades after his appearance before the committee, and with this new information in hand, he publicly stated, "I freely admit that I was unnecessarily harsh in my language at that time."[17] While these admissions are admirable, they came long after the course of history had been set and the anti-Meade elements of the story well entrenched in the literature.

Following Doubleday, the next committee witness was Albion Howe, who commanded a division of the Sixth Corps at Gettysburg and was barely engaged in the fighting. Howe contributed to the committee's arsenal by saying that Meade lacked an "earnestness of purpose," was a McClellan sympathizer, and did not have the confidence of the rank and file of the army.[18]

This was all the ammunition the committee felt it needed. On March 3, 1864, Senators Wade and Chandler headed down Pennsylvania Avenue to pay a call on President Lincoln and Secretary of War Stanton. They had every reason to expect an attentive ear in these two, since Sickles had been whispering his tale to Lincoln for months and Stanton had served as Sickles's defense attorney in 1859, when the two successfully pulled off the first "temporary insanity" defense.[19]

The next day, Chairman Wade ordered the committee's stenographer to record that he and Chandler had made a call on President Lincoln and his war Secretary to demand Meade's removal, "having been impressed with the exceeding importance of the testimony taken . . . more especially in relation to the incompetency of the general in command . . . in behalf of the army and of the country. . . ."[20] That same day, George Meade arrived in Washington "greatly surprised to find the whole town talking of certain grave charges of Generals Sickles and Doubleday."[21]

Meade did not let an entire day pass before he testified, at his own request, before the committee. He later wrote to his wife that Senator Wade was the only member present at the hearing and that Wade's demeanor gave Meade no reason to suspect his intentions. But just twenty-four hours after entering into the *Congressional Record* his assertion to the commander in chief that Meade was incompetent and must be removed, Wade told the commanding general that no one had made any charges against him. The committee, Wade assured him, was only collecting information for a "sort of history of the war."[22]

After testifying, Meade went to Secretary Stanton, who gave him the whole story, including Sickles's role as its driving force. Meade now had to face the reality that in the eight months since Gettysburg, while he had been off fighting the war, Dan Sickles had focused his boundless energy on a plot to save his own reputation at the expense of his former commander.

Though word of the plot had originally been slow to reach Meade, it was now so far in the open that it quickly reached the army in Virginia. Shortly after Meade reached the Capitol, an artillery officer in the field pondered in his diary, "The New York Times says that General Meade has been summoned to Washington to answer charges brought against him before the Committee on the Conduct of the War about Gettysburg, by Sickles and Doubleday. A pretty team!—Rascality and Stupidity. I wonder which hatches the most monstrous chicken."[23] Had Wainwright asked himself the same question a week later, he would surely have concluded that Sickles did the hatching.

The very day Meade testified a second time before the committee—it was March 11—adding more evidence to his defense, a letter appeared at the office of the *New York Herald* that the editor gladly published the following morning. Atop the letter he printed the wordy headline "The Battle of Gettysburg—Important Communication From an Eye-Witness—How

the Victory Was Won and How its Advantages Were Lost—Generals Halleck's and Meade's Official Reports Refuted, etc." The letter ended with a
single word in lieu of the author's signature. It read simply, "Historicus."[24]

Anonymous though it may have seemed to many readers, George G.
Meade, among others, had no doubt that the letter came from Dan Sickles. As he had avoided a duel with his wife's lover five years previous,
Sickles, they surmised, now dodged an open confrontation with Meade
by hiding behind a pen name. Meade was furious. The letter furthered the
claims that the one-legged general had made before the committee,
including Meade's unwillingness to fight, and gave all of the credit for
victory to Sickles's Third Corps.

From Virginia Meade sent a copy of the article to the War Department,
stating "I cannot resist the belief that this letter was either written or dictated by Maj. Gen. D.E. Sickles."[25] He requested a court of inquiry or
some other official venue in which he could defend himself. Halleck
agreed that Sickles was the culprit but advised Meade to let the matter
drop, saying "you will not be able to fix on him the authorship, and nothing would suit him better than to get you into a personal or newspaper
controversy. He would there be perfectly at home, and, with his facilities
for controlling or giving color to the New York press, would have greatly
the advantage."[26]

Lincoln agreed, or at least he preferred that his commanding general
did his fighting in the field against the enemy rather than in a courtroom
against Sickles. "The country knows that at all events you have done good
service," he assured Meade, "and I believe it agrees with me that it is
much better for you to be engaged in trying to do more than to be
diverted."[27]

Ever the good soldier, Meade accepted the judgment of his superiors.
"I am not as philosophical as you are," he wrote Halleck in reply, "nor do I
consider it good policy to permit such slanders as have been circulated to
pass entirely unnoticed . . . if you and the Secretary think it better policy
for me to keep quiet, I will withdraw the letter I have written, or remain

satisfied with an official reply that the Department cannot interfere or take action on an anonymous communication."[28]

If he could not have it out in a public forum against Sickles, Meade must have taken some solace in the responses of friends and colleagues to Historicus. Within about two weeks several letters appeared in the *New York Herald* firing back at the charges leveled in the press. Letters signed by "Another Eye Witness," and "Staff Officer of the Fifth Corps" appeared before anyone actually used his real name in print. In an article titled "The Battle of Gettysburg" General James Barnes, who commanded a division of the Fifth Corps at Gettysburg that rescued Sickles on the field, entered the fray.[29]

Historicus raised Barnes's dander by stating outright that his division had collapsed and only a quick-thinking Sickles prevented the demise of the entire line when Barnes declined to do so. As Historicus's letter described it, "An alarming incident, however, occurred. Barnes's division, of the Fifth Corps, suddenly gave way; and Sickles, seeing this, put a battery in position to check the enemy if he broke through this gap on our front, and General Birney was sent to order Barnes back into line. 'No.' he [Barnes] said; 'impossible. It is too hot. My men cannot stand it.'" Historicus went on to say that Sickles sent for other troops under General Zook instead, and Barnes then got in the way of this relief. Historicus continued: "When they reached the ground, Barnes' disordered troops impeded the advance of the brigade. 'If you can't get out of the way,' cried Zook, 'lie down, and I will march over you.' Barnes ordered his men to lie down, and the chivalrous Zook and his splendid brigade . . . did march over them and right into the breach."[30]

In a reply to Historicus headlined "The Battle of Gettysburg" in the *Herald*, Barnes denied the description in brief yet forceful language.

All this is pure invention. No such occurrence as is here related took place. There is not a particle of truth in it. No order was given to me by General Birney. None was received by me through any one from General

Sickles. I did not see or hear from General Zook. I did not meet him in any way. I did not know he was there, and the article above referred to is the first intimation that I have had that any one pretended that any such event took place.[31]

As for the Historicus letter as a whole, Barnes was quite professional in his dismissal of it, saying, "So far as I am able to judge, and I saw something of the movements of that day, I think it filled with errors, detracting from the merits of some and exalting the moderate claims of others to a ridiculous excess."[32]

The following day the *Herald* published a letter that Colonel Tilton had written to General Barnes a week earlier. Tilton described the credit given to Sickles as "sickening" and wrote that "had Sickles' orders to some of Sykes [Fifth Corps] Brigade Commanders been obeyed, the rebels would surely have had both Round Tops early in the fight." In addition, he said that Historicus had it backward. Sickles's Third Corps, not Barnes's Fifth Corps, had fled. "I had men injured too by being jumped upon by fleeing Third Corps men as we lay behind a stone wall."[33]

In an edition of the *Herald* published a few weeks later, Historicus replied to the group of Meade defenders making small points here and there in the debate before he lashed out again at Meade. The testimony before the committee, he said, "is known to be so ruinous to the Commander of the Army of the Potomac that it will be a singular indifference to public opinion on the part of the government if he is allowed to remain longer in that important post."[34]

While this war of words flared across the pages of the *Herald*, testimony before the Committee on the Conduct of the War continued as well, and there is no doubt that Dan Sickles was pulling at least some of the strings. Early in the committee's testimony gathering, Sickles corresponded with General Dan Butterfield, who had been Meade's chief of staff at Gettysburg. Meade inherited Butterfield at that post when he took command of the army and retained him to reduce the confusion that would naturally follow a change of army commander so close to a major battle. Since the Gettysburg battle—in which Butterfield was wounded—Meade had chosen to replace him, and he was now serving as a division commander in the Western Theater of the war in Tennessee, a step or two down in prestige. As a result, his mood hardly favored Meade and this made him a valuable ally in Sickles's plotting. At Sickles's request, Butterfield came to Washington without the permission of the War Department, and Sickles now sought to put him before the committee. A private letter to Senator Chandler demonstrated how firmly Sickles's fingers plied the puppet strings of the situation, using the committee to his own scheming ends.

(Private) My dear Senator:

Butterfield is at Willards—He has not received permission from Genl. Halleck to come here and apprehends it will be refused— Allow me to suggest that, as in Birneys Case, he be subpoenaed regularly—He comes now only by *request* from Senator Wade.

It is very important that you have Brig. Genl S. Williams Ast. Adjt. Genl Army of the Potomac here *with all orders and communications* bearing on the Gettysburg campaign—original drafts and Copies as received at Headquarters—this is *all important* for you to have before you *when Butterfield is examined*—Then you will get the *real history* of the Campaign.

Truly Yours
Sickles[35]

Sickles's biographer W. A. Swanberg later assessed this letter and its underlying meaning when he wrote, "So Butterfield was regarded as such a vital witness that he sneaked into town secretly and special steps had to be taken to make his appearance there within regulations. All this has the conspiratorial air of low-grade melodrama. And Butterfield, when he appeared as a witness proved to be the biggest blunderbuss aimed at Meade's head."[36]

Butterfield painted Meade as hesitant and far from forcefully in control of events with no plan for the campaign save Hooker's original strategy that Butterfield provided him. Recalling Meade's original plan to organize the army around Pipe Creek and await a Confederate attack, Butterfield, like Sickles before him, depicted Meade as wanting to withdraw from Gettysburg. "General Meade," he testified, "then directed me to prepare an order to withdraw the army from that position." He further implied that Meade intended to retreat from Gettysburg as late as the morning and again on the evening of July 2 but that Confederate attacks prevented him from doing so.[37]

On the heels of this latest damning testimony, Meade returned again to Washington to defend himself before the committee, but it was effort wasted. The committee heard testimony well into April, recording the opinions of eighteen generals who provided 229 pages of testimony. While they held off formal publication of their report and its damning testimony until the war ended, their work had its effect on Meade's reputation long before it reached print.[38]

Throughout the Meade-Sickles controversy the key players in the drama were well aware of the stakes involved, which had nothing to do with winning the war against the South. From the moment Sickles formulated his defense and passed it to the ear of President Lincoln, until the committee ended its inquisition and moved on to other radical issues, this was a battle for the opinion of future generations—a struggle over history and memory.

George Meade claimed that he found solace "in the firm conviction that the day will come when the secrets of all men will become known. . . ."[39] While Meade placed his faith in facts, however, Dan Sickles knew better. He understood that the facts of history are malleable and subject to the influence of those who seek to shape them. Those who took Meade's passive approach to the record of the past were doomed to fall under its shadow, while those who worked tirelessly to shape history to their advantage found their image cast in the warm glow of fame. To the extent that Sickles may be remembered as an able commander on the battlefield, this reputation, as one New York paper described it, had little to do with what he actually did on the field. With the committee still in its early stages back in 1864, New York's *Round Table* assessed Sickles's skills: "We know that he has accomplished more by personal address, adroitness and cunning management of the newspaper correspondents, than by actual display of military ability."[40]

In his letter to the *New York Herald* the "Staff officer of the Fifth Corps" pointed out that Historicus's letter was "manifestly intended to create public opinion," and nearly a century later, Sickles biographer W. A. Swanberg understood that this battle was over how the future would view Sickles's version of the Gettysburg story. "Historicus was intent on getting his particular propaganda before the public as strongly as possible, well knowing that many undiscerning readers would accept it as fact."[41]

IN A LETTER DISCUSSING THE GROWING LEGEND of Custer's fight at Little Big Horn, Gettysburg veteran Robert G. Carter warned a friend about the fallibility of history. "It is perpetuating that kind of history (his—story) which, in my judgment ought to be corrected *now*, for probably no one will ever write it up again for future generations."[42]

This warning grew from a lesson Carter learned while observing the Meade-Sickles controversy. As late as 1925, though he mistakenly blamed Gettysburg historian John B. Bachelder for the Historicus letters, he still remembered it.

> The same applies to Waterloo, Gettysburg, and other great battles, much of the history of which—to my own knowledge—has been the purest *bunk*. Sickles should have been tried for advancing and posting his Corps

in a false position in disobedience of General Meade's orders on the field, thereby jeopardizing our left on July 2, 1863, and he probably would have been if he had not lost his leg. But John Bachelder, a loud-mouthed, blatant photographer, artist at Sickles' headquarters, and *henchman* of Sickles, made the people believe by an avalanche of propaganda that Sickles held back Longstreet, and all *writers began to believe it* and praised Sickles' act. They know better now and that part of the battle of Gettysburg has been corrected.[43]

While Robert Carter's belief that a few people and an avalanche of propaganda can rewrite history may be at least partly true, his conclusion that the story of Gettysburg was ever truly corrected in regard to General Meade may have been a bit hasty. A later historian summed up the controversy by saying, "The committee, with the aid of General Historicus and other interested parties, had laid down a blistering barrage of whispers, rumors, newspaper publicity, and weighted testimony, all aimed at the head of General Meade. The question was, would they get their man?"[44]

In the short term, they did not, as Lincoln refused to remove Meade as commander of the Army of the Potomac. But Robert G. Carter's belief that "that part of the battle of Gettysburg has been corrected," was premature. The Sickles controversy affected popular history for decades afterward. Edwin Coddington, among the most respected of all Gettysburg historians, believed that the study of the battle would be forever troubled because "an abundance of polemical tracts furiously attacking and defending Meade's record at Gettysburg have cluttered up the literature of the battle."[45] One particular example, among countless others, helps illustrate this process.

Nineteen years after the end of testimony before the committee, Abner Doubleday, who had been its second witness and one of the most damning, explained how and why he erred in criticizing Meade and contributing to the agendas of both Dan Sickles and the Radical Republicans.

I freely admit that I was unnecessarily harsh in my language at that time. The fact is, that just before the battle of Gettysburg I was applied to by an officer of high rank, a confidential friend of Gen. Meade, to give him a list of such officers of my division as had made strong demonstrations when Gen. McClellan was removed from command. The object of the inquiry was to promote these men over the heads of others equally deserving. I looked upon this as a plot to change the army of the Union into a partisan force, which was to become the personal appanage of an individual. Believing Gen. Meade to be a party to this arrangement, I thought he intended to carry out this policy, and testified accordingly. I afterward ascertained that I was mistaken in this respect; that he had no intention of reorganizing the army in the interest of Gen. McClellan.[46]

Two decades after his testimony as the second witness before the congressional committee gave Meade's enemies all they needed to demand that Lincoln remove him, Doubleday realized that he had been mistaken, and he regretted it. For nineteen years his testimony and its damning charges existed as part of the Gettysburg literature, affecting the accounts of others and shaping the history to Meade's detriment. Eleven years had passed since Meade's death in 1872 and only now did Doubleday explain that his statements were tainted and based on a complete misunderstanding of Meade's motives, long after the damage had been done both to Meade and to the historical record. Nearly twenty years after the controversy began, Charles Wainwright's early assessment now seemed a premonition. Dan Sickles's rascality used Abner Doubleday's stupidity to hatch a monstrous chicken that helped Sickles escape the blame for his blunder at the cost of Meade's place in history.

Two other important factors greatly diminished the credit that George Meade received for his work at Gettysburg. The first was the arrival of Ulysses S. Grant in the eastern theater of the war. In addition to its position as the population hub of the nation, the East held the dominant media center for each of the contesting sides—New York and Richmond fairly controlled the information that reached the public mind in their respective regions. In the many years that have passed since the Civil War ended, the eastern theater has received a highly disproportionate share of the attention. Consequently, when President Lincoln made General Grant commander of all Union armies and Grant chose to travel with the Army of the Potomac in the East, his presence cast an enormous shadow over George Meade. Though Meade remained commander of the army he had led since Gettysburg, General Grant's presence in the field as his overall superior, with his headquarters often less than a mile from Meade's, has left the impression that Meade was no longer a force in the Union operations. The higher Grant's star rose, the further into oblivion fell the reputation of George Meade.

Meade died in 1872, several years before veterans began to fill the pages of newspapers, books, and periodicals with recollections and the accompanying debates that shaped history, which cost Meade's reputation greatly. Not surviving long enough to join in the fray denied Meade the opportunity to participate directly in the struggle to establish his importance to the Union effort in Gettysburg literature. Nor did the controversy that Sickles wrought die with Meade. Sickles outlived his old commander by more than four decades, as did his energy and predilection for the unusual.

Following the war, he became military governor of the Carolinas before President Johnson replaced him in 1867 because of "overzealousness." Two years later, President Grant made him minister to Spain, where he remained four years. His relationship with Queen Isabella led to his nickname, "Yankee king of Spain." In 1886 the governor of New York appointed him chairman of the New York State Monuments Commission, a position that gave him great influence over how the New York story would be told on the Gettysburg battlefield. Despite his lurid past, New Yorkers elected him to Congress again in 1893 on the sole campaign promise that he would make the Gettysburg battlefield a national park, wresting it from state and private control. During this trip to Washington, however, he refrained from murdering anyone.

Even old age did not dampen his ability to find the center of controversy. Well into his nineties Sickles found himself in charge of the fund set aside for New York's Civil War monuments. But in 1912 the state controller discovered that more than $28,000 was missing from the coffers. Though he was now ninety-three years old, authorities issued a warrant to arrest the one-legged general for embezzlement. When the sheriff arrived to take him in, however, Sickles showed him a telegraph stating that friends had agreed to raise the money to pay the state and a surety company had issued a bond accordingly. Sickles had dodged retribution once again. Ironically, one of the projects that the missing funds had been set aside for was a tribute to Sickles by the men of his old brigade. To this day the Excelsior Brigade monument at Gettysburg has a conspicuously vacant spot at its center, where a bust of Dan Sickles was supposed to stand.[47]

Through all his escapades in later years, Sickles's thoughts and words were never far from Gettysburg. When the sheriff returned to his office without the prisoner he had gone to arrest, he found a note from Sickles, reminding him that the general had once been criticized for his actions at that great event. Though this had nothing to do with that day's events, Sickles seemed intent to bury his later misfortune under the glory he still held for himself from that field long ago. "You will see from the statement of General Longstreet," he wrote to the sheriff, "that I won the great and decisive Battle of Gettysburg."[48]

As one historian has described it, his continued blundering only made him more determined to seek the laurel wreaths of Gettysburg. "In effect, the continued postwar failures made Sickles more determined than ever to protect what he thought was his greatest achievement of his career—his role at Gettysburg."[49]

Modern historians have great interest in Dan Sickles but little sympathy for him. The conventional wisdom today is that—poor play on words though it may be—Sickles did not have a leg to stand on. Looking back at Sickles's decision to move his Corps forward at Gettysburg without orders from Meade—which lay at the core of the entire controversy—Sickles biographer W. A. Swanberg expressed the opinion of many when he wrote, "A commanding general might as well go fishing if his corps leaders are to be allowed to choose ground of their own liking without regard to the rest of the army. Sickles's error in command is clear as crystal."[50]

Nevertheless, a powerful and energetic politician, known for his outrageous, even criminal past, conspired to cover his own mistakes at Gettysburg by attacking the military behavior of his commanding general. This played into the plans of two radical U.S. senators and their committee bent on destroying George Meade's career. Add to the mix a general who sneaked into town against his orders so he could lie to the committee, and the testimony of another who later regretted his words as "unnecessarily harsh." And then consider that both of them had scores to settle with Meade—a soldierly sort who, in deference to his role in the ongoing war, chose not to defend himself as vigorously as he should have, and he was soon subjugated by the new general in chief, U.S. Grant, who chose for the balance of the war to travel with the army that Meade still technically commanded, casting a long, dark shadow over the latter's reputation. Consider then that Meade had the bad fortune to die in 1872, a decade prior to the history-shaping veteran discussions of the 1880s, and it is no wonder that popular history has not widely celebrated the man who, only three days into his term as commander of the Union Army, soundly defeated Robert E. Lee.

CHAPTER 5

THE SELF-FULFILLING PROPHECY OF JOHN BADGER BACHELDER

In all this matter I have the disadvantage of not having been present at the battle, and of having obtained all my information second hand. But on the other side I have the advantage of having questioned the actors so soon after the occurrence that the details must have been fresh in mind and for at that time no side issues had arisen.

JOHN BADGER BACHELDER[1]

I n 1880 the U.S. Congress appropriated $50,000 for one man to write a history of one Civil War battle—Gettysburg. In hindsight, it was a remarkable endorsement from the nation's highest governing body, even in light of the fact that Civil War veterans then controlled Congress, many of them Gettysburg heroes of both sides. Based on the 1880 tax valuations of the Borough of Gettysburg, the recipient could have used the money to purchase the county prison building five times over, the county courthouse two and a half times, all of the major hotels in town combined, or the entire Pennsylvania (now Gettysburg) College campus.

Even by today's monetary standards, this is a hefty sum to bestow on the single literary work of one individual. Even more unusual is that fact that the man on whom Congress bestowed this remarkable honor was not a veteran of the Civil War, nor even of the U.S. military. He was not present at the battle and had never before produced a single historical work. Nonetheless, through a concerted effort on his part, he had a more profound effect on the story of Gettysburg than any other historian.

John Badger Bachelder was a portrait and landscape painter in New England prior to the Civil War. In the early 1850s he served as a professor and principal at the Military and Scientific Institute at Reading, Pennsylvania, which caused the governor to appoint him a lieutenant colonel in the state militia, his only military connection of any kind.[2] Within a few years, however, he was back in his native New Hampshire painting landscapes. At the time of the outbreak of the Great Crisis, Bachelder was trying to collect historical data for a painting of the Battle of Bunker Hill from the Revolutionary War. Less than a decade after Emanuel Leutze painted his *Washington Crossing the Delaware*, Bachelder likely hoped to equal the painting, and no doubt its popularity, with a similar subject. Unable to collect the descriptive information to his satisfaction, however, he happened upon an alternate plan. In place of Bunker Hill and its three-quarter-century-old memories, he would find a subject of equal importance about which he could more easily gather the details. Key to his plan was the fact that the greatest war ever fought on the continent was under way. He would, as he described it, "wait for the great battle which would naturally decide the contest; study its topography on the field and learn its details from the actors themselves, and eventually prepare its written and illustrated history."[3]

In search of this decisive battle, Bachelder traveled with the Union Army through the Peninsula Campaign of 1862 before taking ill and returning home with assurances from officers in the army that they would notify him if a battle of his desired significance seemed imminent. Within days of the end of fighting at Gettysburg in July 1863, Bachelder was on the scene.[4] "I first rode on horseback around the Field in order to determine its limits," he later recalled. Then he obtained a three-foot-long drawing board and began walking the field while making a sketch of the landscape. He continued this work "until the whole territory had been sketched for a distance of nearly four miles."[5]

The kinds of details he had been unable to gather about Bunker Hill he set out to collect about Gettysburg, finding many eyewitnesses and fresh memories. He began in the hospitals, where recently wounded soldiers had many stories to tell. Using his sketched map of the field, he began filling in the battle positions of troops as relayed by the participants. After eighty-four days at this work, he completed a visually intriguing drawing that served as a topographic map of the battlefield, onto which he placed lines representing troop positions. With this in hand, he obtained permission from General George G. Meade, commander of the Army of the Potomac, to visit the troops in the field in Virginia, where he continued his industrious effort.

He later recalled his strategy. "I spent the entire winter of 1863 and 1864, visiting every Regiment, holding conversations with its officers and with privates in many cases, submitted to them the drawings I had made of the Field and had them corroborate and complete the position of the troops upon it."[6] When he had conducted as many of these personal interviews as he could, he obtained a roster of the army and sent mass mailings, complete with outline drawings of his map, to the commanders of all the batteries and regiments in the army. With these he requested the location of each unit in the "line of battle" as well as their movements through the conflict. In the spring of the following year he published the map as a lithograph, complete with the signed endorsements of General Meade, most of the Union Army corps commanders, and even the most prominent citizens of Gettysburg, all of whom attested to its authenticity.[7]

With copies of this print now circulating widely throughout military and private communities, Bachelder had two important accomplishments: he began establishing himself as the leading historian of the battle and placing his unique imprint on the story—or history—of the battle.

Within hours of its conclusion, Bachelder decided to himself that Gettysburg was that "great battle which would naturally decide the contest"—even with the war a little more than half over. Once he had chosen this battle as the war's decisive event, he endeavored not only to chronicle it but also to elevate its importance and thus confirm his choice by making sure that generations to follow agreed with his assessment. If posterity did not come to see Gettysburg as the greatest battle, then all his work would be for naught and the painting he proposed to create would have little value. So Bachelder became a sort of cheerleader in chief for the idea that this was the deciding event of the war. Through his own tireless efforts at promotion, a landscape painter from New Hampshire striving to prove himself right took his place as the most important of all Gettysburg historians and had a profound effect on virtually anything ever written about it afterward.

Bachelder's work did not end with the publication of the map. In fact, it had scarcely begun. When the war ended, he continued his quest for information by inviting veterans to return to the field with him on "excursions" during which they walked the ground and pointed out areas of activity and interest. As early as 1867, he could boast to U.S. Grant of "a visit to every regiment and battery of the Army of the Potomac" and having "visited the field with twenty-six Generals and a large number of other officers engaged in the battle."[8] On the field, Bachelder framed the general action in an area, setting a tone or idea, before veterans added their recollections in relation to what he had said. Thus the veterans got much of their history of the action from Bachelder and then recollected their part in the fight within his framework.

In time, veterans of both sides revealed Bachelder's influence as an authority in their letters. Confederate General Joseph Kershaw, for example, explained that his own view of the battle came largely from Bachelder's descriptions of the fighting around him: "I think I see the whole matter very clearly after reading your statement of operations in my front."[9] Others became so convinced of Bachelder's knowledge that they simply deferred to him on the details, as Union General Joseph Carr did when he wrote, "I therefore think you know as much about the location of my command as I do."[10]

While many seemed content to leave Bachelder to his work, many more felt compelled to introduce their particular version of events in hopes of seeing it published. They did so while pointing out the poor quality of the historical record as a whole. A Vermont veteran made this an issue: "I discover not only an unwarrantable spirit of exaggeration on the part of some officers but a disposition to detract from others what rightfully belongs to them, so I shall not be surprised if you are led into errors."[11]

Another echoed the same sentiment. "Much has been written on the subject of this battle . . . Much of which have contained exaggerated statements, and distorted facts, for the ostensible purpose of making heroes of their favorites and giving the world the wrong impressions of the true history of these eventful times. . . ."[12]

By 1880 Bachelder had furthered his reputation while accumulating an enormous cache of firsthand accounts from nearly every unit that had been on or near the battlefield. It was this reputation and information that many in the Federal government sought to preserve. The generous endorsement of Congress that followed further cemented his reputation as the singular expert, leading many veterans to loosely describe him as the "official government historian."[13]

Official government endorsement aside, Bachelder had no formal training as a historian or even a writer. Landscape paintings require little research, and despite his noble desire to gather only the most accurate details of Bunker Hill and later Gettysburg, his work had many flaws, both in methodology and the influence of his ego. Without any formal training or experience, the painter sought to sort through the problems inherent in dealing with imperfect human memory and then tried to combine an enormous collection of often conflicting accounts into a single history. Considering this, one can quickly see how Bachelder's hand may have swayed either the most or least accurate description of events into the accepted version in public memory.

Ambitious though he was for accuracy, his project was scarcely under way when he began to realize the weight of the challenge he faced. While visiting the Union Army in Virginia during the winter of 1863–1864, Bachelder began to see the difficulty in merging the varying and even contradictory recollections of the veterans into an understandable whole. After one particularly frustrating day at his task, he returned to a tent where he was lodging with some officers. In response to inquiries about his progress he gave this lament. "Well, I have been to the Second Corps to-day, and I believe I have discovered how Joshua made the sun stand still." He based his revelation on the testimony of several regimental commanders who entered the fight as part of the same brigade, yet each gave him a different time for that entry. When the aspiring historian concluded aloud that some of them might be mistaken, he was met with polite reminders that they had been present at the fight, and he had not.[14]

Years later, he was still receiving feedback in regard to the task he had taken upon himself. Two years after the congressional appropriation, for example, a veteran wrote to Bachelder to offer his congratulations and condolences. "What a Herculean task," he told the historian, "to separate the truth from the falsehood in the multitude of reports that have rained down on you since 1863."[15] This was a challenge with which Bachelder had become all too familiar.

Many of the accounts that veterans sent his way contained warnings or disclaimers regarding their potential reliability. "I am unable to give any information that can be considered very important. The dust of twenty years is upon the memory of our Gettysburg fight; and for many of us, only the shadow and outlines are left."[16] These outlines filled the next five pages describing his part of the fighting.

A statement from Union General Abner Doubleday is both typical and contradictory. "It is difficult in the excitement of battle," he wrote to Bachelder in 1885, "to see every thing going on around us for each has his own part to play and that absorbs his attention to the exclusion of every thing else. People are very much mistaken when they suppose because a man is in a battle, he knows all about it."[17] Doubleday revealed this thought just three years after he published his own history of the battle in book form. Not surprisingly, he did not use this testimonial about accuracy on the back cover.

Other recollections that came under Bachelder's eye were framed in strong doubt that rendered them useless to any good historian. In an account of the battle he wrote in 1885, Union artillerist Gulian Weir seems consumed with doubt as to its authenticity. "For the past *night* or *two* another 'recollection' comes back to me as a story I used to tell, (it may be an imagination on the brain) such things do come upon us, I believe, at times as truths, which in reality are built-up imaginations—(so I won't hold up my hand to this)."[18]

Through his long struggle for the truth, Bachelder received both praise and damnation from veterans, and their expressed opinions were usually based on whether his version of events agreed with theirs. Many found his original isometric drawing of the field so visually intriguing that it somehow lent credibility to his skills as a historian.

Having seen his map while still in the field with the Union Army, General Alpheus Williams declared, "Your drawing, in addition to its present interest to all who were engaged in the battle and its artistic beauty will have a future historic value which can hardly now be appreciated."[19] More than ten years later, the colonel of an Illinois regiment furthered this argument. "No man is more able than you," he wrote, "the author of those excellent maps, to write the history of that great battle."[20] Creating the most unusual maps they had ever seen seemed to convince many veterans that he was also a great historian of the battle.

As early as 1865, Bachelder seemed to have developed a positive reputation among Union officers. General John Geary expressed this sentiment: "I am content to leave the whole matter of the history of that great battle in your hands, feeling confident that you will do that *justice* to all concerned, for which you are already so eminently characterized."[21] Others simply heaped praise on him when they began to realize the power he would likely have in shaping the history. Union General Samuel W. Crawford, never shy in his efforts to get credit for his work at Gettysburg (whether deserved or not), stated it plainly in a request: "I want to know what I must do to be in your book and to be like the other officers . . . Tell me just what I must do."[22]

In time, Bachelder's name became inextricably linked with the battle and its history. In 1888 a Wisconsin captain spoke for others when he wrote, "your untiring zeal and efforts to perpetuate the memory of the great sacrifice at Gettysburg is highly appreciated and your name will ever be associated with the great work there accomplished."[23]

Interspersed among the letters of praise, however, were less flattering evaluations of Bachelder's work. General Crawford, probably seeking to get on Bachelder's good side, intimated his opinion of these critics. "There has not been that cordial appreciation of your great work that is due to you and it is because some of them think that you do not like them and fear that you will not do them justice."[24]

A Confederate cavalry commander minced few words when describing the government maps to which Bachelder had applied troop positions in 1883, publishing one map for each day's action. "The truth of history," he wrote, "as well as a solemn duty to my immediate command compels me to say from an examination of the maps of the battlefield of Gettysburg sent me by the Engineers department is entirely inaccurate . . . I write this simply for the truth of history and to put on record my earnest protest against such monstrous and absurd inaccuracies."[25]

Even veterans who registered a dislike for him recognized the power of his work to shape history. One Union veteran decried Bachelder as a "loud-mouthed, blatant photographer, artist at Sickles's headquarters and henchman of Sickles, [who] made people buy an avalanche of propaganda that Sickles held back Longstreet, and all writers began to believe it and praised Sickles's act."[26]

Bachelder biographer Richard Sauers summed up his opinion of Bachelder's relationship with the veterans and their history.

As a result of his lifetime of work at Gettysburg, Bachelder became more and more confident in his ability to understand what had happened on the battlefield, but his self-confidence was easily mistaken for arrogance. Thin-skinned veterans often complained that they knew more than Bachelder—they had seen the battle itself; he had not. Bachelder himself was as stubborn as the veterans. Southern officers claimed he had not collected enough material to accurately place their units, while the mass of conflicting testimony on the Northern side made his task more difficult.[27]

One revealing example of Bachelder's assuredness involved the spot where Union General Winfield S. Hancock was wounded during the climatic charge on July 3. As commander of the troops who repulsed Pickett's division, Hancock was both certain of the location and not used to having people tell him he was wrong. Thus, when Bachelder marked the spot where he believed Hancock fell, the old general was neither pleased nor afraid to say so. "I am satisfied that the position indicating where I was shot, is incorrect," Hancock wrote in 1885. "It was established in 1866 in your presence . . . but is not placed as indicated on that field, on my last visit, by a sign-board. You were present, and in due time, I would be pleased if you would mark with a stake or small boulder (in such a way that it cannot be moved again) the spot. . . ."[28]

Beginning less than a week after the armies left Pennsylvania, Bachelder slowly became the recognized authority on the battle's history largely because the veterans who might have done so were still fighting the war while he was out collecting testimony. His increasing prominence as the perceived "official" historian—a perception based largely on his visually attractive map—gave great power to his data to shape the commonly accepted history of the battle. Clearly, however, there were problems inherent in his particular view of things. A key issue that skewed, perhaps dramatically, Bachelder's view of the battle's action, for example, was his inability to collect any significant accounts from Confederates in the first years after the event.

Bachelder spent the first ten years after the battle forming a vision of it based almost exclusively on the accounts of Federal officers. When Confederate officers finally began submitting their recollections—slowly at first—Bachelder had to merge these new Southern perspectives into his preconceived ideas of the battle, which he had formed from Yankee reminiscences. This shortcoming, however, was certainly not of Bachelder's making. In 1867 in a letter to U.S. Grant, the secretary of war, he unsuccessfully requested permission to see Confederate battle reports that the War Department had in its possession. When he finally sought out Southern perspectives, he found little assistance.

Writing from Augusta, Georgia, while the war continued to rage, Confederate General Lafayette McLaws declined a request from Bachelder to offer his recollections: "I do not think it proper to give an extended account of the operations of my command. . . ."[29] A few months after the war, McLaws criticized Bachelder's facts but declined to correct them, explaining through a third party that "the day for the history of that battle is not yet. It will come. It may be best to state here that the facts expounded or implied in the questions Col. B. proposed to me in reference to the movements of division and brigade are almost wholly imaginary and mythical."[30]

Bachelder pressed on in his attempt to gather the details about Gettysburg that had eluded him at Bunker Hill. Strangely, though his desire to create the great painting of the greatest battle had initiated his quest, when the time came to create the great masterpiece in 1870, he chose not to paint it. Instead, he hired a well-known artist named James Walker to create the painting under his strict guidance while he himself created a guidebook to accompany it. Most likely this was a business decision. Thanks to the commercial success of his isometric drawing of the field, Bachelder had established a business as a lithographer, creating prints of his work and selling them at a significant sum. Having Walker do the painting not only capitalized on the artist's fame but freed up Bachelder to run his business and continue his research for what he now hoped would become an illustrated history of the battle in book form. A lithographic print of Walker's painting *The Repulse of Longstreet's Assault* sold for $50, a hefty sum in the financially racked 1870s.

The Battle of Gettysburg profited Bachelder in a number of ways. He not only derived income from his maps and the Walker painting, but he became well-known for creating printable engravings of portraits and selling them to publishers. His work was so good that he received the ringing endorsement of Abraham Lincoln's son. In 1868 he published an engraving of the martyred president that Robert Todd Lincoln described as "the best and most pleasing likeness that I have yet seen engraved."[31] The engravings he created for many of Gettysburg's leading Union officers also helped him develop strong ties with these key participants whose help in gathering historical data was essential.

Though Gettysburg helped him make a comfortable living, this was nothing compared to the stroke of luck he experienced in 1878. It occurred to him that the information he had collected was of great value as an official history sanctioned by the government, not just in a commercial publication on the battle. With the help of many of the Union officers he had befriended, he petitioned the U.S. Congress for an appropriation to write such a book, and in 1880 he received $50,000. This was essentially a declaration that Bachelder was the official government historian and his work would be accepted, recorded, and distributed to posterity. As soon as this news reached the veterans, their recollections began to pour in and the watercolor painter-turned lithographer-turned historian had his work cut out for him. More importantly, he now had the power of the Federal government behind whatever version of events he chose to record.

AT THE CORE OF GETTYSBURG MYTHOLOGY is the idea that this battle was the turning point of the entire Civil War, the "Waterloo of the Confederacy" as veterans often described it. In lore, it has become the point at which Southern culture and military strength, as well as everything for which it stood, peaked and then ebbed like a tide. It did so symbolically at what is now known as the High Water Mark, a place that draws millions of visitors from every corner of the globe. Now the focal point of the Gettysburg National Military Park, this area, often referred to as "The Angle," is now littered with monuments, markers, cannons, and interpretive signs—even an iron fence and a special commemorative monument placed to perpetuate the memory of the site itself. But this small parcel of land has not always been such a big attraction.

In the years immediately following the battle, the thousands of visitors to the field spent most of their time in places where the battle left its mark on the landscape. In the same way that no one goes to the scene of a hurricane to look at the buildings left undamaged, curious onlookers who rode their carriages around the scene of battle focused their attention, for example, on the remnants of earthworks and logs that soldiers used as protection. They paused reflectively at areas that allowed a scenic or wide view of the surrounding countryside, or inspected bullet and shell damage still evident on buildings and trees. In all of these attractions, the simple crop fields in the center of what had been the Union line of battle were sorely lacking. Within a year or two after the fighting, one could scarcely envision where anything had happened on this mostly flat, bare landscape reachable largely only on foot. Not until the battle scars of other areas had healed and trees had grown over many of the open spaces did the area where the last major attack of the battle occurred become of great interest. It did so as much by design and invention as by any natural shift in interest or curiosity.[32]

Historian William Frassanito has lived in Gettysburg and studied the battlefield for decades; his work on the photographic history of the battle is legendary. In writing his book *Early Photography at Gettysburg* in the early

1990s, he happened upon something that struck him as curious. In none of the historical data from the first six or seven postbattle years could he find the kind of celebration of Pickett's Charge and the place where it ebbed that is prevalent today.

> . . . the current attraction to the scene of the battle's climax was not always strong, particularly from the perspective of the tourist trade. In fact, I have yet to uncover a single pre–1870 tourist account that even mentioned, directly or indirectly, the specific terrain features we today know as the "Bloody Angle" or the "Copse of Trees." Moreover, it is not uncommon to read early accounts which paid little or virtually no attention to the entire subject of the July 3, 1863, Confederate assault against the Union center.[33]

If this interest in the battlefield changed around 1869, there is at least one significant explanation. Seeking to self-fulfill his prophecy of Gettysburg's supreme significance—and in so doing elevate the importance of the thing about which he had become the recognized expert—John Bachelder stumbled upon a way in which he could communicate his idea to generations to come. As he later recalled it, at least, the concept began in the summer of 1869 as something of an epiphany.

> Soon after the close of the war I met Colonel [Walter] Harrison at Gettysburg, who was General Pickett's assistant general, and was with him at the battle. I invited Colonel Harrison to visit the battlefield with me, and we spent several hours under the shade cast by the Copse of Trees, when he explained to me what an important feature that copse of trees was at the time of the battle, and how it had been a landmark towards which Longstreet's assault of July 3d 1863 had been directed. Impressed with its importance, I remarked, "Why, Colonel, as the battle of Gettysburg was the crowning event of this campaign, this copse of trees must have been the high water mark of the rebellion." To which he assented, and from that time on, I felt a reverence for those trees.[34]

After a recitation of his attempts to memorialize the area around those trees, he concluded by taking credit for recognizing and perpetuating the importance of the site. "The thought of naming the copse of trees the 'High Water Mark of the Rebellion,' and the idea of perpetuating its memory by a monument, was mine."[35]

What Bachelder set out to do—and later succeeded in doing—was to literally shape the battlefield to prove his own point. If he could identify just one small area of the field as the exact spot where the entire Civil War was lost and won, then surely people would come to view this battle as the decisive event of that war, as he had concluded for himself back in 1863. In the vast fields of corn, hay, and wheat that now made up the surrounding scene, a small clump of trees provided a natural landmark on which he could focus his idea. This small grove of trees, conveniently located at the geographic center of the battlefield as a whole, could represent the exact location where the greatest nation on earth was saved, and Bachelder set out to enshrine that location.

Copse—a funny word. The average person might live a whole lifetime and never hear it spoken or see it written. Yet it is so entrenched in the lexicon of Gettysburg that scarcely a student of the battle has seriously considered what it means or where it came from. It is a single word that has come to describe a particular group of trees, about two hundred feet in circumference on the Gettysburg battlefield. Ask a Civil War buff where the copse is and he or she will likely have no trouble directing you to it. It is the group of trees that is said to be the spot on which the men of Pickett's Charge directed their attention on July 3, 1863, the aiming point of the assault and the place where it failed.

One of the essential keys to Bachelder's public relations endeavor was to give the place an unusual name in order to set it apart in literature as well as imagination. Any group of trees could be a clump, and grove was all too commonly used. This unique place needed a unique name. In search of a more unusual label, Bachelder borrowed an old English word that Britons use to describe a thicket or grove of some reverential importance. Early on, he began to refer to the feature as the "Copse of Trees."

Webster's dictionary defines the word copse as "a thicket of small trees or shrubs; a coppice." Coppice is "a thicket or grove of small trees or shrubs, especially one maintained by periodic cutting or pruning to encourage suckering, as in the cultivation of cinnamon trees for their bark." Although Bachelder could have used either word or another as simple as "clump," he chose instead one more familiar to landscape artists.

This word, rarely used in any non-Gettysburg context, is a distinct indicator of Bachelder's influence on the story of the battle. Often with myths and legends it is difficult to trace an element of the story back to its first original source, but in this case, Bachelder's unique use of an obscure word left an indelible marker of his influence. Since "copse" is a word virtually unheard and unread, especially in modern parlance, it is safe to say that wherever it occurs in Gettysburg literature, it leads directly back to Bachelder. Thus wherever the word "copse" appears, it is a clear sign of Bachelder's influence on the story—a sort of "Bachelder was here" mark.

The old historian succeeded in planting another name on the area beginning with the 1870 publication that accompanied Walker's painting. In it, he referred to the "the copse of trees in the center of the picture, the 'High Water Mark' of the rebellion." While this name occasionally inspires visitors to Gettysburg to inquire what year the flood occurred, Bachelder meant it as a symbolic label representing the highest point of success and possibility for the Confederate cause. Before they reached this mark their hopes were rising; afterward, they did nothing but recede.[36]

The story of John Bachelder may have come to an inglorious end in the fall of 1869 when he visited his beloved copse and was struck with a horror so great it is a wonder it did not cause a permanent stoppage of his heart. To his disbelief, the local farmer who at that time owned the land on which the copse stood was fetching firewood and fence rails for the coming winter and, being a frugal Pennsylvanian of limited means, decided he should begin with the trees nearest his house rather than travel an unnecessary distance to a far-off woodlot. By the time Bachelder arrived on the scene, Basil Biggs and his ax had quite significantly reduced the size and prominence of what he most likely looked on as merely a clump of trees.

"I expostulated with him," Bachelder later recalled, "but without effect, until I suggested to him that if he cut them then he was only getting for them their value as rails, whereas, if he allowed them to stand to mark the spot he would eventually get ten times as much for them, and he spared them."[37]

While Bachelder did not explain why he thought it would be appropriate for Biggs to cut the trees at some later date but not then, he was right about the value that they would bring after his promotional efforts bore fruit. Years later the various governing bodies who oversaw the care of the battlefield struggled with the practice among veterans and other tourists of taking pieces of wood from the trees as souvenirs. There is no telling exactly how many copse-ian canes, walking sticks, and other mementos came from the precious trees, but it is a good bet that Basil Biggs never saw any profits.

While he managed to convince the wood-starved farmer of the trees' importance to posterity, Bachelder had a much harder time convincing anyone else. Terrified by the idea that the timber in his copse might end up framing some local hog pen, Bachelder sought to have them protected until he could raise the level of attention that veterans paid to them. Seventeen years after he rescued them from the felling ax, he was still struggling to convince the Gettysburg Battlefield Memorial Association—the board that oversaw the battlefield at that time—to take protective action. It was not until 1887, after they twice voted down the idea of preserving the trees, that he finally convinced them to build an iron fence around them.[38]

Once the fence surrounded the trees, however, Bachelder was still not satisfied. Preserving the trees was only a part of his goal; the more important step was to create a permanent marker that would explain in words why the site was the "High Water Mark of the Rebellion" surpassing in importance all others. At a meeting of the association the following year he proposed "that a bronze tablet be prepared indicating and setting forth the movements of troops at the copse of trees."[39]

Weary of his dogged persistence—a trait that gave double meaning to his middle name, "Badger"—the board voted to allow Bachelder, as a committee of one, to go ahead with the project. Facetiously, the chairman remarked aloud that "there were no funds in the treasury for that purpose." Besides, as another member remarked, "only a small tablet bolted to the fence would be required."[40] Again they underestimated his drive to ensure that future generations saw this battle, and this small part of it in particular, as the turning point of the nation's history.

Rather than a small bronze tablet bolted inconspicuously to a fence, Bachelder set out to create a monument whose footprint alone would measure nearly eight feet by ten feet, and he estimated that such a tribute would cost nearly $5,000. In no time, however, his desire to stamp his idea squarely and permanently on the field grew. "As the worked progressed," he later remembered, "and the subject was more fully considered, its importance grew upon me, and I felt that the tablet to be erected should be commensurate with the event to be commemorated; particularly when such beautiful, and expensive monuments had already been erected to mark events of far less importance."[41] While the rest of the board—and many veterans as well—saw little value in it, Bachelder's vision of the High Water Mark and its importance grew steadily, as did his sense of ownership. "I prepared the design," he later reported, "(more than twenty of which were discarded) made the contracts, visited legislatures, secured appropriations and paid bills precisely as though it was my private enterprise."[42] In time, he created a design that included a huge bronze "book of history" symbolically laid open to its most important page, listing the names of the units that had participated in repulsing Pickett's Charge on July 3, 1863. The pedestal supporting the book grew to occupy a footprint exceeding eighteen feet by forty-eight feet.

This design did more than just supply Bachelder with a means of casting his image on the field; it gave him a means to pay for the structure. By petitioning the legislature of each state whose troops would be listed on the tablet's pages, he raised the $5,000 he had originally planned to spend. Recognizing the influence that Bachelder had gained over the story of Gettysburg, and understanding the effect that such a monument would have on future generations, the states seemed eager to pay their share. When he reached the final stages of planning, however, the old historian realized that his costs had grown nearly as quickly as the monument's size, and he was personally in debt to the project by $4,000.

After running up the costs and paying the overrun out of his own pocket, Bachelder did not see the expense as his responsibility, reporting that "I did not feel that it was my duty to incur an expense of $5,000 . . . And yet I had but myself to blame. I had incurred these expenses without the advice of, or even consultation with the Memorial Association; hence I could not ask the Association to help me out."[43] Despite the fact that this was entirely his project, an idea supported by no one else on the governing board, and that he had escalated it at every stage, he felt he should bear no responsibility for its expense. "It occurred to me," he recalled, "that there really was no reason why I should personally sustain this loss."[44]

Just as the bills came due, Bachelder received a letter from Hiram Berdan, the officer who had commanded two regiments of sharpshooters at Gettysburg, complaining that his units had participated in the repulse of the great charge but were not listed on the tablet. This was a stroke of good luck and better timing. Since Berdan's regiments were made up of companies of men from separate states, Bachelder now had several more reasons to go back to the respective legislatures, hitting them up for more historical advertising space on his great monument. The states complied, the tablet was recast to add new troops, and the High Water Mark monument, representing the idea of what one man felt Gettysburg should mean to a nation, still stands today at the most prominent spot on the field—a spot made prominent by the same man who conceived the idea.

All of this public relations work promoting Gettysburg and its central point paid off for Bachelder and in time the battle became widely known as the most important of the war. A Pennsylvania veteran summed up the success of Bachelder's efforts. "Public opinion has decided that the battle was the culminating point of the war. I feel that for the history of our whole Country it is advisable to hand to posterity the details of that memorable trial."[45]

Successful though it was in elevating the charge of July 3 to immortality, Bachelder's work was not without its detractors, particularly men who fought elsewhere at Gettysburg. A New Hampshire private summed up the opposing view. "I went to see the Cyclorama [painting] and the lecturer only gave an acct of the 1st and 3rd days battle. I asked him if there was any battle fought July 2nd. He said there was, but the main one was the 3d day all the heroes he told us was Hancock and the Reb. Generals Pickett and Armistead."[46]

Despite those who challenged it, the idea that Gettysburg was the High Water Mark of the war grew in popular American folklore, elevating the name of the losing general, George Pickett, to immortality as the leader of Pickett's Charge.

More surely than Basil Biggs's field ax, recent scholarship has begun to tear down Bachelder's idea that the Battle of Gettysburg determined the winner of the Civil War. In his book *Pickett's Charge: The Final Assault at Gettysburg*, for example, Earl Hess argues that even if Pickett's Charge had succeeded on July 3, at the Copse of Trees or anywhere else, a Southern victory was anything but a foregone conclusion. "Not only is it nearly impossible to believe," argues Hess, "that a tactical success on July 3 would have resulted in a strategic success in the campaign, but it is also extremely difficult to believe that there was ever a possibility of any kind that Lee's raid into Pennsylvania would have resulted in a decisive blow for Confederate independence."[47]

In addition, the High Water Mark was not even the scene of the largest assault of the battle; the bulk of the attack on the battle's second day, a mile or more to the south, included as many if not more men and lasted at least twice as long. Whether Bachelder did, as he claimed, invent the label and the idea of the High Water Mark or simply adopted it from a growing theme among veteran memories, he certainly advanced it until it become engrained in the popular memory. If the idea was not his, the permanence of it certainly was.

As for the Copse of Trees, it probably had no significance at all to the men in the charge. In 2000 Troy Harman, a National Park Service historian at Gettysburg, published his book *Cemetery Hill: The General Plan Was Unchanged,* a detailed historical study concluding that Robert E. Lee's objective throughout the battle was to drive the Federal army from its superior position atop the vast Cemetery Hill. This goal, Harman explains, was not altered when Lee developed his plan for the massive assault on the battle's final day. What later became known as Pickett's Charge was directed, he argues, at Cemetery Hill in general and not Bachelder's Copse of Trees. Later scholarship seems to agree. In 2002 Earl Hess concluded, "There is no creditable evidence that anyone pointed to the angle in the stone fence or the copse of trees before the assault and told someone to head there."[48]

While the "High Water Mark of the Rebellion" has served as an enticing label for the spot where soldiers actually decided the Civil War, it is nearly impossible to justify as a statement of fact. As much as Bachelder may have wanted future generations to accept his view of the site's importance—and he succeeded grandly—it is difficult for any sober historical study of the facts and the circumstances to conclude that William Faulkner's imagery was accurate and that the South was ever so close to independence at that little clump of trees. Nevertheless, the fact that this notion is now accepted as reality in the popular mind is testimony to the dogged persistence of a New England landscape painter.

In many other ways, both prominent and subtle, Bachelder made his influence felt on the history of the battle. For a period in the 1880s, when monuments seemed to sprout up on the battlefield as plentifully as spring weeds, he served on the board of the Gettysburg Battlefield Memorial Association and as its superintendent of tablets and legends, a position that gave him full authority over not only the location of monuments but also the wording of each. Anyone who was going to carve in stone the pieces of the battle's history would have to go through John Bachelder. Not surprisingly, he perturbed more than a few veterans who were as sure of their unit's position in battle as General Hancock was of the spot where he was wounded.[49]

All this authority and influence eventually seemed to get the better of him. In 1889 he boldly petitioned Congress to mark the Confederate battle lines on the field, put him in charge of the project, and pay him another $50,000 to do so. As he had done the first time he got Congress to fund his work, he sent a circular letter asking veterans to support the petition. At first he received positive responses from congressmen and many letters of support from veterans. By the spring of the following year, however, the necessary bill had stalled in both houses of Congress and Bachelder learned that the holdup was of a personal nature. It was not marking Confederate battle lines that Washington balked at, but rather the personal fortune they seemed to be providing for a battlefield historian who had yet to truly produce the results for which they had hoped.[50]

Governor James Beaver of Pennsylvania finally broke the news. "I have ⌐d incidentally," he wrote, "that there has been objection in some ⌐d some feeling in others on the ground, first, that it fixes what ⌐n exorbitant compensation for your personal services." ⌐e subject as softly but frankly as he could, Beaver ⌐f Bachelder's reputation with Congress.

⌐ached me on the subject, stating that the ⌐ had already been paid for your knowledge and services in connection with the battle of Gettysburg, and that this additional appropriation for the same object was hardly fair. The language used was somewhat stronger than this, but I wish to state the fact to you frankly so that you may understand something of the feeling in both House of Congress as I have learned it confidentially.[51]

A month later, a veteran who supported Bachelder reiterated Beaver's concerns, writing, "Fifty thousand dollars is a very large amount and is the full compensation of a United States Senator for ten years. I suppose it would hardly be claimed that this work could occupy one half of that time."[52] By comparison to modern Senate salaries, Bachelder's requested appropriation would today be nearly $1.5 million.

Rather than scrap the idea of marking Confederate lines, however, Congress came up with an alternative plan. After the bill languished without action for two years, Congress created a commission consisting of three people, at least two of whom would be veterans of the battle and one a Confederate veteran. The first chairman of the commission was John P. Nicholson, a veteran of the 28th Pennsylvania, who served along with William H. Forney of the 10th Alabama, and Bachelder. This board was answerable to the Secretary of War through the War Department with each member receiving a stipend of $10 a day "when actually employed."[53]

Within two years of the commission's first meeting, John Bachelder was laid to rest in his native New Hampshire, far from the field on which he had spent his life's energy. He never published an illustrated history of the Battle of Gettysburg as planned and promised, nor did he paint the great masterpiece that had lured him to the field three decades earlier. Very few people know of his life and work at Gettysburg despite his profound influence on the battle's story. But for this he has only himself blame. Perhaps the greatest lesson of all to be gained from the Bache legacy lies not in what he did, but in what he failed to do. Few, if a torians ever had more information, support, and funding for th

He was not present at the battle nor was he a military man. He had no formal training as a historian but, though little known today, John Badger Bachelder (shown here with his wife in Devil's Den) had a more profound effect on the story of Gettysburg than any other person.

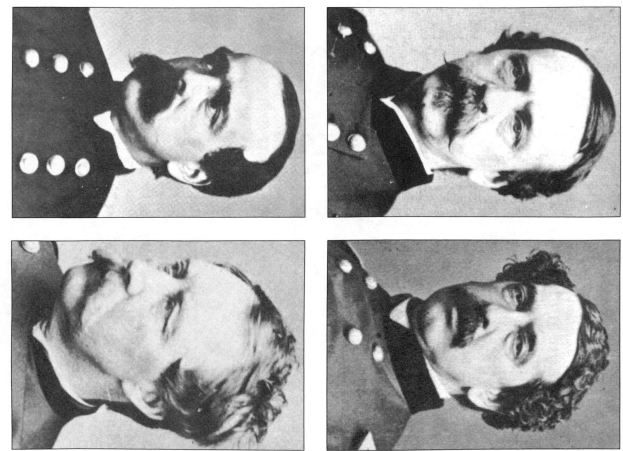

Beyond their similar tastes in mustaches and poses, Sickles, Doubleday, Butter-field, and Howe shared a point of view that doomed the reputation of their commander at Gettysburg, George G. Meade. "Rascality" Sickles (top left) duped "Stupidity" Doubleday (top right) while getting help from Meade's Chi-duped "Stupidity" Doubleday (top right) while getting help from Meade's Chi of Staff Daniel Butterfield (bottom left) and General Albion P. Howe, who not involved in the Sickles maneuver but testified against Meade anyway.

In 1938, President Franklin Roosevelt (above) arrived at the same Gettysburg train station that Lincoln used seventy-five years prior. Two hundred thousand people, including two thousand veterans of the battle, watched his speech at the dedication of the Eternal Light Peace Memorial (below) in the same field on which the Ku Klux Klan had rallied twelve years earlier. One hundred thousand people were still on the roads trying to reach the site. As with Lincoln's, FDR's speech at a Gettysburg dedication allowed him to express his own political perspective on a war. Though the memorial was conceived as a reaction against the growing violence in Europe, the U.S. entered World War II just three years later. Two decades later, President John F. Kennedy visited the memorial with its eternal flame. Legend has it that this was the inspiration for a similar flame at his grave.

At the Fiftieth Anniversary Reunion of the Blue and Gray in 1913 on the Gettysburg battlefield, heeding the disquieting unease on the European continent, President Woodrow Wilson (third from left) spoke of peace while furthering the theme of national reunion. "The previous half-century," he said, "has meant peace and union and vigor. . . . How wholesome and healing the peace has been." In summation, he praised "the nations of the world in peace and righteousness and love." One year later Europe exploded into the "Great War" in which more than 10 million people perished.

Though a sour-faced President Dwight
Eisenhower probably wanted to forget
Field Marshall Montgomery's visit
(right), he enjoyed touring the battle-
field with visiting dignitaries such as
British Prime Minister Winston
Churchill (below), French President
Charles de Gaulle (bottom), and even
Soviet Premier Nikita Khrushchev.

Since the battle, many groups have used the symbolic backdrop of the Gettysburg battlefield to elicit an "American" image. In 1926, more than 10,000 members of the Ku Klux Klan from six states held an annual gathering on Oak Ridge. Draping themselves in their robes and American flags, Klan members used the image of Gettysburg to symbolize their own vision of America. Warming to their arrival, the community cheered and applauded a Klan procession and the local newspaper editions included stories of interracial crimes by African Americans from places as far away as Ohio and Delaware.

Looks can be deceiving. Civil War photographer Mathew Brady took this well-known photograph of three Confederate prisoners at Gettysburg. It is often described as a depiction of the good character of Confederate soldiers—stalwart and upright, even in defeat. While used as models of positive Southern traits, the time and place of their capture reveals that these three were likely stragglers or deserters rather than heroes.

Was this a "sharpshooter"? Are these pictures of the same soldier or two different bodies? Battlefield photographer Alexander Gardner described his famous photograph (top) as a dead Confederate sharpshooter at Devil's Den. Though clearly his weapon is of no special "sharpshooter" quality, this photo helped perpetuate the myth that special Confederate snipers killed Union soldiers hundreds of yards away on Little Round Top. In 1974, renowned photographic historian William Frassanito argued that Gardner had staged this photo, dragging the dead body from seventy yards away (where he took the photo below) and posing it for the picture. In 1988, however, Richard Pougher, an expert in Confederate military uniforms, pointed out "significant differences" between the two bodies. This continuing debate demonstrates that even photographic evidence can be interpreted in various ways leading to multiple histories of the same event.

French artist Paul Philippoteaux based his "Gettysburg Cyclorama" on a panorama of black and white photographs taken especially for his work by local photographer William Tipton in April 1882. A composite of part of Tipton's panorama (above) shows the landscape in its barren wintertime form. In addition to the painting's factual errors, the use of these photos led to understandable flaws in Philippoteaux's rendering on canvas (below). The Round Tops appear at the center distance while the Copse of Trees appears at right.

Bayonet! by Don Troiani (1988). Historical artist Don Troiani created this image in 1988 but left the main subject of the painting, Colonel Joshua Chamberlain, without a hat. He did so because he could not determine with enough certainty what kind of hat Chamberlain had worn. Troiani's passion for historical accuracy led to a series of other images with hatless Chamberlains, including a pivotal scene in the movie *Gettysburg*.

Veterans of the 1st Minnesota Infantry wanted to commemorate their service at Gettysburg with "something that will attract attention therefore *odd* in design," so they first submitted the design at left; a soldier destroying the serpent Secession. In contrast, the Gettysburg Battlefield Memorial Association, which controlled the field, wanted "chaste, artistic structures," so the Minnesotans had to settle for the depiction of a soldier running to meet the enemy (right).

Some monuments are notable for what they do not contain. The 4th Ohio monument (left) was originally topped by a statue standing atop a tall column but when the new "white zinc" metal proved too soft, the soldier tilted to one side and had to be removed. Within the columns of the Excelsior Brigade monument (right) there is a space where the bust of General Daniel Sickles was supposed to be placed. When Sickles embezzled money from the State of New York's monument fund, there was not enough left to afford his likeness.

John Bachelder's lifelong struggle to establish the scene of "Pickett's Charge" as the crucible of the Civil War led him to name it the "High Water Mark of the Rebellion" and to place (at his own expense) the "High Water Mark Tablet" monument. He also preserved the "Copse of Trees" to serve as a highly symbolic place to visit. As a result, it is now the most visited area of the battlefield, as demonstrated by this 1902 photo of Gettysburg tourists.

Veterans of the 1st Minnesota Infantry wanted to commemorate their service at Gettysburg with "something that will attract attention therefore *odd* in design," so they first submitted the design at left; a soldier destroying the serpent Secession. In contrast, the Gettysburg Battlefield Memorial Association, which controlled the field, wanted "chaste, artistic structures," so the Minnesotans had to settle for the depiction of a soldier running to meet the enemy (right).

Some monuments are notable for what they do not contain. The 4th Ohio monument (left) was originally topped by a statue standing atop a tall column but when the new "white zinc" metal proved too soft, the soldier tilted to one side and had to be removed. Within the columns of the Excelsior Brigade monument (right) there is a space where the bust of General Daniel Sickles was supposed to be placed. When Sickles embezzled money from the State of New York's monument fund, there was not enough left to afford his likeness.

John Bachelder's lifelong struggle to establish the scene of "Pickett's Charge" as the crucible of the Civil War led him to name it the "High Water Mark of the Rebellion" and to
place (at his own expense) the "High Water Mark Tablet" monument. He also preserved
the "Copse of Trees" to serve as a highly symbolic place to visit. As a result, it is now the
most visited area of the battlefield, as demonstrated by this 1902 photo of Gettysburg
tourists.

He did not enlist in the Union army until four months after Gettysburg and then served as a drummer boy in a regiment stationed in Tennessee that never saw any action. Yet Albert Woolson's image is cast in "heroic size" bronze in a prominent location on the Gettysburg battlefield, where it is the focus of the annual Remembrance Day ceremonies.

Erected in 1925 by New Yorkers who sought to claim their state's share of credit for success in the battle, the New York Auxiliary Monument stands "in recognition of the services rendered by those corps, division, and brigade commanders at Gettysburg not elsewhere honored on this field."

Once John Bachelder succeeded in making his "High Water Mark" the symbolic focal point of the battlefield, veterans adorned the "Bloody Angle" at Gettysburg with numerous monuments and markers. Within a short distance of the "Copse of Trees" (left) are the controversial 72nd Pennsylvania monument (right), the Armistead marker (center just in front of cannons), and the North Carolina advance marker, intentionally placed several paces closer to the enemy than Armistead's symbolic Virginia high point.

Inspired by a sympathetic portrayal in the movie *Gettysburg*, a less intrusive monument to much maligned General James Longstreet takes many visitors by surprise as it lacks the huge pedestal and statuesque design of earlier equestrian monuments. The statue has been criticized for resembling the film character more than the general himself.

than Bachelder did in writing a history of the Battle of Gettysburg. After gathering thousands of firsthand accounts, taking hundreds of battlefield strolls with veterans, and developing an intimate knowledge of the terrain and topography, when the time came to produce his $50,000 tome, apparently Bachelder agreed with those who had pointed out the difficulty. Despite years of written and oral conversations with hundreds, if not thousands, of eyewitnesses, the final product of his endeavor was an eight-volume, 2,000-page summary of the battle taken largely from the already published official reports of the battle. Less than 10 percent of this work makes use of the vast body of knowledge he collected.

The Gettysburg volumes of the *Official Records of the Union and Confederate Armies in the War of the Rebellion*, published by the War Department in the 1880s, rendered the Bachelder history relatively useless as a well of historical information. Why Bachelder failed to make use of his mountain of evidence is unclear; when he chose to rely almost exclusively on the official records, he did so despite numerous warnings from both sides. On many occasions, veterans had reminded Bachelder not to place too much importance on them. Confederate General Joseph Kershaw was one who lamented the difficulty of building war histories at all. "Few men *can* describe these matters accurately," he wrote. "Many *will* not. Official Reports are the best data, but even these are not always reliable, indeed are mostly not."[54]

An even stronger warning came from a Michigan cavalry commander who wrote, "I am aware that so far as I was concerned the reports of my regiment for the Gettysburg campaign were very deficient in detail: indeed, we thought or cared very little about reports, what we wanted at the time was to finish up the war and get home, and for that reason I know that great injustice had been done to my officers and men for such neglect."[55]

Historians have speculated on why a man with such an enormous advantage failed to make use of it. The general consensus is that the numerous controversies and disagreements among veterans over what

happened in July 1863 made it difficult for Bachelder to create a history that would stand as the most important work without simply generating endless arguments among those who contributed their recollections to it.

In reality, when it came time to put pen to paper and commit to one version of the truth over another, Bachelder came to the realization that so many Gettysburg historians have since followed him to. There is no "what really happened" at Gettysburg; only a mountain of varying, often contradictory accounts that are seldom in accord, all tainted in some way or other by memory, bias, politics, ego, or a host of other factors.

In an enlightening exchange a Michigan officer responded to a comment by Bachelder that writing a truly factual history from all of the veteran recollections was impossible. "I already knew the truth of your statement that it is impossible to harmonize these different visions of the same engagement. Hardly any two of the same regiment can agree. And this leads me to say Colonel that I wonder you are still alive after the pulling and hauling for it nearly five years over this Gettysburg history."[56]

Despite its apparent failure to produce the intended single work of history, the congressional investment paid great dividends, perhaps justifying the outrageous expense. While assembling the history, Bachelder collected a storehouse of data, most of it firsthand accounts, that rivals any collection of information on a single event in American history. Beyond the value of what he collected on his own, his work spurred countless discussions, debates, and recordings of thoughts, ideas, and memories by thousands of veterans, even though these were tainted in some way by Bachelder's influence. Based on the lasting affect that his work had on the story of the battle, he is without question the single most important Gettysburg historian of all time.

Civil War veterans focused their postwar attention on Gettysburg mainly because Bachelder provided them a hefty base of information on which to exchange opinions and arguments. At the same time, his ongoing effort to extract details and recollections from them kept a myriad

This early view of the summit of Little Round Top shows the original monument placed by the 91st Pennsylvania as a memorial to their commander, General Stephen Weed. Years later, as the legend of the deaths of Weed and Lieutenant Charles Hazlett grew to prominence, the veterans of the 91st moved the marker back to a rock (B) where legend said that Lieutenant Hazlett had died, physically bringing the two death sites together and in line with the legend. Today a larger, more prominent monument to the regiment marks the original site. The statue of General Warren "discovering" the Confederate advance was placed on the prominent rock (A) in 1882, and the cannons representing Hazlett's Battery were moved back to accommodate a new pathway and observation area.

of discussions and debates alive in postwar literary circles that might otherwise have drifted into relative obscurity. Bachelder's work kept the story of Gettysburg alive so that it achieved a status greater than any other conflict in the war. Whether it actually was the decisive event he had sought to study, or just one of many key episodes of the war that he inflated to that place of importance, clearly in the popular mind Gettysburg became, and remains to this day, the pivotal moment of the Civil War. It is important to remember, however, that this is not only the result of its magnitude as a military event or the numbers of soldiers who fought and fell compared to other fights; no other fight had a John Bachelder. The legend of Gettysburg had what no other battle had—the tireless energy of a New Hampshire landscape painter armed with a massive appropriation from the Federal Treasury and determined to make others believe that this was the greatest story of the war and perhaps the nation.

Despite the fact that leaders like Napoleon Bonaparte and Alexander the Great took historians along on campaigns to record their triumphs, Bachelder may well be the most influential historian of a single battle in military history. No other ever returned to the field with thousands of officers of both armies with the specific purpose of aiding in the establishment of a single history. No other ever actively sought information on commonly accepted maps of the field. None was supported by a huge stipend from the government that eventually served over both sides. Despite all of these advantages and all his years of endless toil, he simply could not sort out the truth and would not choose one version over another and promote it as the official history. Since his death in 1893, however, thousands of historians with substantially less advantage have written and published historical works that have helped shape, reshape, and define what society collectively thinks of as the ever changing story of Gettysburg.

CHAPTER 6

LOST IN THE LOST CAUSE

We went to war on account of the thing we quarreled with the North
about. I never heard of any other cause of quarrel than slavery . . .
Men fight from sentiment. After the fight is over they invent some fan-
ciful theory on which they imagine that they fought.
JOHN SINGLETON MOSBY[1]

It is likely that never before had an army of soldiers focused more on
their own sins than did the men in gray who followed Robert E. Lee
away from Gettysburg and home to Virginia. Georgia private Azariah
Bostwick penned the feelings of many of his comrades in Lee's army
when he wrote: "I believe we as a nation have incurred the displeasure of
a just God, and have been exceedingly wicked . . . and the reverses we
have met of late have all been for our good, and to make us more humble
and to have a firm reliance in Him."[2]

Confronted by the stark reality of their first clear-cut defeat of the
war, soldiers of the Army of Northern Virginia strained to find an explanation why they had been whipped by a Yankee army that they had so
magnificently trounced on so many previous fields. For many of them,
the answer lay in their own sinful behavior and, in repentance, they created the largest religious revival movement of the entire war.

As for what their transgressions were, each soldier had his own opinion, often at variance with his comrades, but the *Richmond Advocate* took the time and space to list the sins then gripping the Confederate capitol, namely "profanity, dancing, theatre-going, frivolity, a harsh temper, croaking, pimping and operating in money, Sabbath breaking, liquor, snarling, and especially extortion."[3]

Historian Troy Harman explored the late 1863 revival in Lee's army and saw that it led directly from their losses. "After Gettysburg," he wrote, "the revivals occurred on a much larger scale . . . as there was a general sentiment within the rank-in-file of the need for repentance. There was a sense that the losses at Gettysburg and Vicksburg were the results of God's punishment for ongoing sins in both Lee's army and the Confederate nation."[4]

A similar religious upheaval occurred in the army after Antietam the previous fall—the other battle that they could not claim as a victory—but the revivalist fever that gripped the Army of Northern Virginia after Gettysburg may be rightly considered the largest "Come to Jesus" movement in American military history. "The converts were so numerous," one Southern soldier recalled, "that they were numbered not by tens and hundreds but by thousands."[5]

Historian Bell Wiley also noted the rise in post-Gettysburg Confederate revivalism, attributing it to military defeat. "A series of setbacks that began with Gettysburg and Vicksburg was seen as a rebuke from the Almighty to sin and to overweening reliance on the strength of man," he wrote. "It is significant that evangelism reached its peak immediately after Gettysburg and Vicksburg."[6]

Not all Southerners associated battlefield successes and failures with God's will, of course, but all recognized that their leaders seemed to believe so, and they lamented it. "I think it was a serious incubus upon us," wrote a Confederate soldier, "that during the whole war our president and many of our generals really and actually believed that there *was* this mysterious Providence always hovering over the field and ready to interfere on one side or the other and that prayers and piety might win favor from day to day."[7]

Within this statement lies the taproot of what is probably the most powerful and influential cultural myth in American history. Southern leaders, prominent and educated men who later helped write the history of the war, professed a firm belief that they were fighting for a righteous cause with the full blessing and encouragement of the Almighty. At war's end, however, the stark reality of failure forced them to confront a powerful psychological dilemma. Failing to win the war raised the possibility that perhaps they had not been fighting on God's side after all. To accept this idea was to acknowledge that they had engaged in four years of unimaginable death and destruction, all the while acting *against* God's will. Given that the inevitable outcome of such behavior was eternal damnation in a fiery hell—and worse, admitting that God was on the Yankee side—it is no wonder leading men of the postwar South took on the challenge of devising a different way to rationalize their loss. The result of this understandable human effort is what historians have labeled the Lost Cause.

A Richmond newspaperman named Edward A. Pollard created the label for this cultural phenomenon within a year of the war's end, and writers and historians have penned a small mountain of words on the subject ever since. Among the many tenets of Lost Cause mythology is the reduction of slavery as a cause of the war and an emphasis on other issues, such as state's rights, as the real reason the South went to war. Nearly a century and a half after Pollard labeled the idea, the debates over root causes of the war and the meaning of the Confederacy are persistently popular issues in state and national politics today.[8]

This did not happen spontaneously. It was, rather, the result of concerted efforts by many of the learned and active men of the South who sought not only to find some form of righteousness in their failed cause but also to lash out at the Yankee yoke of reconstruction under which the Southern states chafed for more than a decade after the fighting ceased.

In this climate an elaborate assemblage of groups, organizations, and particularly literary outlets grew to social dominance.

Alfred Taylor Bledsoe, a Virginia professor and Confederate undersecretary of war, founded the *Southern Review* defending the Southern legacy in Baltimore in 1867, a year after former Confederate general D. H. Hill began publishing *The Land We Love* in Charlotte, North Carolina. *Scribner's Monthly Magazine* began publishing in 1871, and along with the *Century Illustrated Monthly* featured Southern writers prominently, though they were not specifically Southern institutions. The Southern Historical Society, which clearly was, began publishing its *Papers* in 1876, while the United Confederate Veterans published the *Confederate Veteran* monthly shortly thereafter, among many others. Various veteran and survivors associations, particularly those in prominent southern cities such as Charleston and New Orleans, led to more substantial and powerful organizations such as the Southern Historical Society (SHS).

As historian David Blight described this group's motivating mission,

> the SHS worked from the assumption that the war's victors would never do them justice in the history books or in the emerging memoir literature. Based on the collection they had assembled in the offices reserved for them in the Virginia State Capitol, the SHS leadership put their faith in the power of documentation. These ex-soldiers demanded respect and would try to argue their way to righteousness before the bar of history.[9]

Though it was officially formed in 1894, the United Daughters of the Confederacy, perhaps the most powerful of these groups, rose to prominence as the self-described "outgrowth of many local memorial, monument and Confederate Home Associations and auxiliaries to Camps of Confederate Veterans which were organized after the War Between the States."[10] Led by literary and social elites, the movement painted a chivalrous, romantic view of the prewar South that was absorbed by the entire culture. Nearly all average Southerners participated in organizations and consumed literature that shaped a particular view of the war and the South as a whole. As historian Gaines Foster pointed out, "More Southerners formed an understanding of their past through the ceremonial activities or rituals conducted by these groups than anything else."[11]

Chief among the learned and active men who led this cultural movement was Jubal Early, a former Confederate general and Virginia aristocrat. Early had opposed his state's secession in 1861, publicly arguing that it was "a great crime . . . against the cause of liberty and civilization."[12] Nevertheless, he was a devoted soldier for his state when secession and then war finally came. After the conflict, Early lived in self-exile in Toronto, Canada, until 1869. Shortly after returning to Virginia, he became financially well-off, having connected himself with the Louisiana lottery in the mid–1870s, and his wealth allowed him to concentrate on shaping the postwar history and image of the Confederacy. He lectured and wrote extensively and eventually rose to the presidency of the Southern Historical Society and the Association of the Army of Northern Virginia, giving him great influence.

Lost Cause historian Gary Gallagher described the reach of Early's dominance when he wrote that "younger ex-Confederates who would hold major state and national offices, as well as political leaders of an earlier generation, turned to Early for advice, took care to explain positions they knew would be at odds with his, and otherwise indicated that he was a man to be reckoned with."[13]

Confederate artillery commander E. Porter Alexander played a critical role in the Army of Northern Virginia during the war, particularly at Gettysburg, and a comment he made to John Bachelder in 1876 serves as a key example of Early's power over the literature of the war and his selective use of the sources he controlled.

> I collected material for some years after the war with a view to publishing a History of Longstreet's Corps, but I could not procure all I required and was unwilling to proceed with less, so I eventually gave to the Southern

Historical Society Hd Qrs. in Richmond all I had collected and they published parts of my own writings and some of the report I had collected,
(not heretofore in print) from time to time in the Southern Magazine of
Baltimore (Turnbull Press) up to July last: and since Jan. 76 in a monthly
publication they are bringing out.[14]

Though Alexander had intended this valuable collection of facts to help
build an accurate history of the war, Early used them instead as ammunition in his struggle to shape the history of Gettysburg and the Civil War.

Since E. A. Pollard's *The Lost Cause* first appeared in print in 1866, historians, scholars, and novelists have amassed an enormous body of literature on Lost Cause mythology, making it a controversial subject through
the decades. Although a review of the long history of this complex historical struggle lies outside the scope of this discussion, it is nonetheless
enlightening to explore some of the ways that Gettysburg figured prominently in the Lost Cause and vice versa.

In the literary form of the Lost Cause, whether a Greek tragedy or a
more modern reiteration, there is a central heroic character who rises
above the failure of his own efforts. For Southerners, Robert E. Lee, or
rather an idealistic exaggeration of him, became the embodiment of that
image. Despite his failure to lead his army and his people to victory, Lee
is revered as the ultimate paragon of virtue and humanity.

Three years after the war, a Southern writer named Fanny Downing
described Lee as "bathed in the white light which falls directly upon him
from the smile of an approving and sustaining God."[15] Several years
afterward John W. Daniel of Jubal Early's staff wrote of him, "The Divin-
ity in his bosom shown translucent through the man, and his spirit rose
up the Godlike."[16] Bathed in white light but translucent, godlike in
spirit, Lee was elevated in postwar literature to a height that no mortal
could ever possibly achieve—indeed to accept the modern image of him
is to believe that the modest Lee would have been embarrassed by the
attention.

This idolization of Lee created a problem for those who recognized or encouraged Gettysburg's growing stature as the war's most prominent battle. It could easily be argued that at Gettysburg, the man they sought to elevate to near sainthood had failed as a commander, leading his army to its most devastating defeat.

In many ways, the story of Gettysburg is both the linchpin of the Lost Cause and a reflection of it. Virtually all of the published history of the battle is tainted by the ongoing struggle among Southerners to rationalize their loss. Since Gettysburg was the first clear-cut Confederate defeat in the prominent eastern theater of the war, it is naturally a major focus of these rationalizations.

The logic of the rationale proceeds by steps. First, the South lost because some great, even diabolical human error at a pivotal point in the war led to the failure of Confederate arms, not because it was God's will. In postwar literature, Gettysburg became this pivotal moment and it is within this context that many soldiers promoted it as the crucial turning point of the war. Having established an appropriately critical moment at which victory in the war could fall either way, Jubal Early and his allies focused on a small group of human errors—none of which were their own—to explain Southern defeat. These naturally gave rise to that other necessary character in the literary form. If Lee was the hero, there must also be a villain or in this case—just to be sure their efforts succeeded— a handful of them.

The first of those who fell under this characterization was General J.E.B. Stuart, Lee's most significant cavalry leader. Despite his role as the "eyes and ears of the army" Stuart failed to remain in contact with Lee or his army for several crucial days leading up to the battle. Thus the cavalry commander helped lose the battle by not providing Lee with the information he needed as to the strength and whereabouts of Federal forces, leaving the Southern commander groping blind across the Pennsylvania countryside. Lacking this information, Lee found himself drawn into battle at a location that favored the Federals, a fact that contributed heavily to the Union victory. Those who put forth this explanation seldom pointed out, among other key points, that Lee had significant cavalry forces, separate from those under Stuart's command, traveling with him throughout the campaign and that they also could have collected the information Stuart is supposed to have failed to supply.

The second target of those who sought to explain the loss at Gettysburg and thus the loss of the war was General Richard S. Ewell, commander of Lee's Second Corps and Jubal Early's direct superior. Ewell's troops were in a position to push the retreating Yankees hard after their line collapsed during the first day of the battle, attack the confused, disorganized enemy gathering on Cemetery Hill and drive them from the high ground, forcing the catastrophic defeat that might have given the South complete victory. Instead of doing so, however, Ewell stopped his advancing troops and declined a strong suggestion from Lee to press on. Seldom do these detractors point out the legitimate and compelling issues on which Ewell based his decision. Instead they argue that by failing to attack at this crucial juncture, when the Federals were on the verge of complete defeat, he bungled and cost them the war.

The third and most often cited target of the Early syndicate was General James Longstreet, for whom they saved their harshest and most destructive attacks, creating the darkest and most vile villain of their enterprise. Fortunately for them, Longstreet had all but volunteered for the role.

Only two years after the war, while Louisiana strained under the overbearing weight of the Federal government's policy of Reconstruction, the *New Orleans Picayune* published a request of numerous Southern leaders seeking advice on how best to cope with their unhappy situation, which amounted to a military occupation. As one of those specifically named in the request, Longstreet offered his assessment.[17]

In his view, the swiftest route to a post-Reconstruction was to cooperate, in appearance at least, or as he put it, "to wisely unite in efforts to restore Louisiana to her former position in the Union through the party now in power."[18] Resting subtly beneath his rhetoric is a political strategy

with some merit. By temporarily acquiescing to the Northern government's policies of Reconstruction, the South could more quickly slip
from under the oppressive yoke and regain political control. Wise though
it may have been, the idea of even pretending to cower under the foot of
Yankee oppression was too great a proposal for most Southerners to bear.
The ink had barely dried on the newsprint before other Southern leaders
began to savage Longstreet. As he wrote:

> The afternoon of the day upon which my letter was published the paper
> that had called for advice published a column of editorial calling me trai-
> tor! deserter of my friends! and accusing me of joining the enemy! but did
> not publish a line of the letter upon which it based the charges! Other
> papers of the Democracy took up the garbled representation of this jour-
> nal and spread it broadcast, not even giving the letter upon which they
> based their evil attacks upon me.[19]

Until his death Longstreet never completely distanced himself from
the negative labels that his former comrades began to attach to him in the
days following publication of this letter, though he bears at least some of
the responsibility. Rather than show sensitivity to the views of his critics,
he seemed almost eager to give them more ammunition. He had a knack
for including Robert E. Lee among those who should bear responsibility
for wartime failures, particularly at Gettysburg, and even committed the
dual sins of becoming both a Catholic and a Republican. He campaigned
for U.S. Grant in 1868 and then accepted Grant's nomination to the Federal post as surveyor of the Port of New Orleans.

All of Longstreet's political missteps helped paint a target squarely on
his back toward which those who sought to explain the loss at Gettysburg
while sparing Lee's reputation could fire at will. This culmination of
events gave rise to what historian Gaines Foster calls the "Longstreet Lost
It At Gettysburg" theory.[20] To deal a crushing blow to Longstreet's reputation, Early and his henchmen chose a tactic that even the rascally Dan

Sickles had not entirely stooped to—though he was certainly not above doing so. They simply made up the facts.[21]

Just as Dan Sickles used his relationship with President Lincoln and congressional leaders to shape the history of Gettysburg by attacking George Meade, Jubal Early used his prominence, free time, and literary power to do the same with James Longstreet. Speaking at Washington and Lee University just two years after Lee passed away while serving as its president, Early, who had only recently returned from his self-imposed exile in Canada, concocted the idea that Lee had issued an order for Longstreet to attack the Union left flank at sunrise on July 2 at Gettysburg. By Early's assessment, Longstreet's failure to do so, and the delay of ten hours or more that he thus created, proved the difference in that pivotal day of fighting. A year afterward, William Pendleton echoed Early's fabrication, claiming he had personally scouted out the Union left flank on July 1, and that Lee had ordered Longstreet to attack the following dawn. His failure to do so, Pendleton argued, caused the Southern loss.[22]

On that crucial evening at Gettysburg, Early was about as far from Lee and Longstreet as a Confederate could get and still be on the battlefield, and thus he likely had no firsthand knowledge of any conversation between them. In addition, according to one of Lee's staff members, Early's comrade Pendleton "suffered some type of paralytic attacks that interfered with his memory."[23] Nevertheless Early's speech appeared in print the following year and the "sunrise attack order" became part of the Gettysburg literature. Lee was dead and could not set the record straight, and many of his subordinates who were in a position to know of such an order were either so angry with Longstreet, so enamored of Lee, or both, that they chose not to challenge Early's assertions publicly. As a result, the idea that Longstreet intentionally disobeyed an order from Lee shifted blame for the loss from the South's chief icon to a subordinate who was not a Virginian and had made himself a target by his own doing.

The idea that Lee would have planned and ordered a dawn attack on July 2 at Gettysburg is easily dismissed with even a brief assessment of the circumstances. Two of Longstreet's three divisions were more than twenty miles from Gettysburg at dawn on that crucial second day, a fact of which Lee was well aware. Further, those members of Lee's staff who did speak up on the subject—some of them years afterward—made it clear that even the idea of such an order was out of the question. Nevertheless, Early and his compatriots succeeded in painting Longstreet as the villain while simultaneously diverting any critical assessment of Lee's generalship at Gettysburg.

Historian Alan Nolan, a critic of the iconic Lee legend, observed concerning the power of the Lost Cause, "I insist that the legend exists and that it is more popularly entrenched than the history of the period. Indeed, it serves as the history of the period."[24] If there is any doubt about the power of the myth to shape a particular image of the Confederacy and its fighting men, we need look no further than the visual image that the literary tradition created, not of prominent men such as Lee or Longstreet but of the average Confederate fighting man.

As the opening of the fifth episode of Ken Burns's film *The Civil War* fades from black, the viewer sees one of the war's most famous images: three Confederate soldiers standing on the grounds of the Lutheran Theological Seminary at Gettysburg. The photo has been romantically described as a symbol of the model Confederate fighting man, upright and stalwart, defiant to the end. The first sounds of this episode come from the voice of Shelby Foote, the Southern novelist whom Burns chose as his central commentator for the series.

There's a photograph I'm fond of. It shows three Confederate soldiers who were captured at Gettysburg and they are posed in front of or alongside a snake rail fence and you see exactly how the Confederate soldier was dressed. You see something in his attitude toward the camera that's revealing of his nature, and one of them has his arms like this; as if he is having his picture made but he's determined to be the individual that he is. There's something about that picture that draws me strongly as an image of the war.[25]

Despite the fondness that many feel for this photo and its idealized imagery, there is a flaw in the logic of this perspective that is as common in the literature of the war as it is easy to discredit. The date of the photo, virtually always listed when it appears in print, is July 15, 1863. Assuming the date is accurate, then these men were still in Gettysburg eleven full days after the Army of Northern Virginia had left the area. Given that the Union Army sent Confederate prisoners south to Baltimore within a few hours of capture, and that none of these men appears to be seriously wounded, it is highly probable that they were captured long after the fighting ended, meaning they were either deserters from the army or shirkers hiding from duty. Nevertheless, starry-eyed romantics of the Lost Cause have continually ignored this underlying defect in their own logic.

This photo also exposes an enduring legend regarding the clothing and equipment of the Southern soldier. One of the key elements of Lost Cause mythology is that the North won because of an overwhelming advantage in industrial capability, not because of any moral superiority. God *was* on their side, former Confederates argued, but the enemy had too many advantages. The Yankees had more guns, more ammunition, more soldiers, more everything, and while this sentiment was based in fact—the industrial might of the North far outweighed that of the South—the image was often taken to extremes. Within this element is the caricature that survives today of a ragged Confederate army, poorly equipped and barely clothed but still proving the match of the Federals in battle after battle. The resulting image of the Confederate soldier as a ragamuffin but a fierce fighter lingers powerfully in the national conscience even today, reinforced by thousands of paintings, films, and novels.

The soldiers in the photo in which Shelby Foote sees "exactly how the Confederate soldier was dressed," don well-fitting uniforms without a patch or tear in view. Their haversacks are full and, despite Foote's contention that they were in Gettysburg to collect the shoes they were so badly lacking, they each have the benefit of substantial footwear. In spite of this photographic evidence and Foote's fondness toward it, he is among the many authors who have perpetuated the myth of the ragamuffin Confederate soldier.

Richard Pougher, a Virginian and former curator at Richmond's venerable Museum of the Confederacy, spent years poring over Confederate uniforms and photographs of Southern soldiers shown nearest to combat events, as well as those shown in photographs taken immediately after the fighting, either the dead or prisoners of war. He sought to determine scientifically just how well equipped the average soldier in Lee's army was while on campaign in the field. His findings exposed the legendary ragamuffin image as faulty.

"The traditional, historic portrayal, reflecting these men as suffering severe privations in terms of uniforms and equipment, is incorrect," he concluded. "Southern enlisted men were, in fact, well appointed throughout the war with proper uniforms and requisite equipage."[26]

Far from a ragged David fighting off the war machine of the Yankee Goliath, "the common Confederate soldier in the Army of Northern Virginia was well dressed in Southern military uniforms, well-shod, and well accoutered with the requisite equipment throughout the war. He was not the ragged, barefoot, poorly equipped individual in nondescript mix-and-match clothing so many have come to see him as."[27]

Without question the most prominent and influential scholar to write about Gettysburg and Lee in particular during the twentieth century was Douglas Southall Freeman. Though Freeman grasped the idea that veterans' memories and the reality of history often diverged, he had difficulty taking Lee to task for failures. Reflecting on Pickett's famous charge, he contrasted the recollections of veterans with the popular perception that grew up later on. "Every emotion there was of vain and costly assault," wrote Freeman, "every one except a consciousness that more than a battle had been lost; the enemy had beaten them back; they could do no more. The rest of it—war's decision, America's destiny, the doom of the Confederacy—all this was read afterward into the story of their return."[28] By downplaying the importance of Pickett's Charge to the outcome of the war as a whole, Freeman, a Richmond native who adored the Robert E. Lee of legend, sought to downplay the importance of what can rightly be described as Lee's biggest military blunder. Nevertheless, he recognized the disparity that exists between what soldiers thought at the time and what history later recorded.

In time, scholars took Freeman to task for what they perceive as an inherent bias toward Lee and the Lost Cause. Alan Nolan argued that "in addition to anonymous, unverifiable anecdotes about Lee the man, Freeman rationalized every blemish, always blamed Lee's subordinates for military failures, and emasculated documents that would mar this characterization."[29] Nevertheless, Freeman's image of Lee dominated Civil War scholarship for decades.

In the twilight years of the last millennium, Lost Cause mythology was the subject of heated and voluminous debate, most of it attacking men like Jubal Early as having white supremacy in the South at heart. The growing backlash against racist literature of the past caused historians to dismiss most or all of the writings left to us by veterans of the war who weighed in on the side of the romantic, chivalrous South. As the twenty-first century dawned, the pendulum seemed to be swinging back toward the center.

Historians such as Gary Gallagher have found room to learn from the literature while recognizing its potential failings as factual record. Regarding the South's chief commanding general, for example, he believes that because of the South's inherent connection to slavery, scholars who react against Lost Cause mythology often discredit Lee's abilities out of hand due to the central place that Early and his ilk gave him in their romantic Southern drama. However, to do so, he argues, is to overlook the fact that despite the overinflation of his stature, Lee was a skilled commander. "In short," says Gallagher, "Lee adapted well to the demands of a conflict that far exceeded in scope and complexity anything he or anyone else could have anticipated in the spring of 1861."[30]

Gallagher also points out that Lee's wartime behavior demonstrated that his views were anything but those of a man waxing nostalgic about a romantic past. "Far from looking back toward the traditional South," wrote Gallagher, "he looked forward to a Confederate nation that in many ways would little resemble the society into which he had been born."[31]

In the most recent work on Gettysburg's much heralded third day, Earl Hess reflects the new path that many scholars have chosen. Instead of espousing the romantic postwar notions of the combatants, his assessment of the South's failure has little to do with Lee. In explaining the failure of Pickett's Charge, Hess argues against one of Jubal Early's postwar henchmen. "Lee's artillery chief Pendleton," wrote Hess, "completely failed to coordinate the army's guns and there was a fatal lack of cooperation between the artillery chiefs of the three corps."[32]

All of the internal Southern debate over which of them was to blame for the loss has led to an interesting phenomenon at Gettysburg. Much of the historical writing on the conflict seeks to explain why the South lost, rather than why the North won. Even in defeat, Lee's army is the center of attention. Though it has taken hold firmly, this is not a recent phenomenon. Debates over the outcome of the battle tend to focus on the question of why the South lost. They stress the South's inferior industrial capacity, the overconfidence of Lee and his soldiers, dissent among Lee's subordinates including Ewell, Stuart, and chiefly Longstreet. This squabbling seems to have distracted attention away from another issue that may be at the heart of the matter. George Pickett, the man for whom the culminating charge was named, seemed far ahead of his time when he supposedly weighed in on the issue years afterward. Asked on a visit to the battlefield why he felt the South lost, he reportedly replied: "I've always thought the Yankees had something to do with it."[33]

Pickett's Charge provided another important element of the Lost Cause mythology in that it served to reduce the entire Civil War to one critical and momentous instant while also depicting a superior quality among Southern soldiers. It provided a critical moment in time when some fatal human flaw, rather than the determining will of God, could and did seal the Confederacy's fate. The more they elevated the importance of the battle and particularly the charge, the easier it was to accept this idea. Further, the more desperate and suicidal the image of the charge became, the greater was the idea that Southern soldiers exhibited bravery, heroism, and commitment to their cause, qualities that they presumably held in ways far superior to the Yankees.

This concept that the Old South represented something more chivalrous and more attractive than the rest of the nation—or for that matter the postwar nation as a whole—was generated by the inventors of the Lost Cause and has permeated Southern literature ever since. William Faulkner, a man whose fiction has come to reflect and represent everything Southern, once summed up this combination of ideas about Gettysburg, Pickett's Charge, and Southern memory when he painted this word picture in his novel *Intruder in the Dust*.

For every Southern boy fourteen years old, not once but whenever he wants it, there is the instant when it's still not yet two o'clock on that July afternoon in 1863, the brigades are in position behind the rail fence, the guns are laid and ready in the woods and the furled flags are already loosened to break out and Pickett himself with his long oiled ringlets and his hat in one hand probably and his sword in the other looking up the hill waiting for Longstreet to give the word and it's all in the balance, it hasn't happened yet, it hasn't even begun yet, it not only hasn't begun yet but there is still time for it not to begin against that position and those circumstances which made more men than Garnett and Kemper and

Armistead and Wilcox look grave yet it's going to begin, we all know that, we have come too far with too much at stake and that moment doesn't need even a fourteen-year-old boy to think This time. Maybe this time with all this much to lose and all this much to gain: Pennsylvania, Maryland, the world, the golden dome of Washington itself to crown with desperate and unbelievable victory the desperate gamble, the cast made two years ago.[34]

Though it is probably impossible to completely assess and summarize the enormous impact that the Lost Cause has had on American culture since Pollard first launched the idea in 1866, it is clear that the mythology as a whole is inextricably linked with the story of Gettysburg. The literature of the battle was deeply affected by the falsehoods and exaggerations of men like Jubal Early and the responses of men such as Longstreet for decades afterward—indeed until the present. Perhaps the most certain thing about the efforts of those who promoted the ideas of the Lost Cause is that, by and large, they succeeded in greatly affecting the history of Gettysburg and in painting Robert E. Lee as a national hero in the midst of his greatest military defeat.

In 1995, when officials at the Gettysburg battlefield suggested that the story told by the National Park Service there should change, the Sons of Confederate Veterans labeled the suggestion an attempt to "modify and alter historical events to make them more 'palatable' to a greater number of park visitors." Their stated goal was that the Park Service "return to its unaligned and apolitical policies of the past, presenting history, not opinions."[35]

What the Sons did not seem to recognize is that the history of Gettysburg is little more than opinion and that the two ideas are irrevocably inseparable. Whether Robert E. Lee was a great or terrible general is as much a matter of historical opinion as the many ideas put forward to explain Southern defeat. There simply *is* no definitive right or wrong. The policies of the past that the Sons would have the Park Service perpetuate are no less political or aligned as any other version of the so-called truth. Society has merely chosen to focus more on the arguments of Jubal Early at one time, for example, and then James Longstreet at another. In the ever changing history of Gettysburg, the ideas of Dan Sickles held sway for a time, and then those of George Meade. At neither period was one history more right or more wrong than the other, but this argument continues to expose our knowledge of Gettysburg as a collection of changing and varying opinions manipulated intentionally or unwittingly by thousands of veterans and historians alike.

This process of creating heroes and villains is, of course, not in any way unique to Southerners, nor has it slowed over the decades. Though grown from very different circumstances, a new literary tradition has helped create another Civil War hero of equally epic proportions and, as with Lee, Gettysburg is at the heart of this new legend as well.

CHAPTER 7

CONSTRUCTING THE CONSUMMATE GETTYSBURG HERO

*By curious paradox, through the very fact of their respect for the past,
people came to reconstruct it as they considered it ought to have been.*
HISTORIAN MARC BLOCH[1]

I n the narrowing light of a late Pennsylvania afternoon on a small rock-strewn hill a half dozen miles above the line that Mason and Dixon drew to separate North from South, the unlikeliest of soldiers found himself thrust into the crucible of American history. He was soft-spoken and careful with words, the result of a childhood struggle with hard consonants that created in him what he called "nervous anxiety." Of small frame and unremarkable height, his one distinctive feature was the long, prominent mustache stretching from below an equally prominent nose, all of it forming a regal profile. Not twelve months earlier he had commanded little more than a classroom full of eager lads at a sleepy college in Maine, his greatest challenge being to form ideas in rhetoric or in revealed and modern religion. Now he stood on a small nubble of land two dozen feet high on which the Battle of Gettysburg would be won or lost. As he once taught young men to reason with books and words, he now led them to kill with muskets and lead—strange work for a man trained as a minister before becoming a professor. Victory, if it came, would be his only when the enemy now approaching had seen enough of the killing and turned away. Just here a nation torn asunder by civil war would persevere or perish, and it was all in his hands.

In moments the enemy came and rushed the small hill again and again, throwing against him four, five, perhaps ten times the number of men he had to defend it. Though twice hit by lead in the melee, calmly and with great poise he held his position, ordering men back here and forward there, until a lull brought unwelcome news. The enemy was organizing again in the thickets below, clumps of men growing larger until they became one long line of gray. Around him he heard the cry for ammunition but found none. A third of his own men were down and the rest were nearly without bullets; his once solid wall of blue was now tattered and thinned by the relentless assaults of the enemy. Behind him was the key to the battle, perhaps the entire war: a boulder-strewn hill with a view that commanded the countryside for miles. From its summit either army could bombard the other into submission. If the enemy seized it, he would throw open the door to Washington, where a triumphant Robert E. Lee could demand his own terms of surrender and the world's greatest example of self-government would falter; the great experiment democracy would end in failure.

At this critical moment the professor-turned-warrior fell back on his intellectual underpinnings and summoned an idea. A maneuver from an old army textbook might be his only salvation. Gathering his officers together, he passed on his plan. The remaining men in the regiment would fix their bayonets and charge down the hill into the still regrouping enemy line and, while swinging "like a gate on a post," the Mainers would sweep the enemy before them, perhaps saving the hill, the battle, and the nation in one fell swoop.

This is the legend of Joshua Chamberlain and his 20th Maine Regiment at Gettysburg, leading his men in an unlikely battlefield assault that held the left flank of the Union Army intact and in control of Little Round Top. When the charge ended—legend tells us—five regiments of Confederates had fled in its path, leaving four or five hundred prisoners in Chamberlain's care, among them some of the most battle-hardened men in Lee's army. Three decades later, the government of a grateful nation awarded the Maine colonel the Medal of Honor for his "courage and tenacity" on that crucial hillside.

If Americans have used the story of Gettysburg to elevate their sense of place in the world to that of other nations and empires, then they have also used it to find or construct their legendary heroes in the same fashion. For every Troy, there must be an Achilles. For every Paul Revere's ride there must be a Paul Revere. In Gettysburg mythology, there are many heroes and antiheroes, loathed or admired for many reasons. In the last decade of the twentieth century, however, one iconic hero emerged above all others to become the single most prominent, and promoted, Gettysburg figure of all. The one person whose story embodies the elements of misunderstanding, miscommunication, and outright invention that the Gettysburg story has become is this Maine colonel—Joshua Lawrence Chamberlain.

A long list of Chamberlain-related items has appeared in the marketing mainstream since 1990. They range from the more subdued tributes such as sculptures and paintings, to the more outrageous such as floatee pens, action figures, and even a Chamberlain night-light. A member of the now enormous Chamberlain fan club can drink Chamberlain pale ale from a Chamberlain coffee mug propped up against a Chamberlain pillow, spying a Chamberlain wall clock or wristwatch. The fan can purchase these and countless other manifestations of cult worship using a Chamberlain Visa card. If we once held our heroes aloft in the writings of Nathaniel Hawthorne and Henry Wadsworth Longfellow, we now measure them largely by the number of times their image adorns a T-shirt. By this measure of merchandise as hero worship, Chamberlain is, for now at least, the unchallenged ruler of the Civil War.

The common popular perception of Chamberlain centers on the hour or so of fighting on the second day of the Battle of Gettysburg, in which he played a key part. His experiences in the fighting on Little Round Top form the basis of his legend and are instrumental in his story. They are the context in which people, including perhaps even the man himself, evaluated his entire life.

This legend has lived and grown for more than a century. It is, for the most part, what the tourists who buy Chamberlain ale and night-lights attest to in the shops around Gettysburg. This is the story that brings millions of people to Little Round Top in search of their American hero. Yet this is a story full of easily disproved details. A story that is as much construction as it is fact. To understand how this story became the accepted version of events, and how Chamberlain became the most marketable figure in recent Civil War history, one must examine the "story of the story" of Chamberlain at Gettysburg. By dissecting its parts, we learn much about Americans and their relationship with their past.

The story of the story of Chamberlain at Gettysburg began in earnest in 1878. In that year, the Southern Historical Society in its *Papers* published a letter written by General James Longstreet to his uncle a few weeks after the battle. The author was the overall Confederate commander of the assaults that reached Little Round Top during the battle. In it, he stated that "the battle was not made as I would have made it," among other descriptions of why the Confederates failed to win a victory on July 2, 1863. A few months later, Colonel William C. Oates, Longstreet's subordinate and the man in command of the Alabama regiment that attacked the 20th Maine at Gettysburg, penned a response to the letter and forwarded it to the same periodical.

Regardless of where his opinions may have fallen in the pro- and anti-Longstreet debate then raging among veterans in various periodicals (and particularly this one), Oates had personal reasons for attaching blame—any blame at all—to James Longstreet. Among his other activities in the war Longstreet offended Oates deeply when he placed Oates's good friend and brigade commander, Evander Law, under arrest—twice. In addition, Oates held Longstreet responsible for preventing his own promotion to general during the war. With this attitude in mind, he set out to refute Longstreet's previously published account with great vigor.[2]

In the midst of his personal and professional refutation of Longstreet, however, Oates took about a page and a half to describe, in minor detail, his fight on Little Round Top. Almost as an aside to the rest of his anti-Longstreet rambling, Oates summed up the gravity of his own personal circumstances at Gettysburg. "Of 644 men and 42 officers, I had lost 343 men and 19 officers. The dead literally covered the ground. The blood stood in puddles on the rocks."[3]

Rather than fall back on the generalized phrases common to military hyperbole of the time and more effective when clouding numbers was a goal, Oates's statement seems to lay out exact statistics. These figures from his regiment alone—686 went in, 362 were lost—plainly indicate that he had a sizable regiment going in, and 53 percent casualties when it was finished. What is more, they point out the terrific effect that the 20th Maine had on its enemy, a fact given great credibility as it is an admission of failure by the vanquished. In essence, Oates was saying, "I was whipped, and badly." And he gave exact numbers to prove it.

Given the wide distribution of Southern Historical Society Papers among veterans of that time, these numbers became commonly available as a baseline by which others could begin to judge the size of the Confederate force that reached the 20th Maine's position. Oates's article was the first widely read account of the fight in which Chamberlain took part, and it is where certain elements of the legend began to diverge from fact.[4]

Not until twenty-seven years later did Oates correct in print a simple error that he made in his mathematical aside in 1878. Intent on damning Longstreet, and less focused on the details of his fight with Chamberlain, Oates's quick and shoddy research about his own part of the fight caused him to be off with his estimate of strength—way off. In 1905 he published a book recounting his experiences in the war and attempted, though far too late, to correct the record. In the latter account, he admitted that the heat, prolonged march, and other factors reduced his force to "less than four hundred officers and men who made that assault." He then explained the nature of his error.

> All these facts I did not know when I made my report nor when I wrote the article for the *Southern Historical Society Papers* in 1878, but close investigation since the war revealed them to me. In the hasty manner of writing my report I took as a basis of the strength of my regiment its last muster before we began the march to Pennsylvania. I also wrote the *[SHSP]* article after the war on the same basis, which was a mistake.[5]

That mistake nearly doubled the number of men believed to have attacked the 20th Maine from his regiment alone and also the number captured by Chamberlain and his men. While modern analysis of records and the report written by Oates within a month of the battle confirm the lower numbers as accurate, Oates's attempt at correction in his 1905 book came long after his errant figures had formed the beginning of the legend.[6]

Ironically, in that 1905 book Oates took issue with a speech he had read in *Maine at Gettysburg* (1898), a book compiling information on all of Maine's batteries and regiments in the battle. In it, the 20th Maine's official historian, Howard Prince, noted that "no less than four hundred prisoners, mostly from the Fifteenth and Forty-Seventh Alabama, were sent to the rear." Failing to understand his own role in the Maine man's calculations, Oates reported that "Captain Prince has but little over half the number of prisoners which he says were taken from those regiments and sent to the rear. General Chamberlain fell into the same error." Explaining these statistical inaccuracies, Oates went on to say that "all of us, on both sides, who were in such hot places as that were made to see double and are disposed to exaggerate in favor of our respective sides, and do it honestly in most cases."

What Oates failed to realize was that the Maine veterans, in their description of enemy strength, had based their calculations on his own 1878 article. As the only unit commander who escaped from Little Round Top alive and aware of how many men had done the same, Oates was the only Confederate in a position to later assess the strength of the attacking force. His erroneous 1878 *Papers* account was the only way men such as Prince and Chamberlain could have known the actual size of the Alabama force that had once opposed them at Gettysburg. Thus it was Oates's error, not the fog of war, that perpetuated the misunderstanding and set in motion a long chain of connected misstatements. With the publication of Oates's first article, the size of the Alabama assault force was firmly set in legend as being at least twice that of the Maine men under Chamberlain. Now deeply entrenched in the literature, these "facts" that he inadvertently contributed to the story would reverberate through the legend for decades.[7]

A former private of the 20th Maine and postwar minister placed the next stone in the foundation of the Chamberlain legend. Theodore Gerrish is among a handful of people in American history who, according to official government records at least, was eighteen years old for three years. On the last day of each calendar year during the Civil War each unit was "mustered for pay." Though they only occasionally received money at these events, they were nonetheless lined up and counted. The point of such formalities was to record the presence of each soldier along with his date of birth, hometown, height, the color of his eyes, hair, and complexion, and other details so that he could officially claim what pay was due him. Lacking photographic identification or the science of fingerprinting, these records provided what passed for proof of identity in the 1860s and left historians with a wealth of minor details on which to dwell.

Among the other features that these records reveal about Theodore Gerrish is that he was from a place so small that it did not warrant a name. Calling it a town seemed an exaggeration. Even the official maps of Maine simply listed it as T5 R3—the designation for the fifth township

along the third range of Aroostook County. These records also reveal that
Gerrish was eighteen years old when he enlisted in the summer of 1862
and failed to age another year until almost 1865. Actually, of course, Gerrish was only sixteen when he enlisted and, like so many other eager and
patriotic youths of the era, he lied about his age in order to meet the min-
imum requirement. He continued to do so until reality caught up with
the ruse and he began to age normally once again toward the war's end.
All of this means that Theodore was probably a scared young private from
a tiny spot in Maine and all of sixteen years old when his regiment
reached the southern slope of Little Round Top in July 1863.[8]

Shortcomings and all, this former private spoke up in print some nineteen years after Gettysburg to tell the story of his regiment from its first
to last day as a unit. He titled the book, *Army Life: A Private's Reminiscences
of the Civil War,* and it is the only full history of the regiment written by any
of the sixteen hundred men who once served in it. His description of the
20th Maine's part at Gettysburg has become one of the two or three most
often quoted sources on the subject. Author and historian John Pullen,
whose history of the 20th Maine is deservedly among the most popular
regimental histories ever written, said in 1995 that "many books are built
upon other books; and in writings on the Civil War, few books have been
built upon more often than those of Theodore Gerrish. . . . Without
thinking very hard at all, I can recall half a dozen recent books on the
20th Maine Regiment, Joshua Chamberlain, and the Battle of Gettysburg
which all use Gerrish as a source."[9]

Gerrish is a source for Ken Burns's description of the action on Little
Round Top in his film *The Civil War.* A narrator repeats the pivotal moment
from the young Mainer's Gettysburg description, though implying that it
is Chamberlain speaking.

How can I describe the scenes that followed? Imagine if you can, nine small
companies of infantry numbering perhaps three hundred men, in the form
of a right angle, on the extreme flank of an army of eighty-thousand men,

put there to hold the key of the entire position against a force at least ten times their number, and who are desperately determined to succeed in the mission upon which they came. Stand firm, ye boys from Maine, for not once in a century are men permitted to bear such responsibility for freedom and justice, for God and humanity, as are now placed upon you.[10]

While any author of the Victorian era can be easily forgiven a few dalliances with hyperbole—*every* soldier's position was "the key of the entire position," for example—one is left wondering how a veteran soldier could so badly misinterpret a fight. The fog of war, the inexperience of youth, and the lapse of memory over time are all understandable elements. A frightened young man of sixteen years might see more of the enemy before him than were actually there, but how could a fight between two units that records show were of relatively equal size blossom into one in which the enemy was "at least ten times their number"?

The vast overstatement has two sources, and a careful reading of Gerrish's book as a whole reveals the first. Throughout the descriptions of his experiences before and after Gettysburg he writes in the first person, using phrases such as "I saw this," or "I did that." In the Gettysburg chapter, however, he frequently uses demonstrative pronouns or the first person plural: "This happened" or "We," meaning the regiment, "went there." As it turns out, Gerrish's rhetorical query, "How can I describe the scenes that followed?" is one that his fellow soldiers might well have asked him in his lifetime, and in fact did.

Elements of Gerrish's Gettysburg account raised the ire of many of his wartime comrades who said so in local newspapers after its publication. The reason for his misinterpretation of the fight is now plain. According to medical and regimental records of the period, Theodore Gerrish was in a hospital in Philadelphia when the Battle of Gettysburg took place. Thus a man who was more than one hundred fifty miles away at the time it occurred wrote one of the most quoted eyewitness accounts on this part of the battle.[11]

The second source of his misstatement of strength is revealed in a question: If he wasn't at Gettysburg, how did he come up with such exaggerated numbers? The answer to this lies in a very simple, understandable, and common set of traits in human behavior. When Gerrish sat down in 1881 to write a book about his regiment in the Civil War, he could hardly have left out the battle for which the regiment was becoming quite famous. In order to fill the void that his absence from the unit had left in the reminiscences, he simply filled in the blanks as well as he could, taking from his memory the accounts of the battle that his buddies had related to him when he returned from the hospital in late summer.

Anyone who has ever been part of a group has likely observed the social phenomenon that takes place when one member misses an event that the others feel is highly important. By the time the absent friend has returned, even a small event may have become the grandest of adventures, growing in scope and importance with each retelling. Since being at this event became a huge source of pride and self-esteem among a group of young men in the close social confines of an army unit, his comrades likely had a high time goading poor Gerrish about missing the biggest battle of the war. The bigger they made the story of their part in it, the more they had on him.

Twenty years hence, Gerrish had only these tall tales, a handful of records with sketchy details, and the mistaken account by Colonel Oates on which to base the Gettysburg chapter of his book. One of the commonly known tidbits then bandying about among the veterans was the fact that at Gettysburg, the 20th Maine captured members of five Confederate regiments. It is unlikely that Gerrish ever knew or realized that their share of prisoners from three of the five was but a handful of men rounded up long after the fighting on Little Round Top ceased. The Maine men grabbed up a handful of men from the 4th and 5th Texas and one wayward member of the 4th Alabama on Big Round Top later that evening, but none of these units likely fired a single round in Chamberlain's direction—and certainly not Gerrish's. Thus he could incorrectly but honestly conclude, based on this data alone, that the 20th Maine fought and defeated five enemy units. If Gerrish then took the number of men that Colonel Oates mistakenly listed in his Alabama unit alone (686) and multiplied it by the five regiments he believed had attacked, the result is almost exactly ten times the "perhaps three hundred men" that Gerrish believed made up the 20th Maine. Hence his claim, and probably firm belief, that the Mainers fought "a force at least ten times their number."[12]

Reaching this point in their research, able historians could lay claim to reasonably definitive proof of the numerical superiority of Chamberlain's enemies, and many have. An eyewitness from each side had given carefully thought-out testimony, including print accounts, and each seemed to confirm the other. An experienced commander and a scared private, a Yankee and a Rebel, each arrived at what appeared to be the same general math.

Within twenty years of the battle, the mortar around the legend's foundation began to cure. In the mid–1880s veterans of the Maine regiment, Gerrish included, placed a granite monument at the crest of the hill they had defended against some number of Alabamians—however many that might have been. On this memorial to their dead, they inscribed a brief narrative of their part in the fighting claiming the prize of more than three hundred prisoners. Oates's mistaken figures regarding his strength surely played a role in choosing that number. When the monument went into place, the mistaken legendary numbers were forever etched in stone.

A modern analysis of the records, soldier by soldier, of Oates's Alabama regiment shows that it lost, in killed, wounded, and captured, 167 men. Even if the sixty-four losses of the much smaller 47th Alabama (of which seven companies fought near Oates and against both the 20th Maine and the 83rd Pennsylvania regiments for about five minutes) are added in, and then the dead are considered prisoners, there simply were not enough men in gray uniforms to equal the legendary claim that the

20th Maine snagged three hundred, and sometimes four hundred or more prisoners.[13]

The stories told by both Oates and Gerrish laid out information, however erroneous it may have been, that crept into the conversations, articles, speeches, and memoirs of the other veterans who read them. In time, the idea that Oates had attacked Chamberlain with a numerically superior force began to take hold. Yet theirs were only the first two of many elements that formed the base of the Chamberlain legend. The third came from the legend himself.

Among the most credible sources when human memory is an issue are those written closest to an event. Memory fades over time and the closer in time to the event one is, the more likely it is that the account given is accurate. With this in mind, historians have given great credence to the first account of the battle written by Chamberlain, which is dated just three days after the battle ended. This account was his official report of the battle, a document traditionally submitted to one's superiors as a matter of military protocol following each action. This account was later reprinted in the *Official Records*, and it became widely available to veterans and historians from the mid–1880s on. Two statements in this published report, however, raise doubt as to its date of origin. First, Chamberlain refers to the hill on which he fought as "Little Round Top" four times in this account. This is revealing in that the hill did not have a name in 1863 and did not become known by that one until years later. Also, Chamberlain's other correspondence at the time refers to the hill mistakenly as "Wolf Hill," a geographic feature more than a mile to the east, but never Little Round Top.[14]

While the first statement can be explained away as the editing of a War Department clerk, the second suspicious statement is far more curious. He writes that "Captain Billings, Lieutenant Kendall, and Lieutenant Linscott are officers whose loss we deeply mourn. . . ." If he had actually written this account on July 6, 1863, he would have had some careful explaining to do to two of these men. While Chamberlain's brother John brought him word on July 4 that Kendall had passed on, Billings and Linscott were alive and not necessarily in serious danger. Billings lived for two weeks after receiving his wound and succumbed on July 15. Linscott was alive on the date of Chamberlain's report, and he recovered so fully two weeks later that doctors sent him home to Maine on furlough. There he died on July 27, most likely of a fever or infection resulting from the wound. On July 17, in a letter to his wife, Chamberlain mentioned that five officers, including Linscott, were wounded, but "not seriously." The following month, while home in Maine on leave he began a letter to the governor with this statement: "I regret to learn indirectly of the death from wounds of Capt. Billings of Company 'C' & Lieut. Linscott."[15] Clearly, there was no way on July 6 that Chamberlain could have known which of his wounded men would eventually deserve his deep mourning, and War Department editing cannot explain away these subsequent statements.[16]

The answer to this mystery lay in a box deep in the National Archives for well over a century. Among the musty shelves of the inner hallways of this building is a group of records that researchers have seldom, if ever, opened. These are the records of the War Department for 1884. In the early part of the 1880s someone thought that the government should gather up all the orders, reports, and correspondence that it could and publish them in bound volumes for posterity. The War Department thus produced more than one hundred volumes known to Civil War buffs simply as the *Official Records*. Contained in these neglected archival boxes are the records of that project, including correspondence back and forth between clerks and veterans trying to assemble the appropriate pieces of information. Deep within this collection is a box containing the data that cover the collection of Gettysburg battle reports.[17]

In March 1884, the War Department got around to the Gettysburg portion of the *Official Records*. A clerk noticed that the report of the 20th Maine Regiment was not in the files, and he wrote to the unit's former commander to see about getting a copy. Chamberlain replied that he did not have one but would be happy to supply something, since "justice to that regiment demands that so important a portion of their listing should be preserved." The War Department agreed and asked for the report along with a formal certificate "that it is an exact copy of the report made by you in the first instance."[18]

Desiring to give his regiment its just mention in these important records, Chamberlain shortly submitted what he called a "copy" or "draft" of his original July 6, 1863, report along with the requested certificate of authenticity and a caveat. "I must also beg indulgence," he wrote, "for expressing something short of absolute certainty as any report being identical in print and letter as this." This copy of his report was in Chamberlain's handwriting and had very few corrections—strange when considering that he wrote it in haste just a few days after the battle while the army was on the march. Despite these conditions, he wrote it in eloquent style comprising just over 2,500 words.

While Chamberlain made plain his firm belief that he was submitting a near exact copy of his July 6 report—he swore to it on his honor—there is ample evidence that he was mistaken. While errors in a few telltale statements belie the accuracy of it, there is a still greater reason to question this memoir of his original thoughts on Gettysburg—the actual original report. While Chamberlain did not have a copy in his possession when the War Department came looking in 1883, the State of Maine did, and still does.

In November 1863 he sent to the adjutant general of Maine what he called "my official report of the battle of Gettysburg." In his letter from the field conveying the report, he noted that it contained little detail, saying, "Had it been written for you I would gladly have given you some particulars which would have made you proud of our noble fellows from the State of Maine." Lacking "particulars," this copy of his report, now in the Maine State Archives, is one thousand words shorter than the 1880s version and makes no mention of Little Round Top nor his mourning of the two not yet dead officers whom he listed here as "mortally wounded."

Contrary to the copy provided to and then published by the War Department, it reads as a brief official army report should—concise and to the point. Since the copy actually written in the 1880s is dated within just a few days of the battle, it is natural for others to assume that he wrote it from a more reliable and recent memory. The period of the 1880s was a boon for Civil War memoirs as veterans of both sides recounted and debated the war in print across the nation. That this misdated version appeared in print and received wide national distribution at this important juncture, meant that it (errors of fact and all) greatly influenced the development of "the story."

Given the value of any source written so soon after an event, it is not surprising that those unaware of its actual origin place great credence on the misdated report even today. By the time he submitted this copy for publication, however, Chamberlain had read the accounts of both William Oates and Theodore Gerrish, in addition to having an opportunity to speak with other veterans of the fight at reunions or at his many public engagements. These outside influences most certainly had an effect on Chamberlain's memory and found their way into his new "official" account.[19]

Since these three seemingly separate accounts corroborate one another on a few key points, one might conclude—and many have—that they had discovered the "facts." Even today, murder trials often hinge on less than the corroborating testimony of three different witnesses. Rather than the separate memories of three men, however, what exists here is the blending of some key elements through three different accounts that appear to stem from independent thought. Instead, the accounts are related, with much of the information in one derived from one or both of the others, poisoning various recollections with errors and compounding their effect. It is now virtually impossible to determine how much of each veteran's memory affected the others or how much of any account is from each author's own memory uninfluenced by the other accounts.

The next stone laid in this legend's foundation appeared in print in 1913 as the fiftieth anniversary of the Battle of Gettysburg drew near. In his article "Through Blood and Fire at Gettysburg" Chamberlain portrayed in lavish detail the fight for Little Round Top from his own perspective. This particular description of events has become the most widely read and quoted account of the fight and has had a profound impact on the legend as people know it today. Like those before, however, there is good reason not to trust this account of events and not just because of the fifty-year-old memories behind it.

A clue to the more serious problem lies in the title of the publication in which the article appeared, *Hearsts* magazine. To even casual students of American history, the name William Randolph Hearst elicits the image of "yellow journalism." Hearst was one of the early masters of sensationalizing the news in print to attract more subscribers to his periodicals. Some have even credited Hearst's imaginary news stories with starting the Spanish-American War in 1898. It should come as no surprise, then, to find that an article submitted to his magazine did not necessarily appear in print as the author intended.

So unhappy was Chamberlain with the article that bore his name that he refused to keep a copy of his own and declined sending copies to friends who inquired. "The Hearst editors mutilated and 'corrected' my 'Gettysburg,'" he told one admirer, "so that I have not tried to get copies." The Maine adjutant general wrote him saying that it was "one of the most striking contributions to war literature that I have ever read." But, in thanking him for the kind words, Chamberlain explained that the article "is much curtailed and changed by the insertion of 'connective tissue' by the editor."[20]

From Chamberlain's own opinion of the piece, the most quoted source from the subject of the legend, it is so far from being his own writing in places that he declared it "mutilated." Which words or descriptions are those of Chamberlain and which are those of an editor at *Hearsts* is difficult to determine, since the original manuscript has not been found. One clue, however, lies in the story of an Alabama sharpshooter who wrote a letter to Chamberlain years after the war to explain an incident at Gettysburg. In that battle, according to the letter, the Southerner recalled having seen the Maine colonel clearly in his sights at least twice but could not bring himself to pull the trigger. The letter closes with the quaint remark, "I am glad of it now and hope you are." This is now among the more often told portions of the legendary story.[21]

The problems with this letter, reprinted in the article verbatim, are many. First, this story does not appear in any of Chamberlain's other writings, nor in the writings of any Alabamian who fought against him. Also, if a story of such human interest warranted inclusion in a nationally distributed magazine, why would he not have used it in one of the hundreds of speeches, interviews, and other reflections that he made on the war? Another curious issue is that Chamberlain saved almost every letter and piece of paper that he ever received, yet none of the large collections of his papers, now held in libraries and repositories across the country, contain this letter. Did Hearst's people simply invent the story out of thin air? Did they perhaps embellish some lesser anecdote that Chamberlain mentioned in the original article? While these questions will likely never be answered, it is revealing to find that the article, given the strength of evidence of being Chamberlain's own writing, is what he described as "mutilated."

For most of a half century these pillars of the Chamberlain legend sat relatively unnoticed and unremarked on as the nation's interest in the Civil War seemed to pass with the aging veterans. For decades, the story of Joshua Chamberlain was forgotten, as people now describe it, amid the clutter of larger historical issues and figures. Then, in the 1950s, novelist Kenneth Roberts, a Mainer himself, wrote the book *Trending into Maine*, in which he included a chapter titled "Maine Stories I'd Like to Write." These were stories so good in reality that he wished he could have such imaginative ability with fiction. Among these was the story of Chamberlain at Gettysburg. While Roberts was most likely unaware of the unusual circumstances behind the sources that made up the Chamberlain story, he knew a good tale when he saw one.[22]

While Roberts's article did little to revive the Chamberlain legend, it brought the story to the attention of an advertising man in Philadelphia named John Pullen. In his line of work Pullen also knew the value of a good story and, being a native of Maine, he set out to write the Chamberlain story in depth. A gifted writer, Pullen reawakened the legend in his book, *The Twentieth Maine*, published in 1957. Many have credited the book with reinventing the way Civil War regimental histories are created, and some military experts have called it "the best military history ever written." As the hundredth anniversary of Gettysburg arrived, Pullen's advertising mind, historical gifts, and considerable writing skills brought Chamberlain's story a measure of national attention.[23]

For nearly two more decades the story of Joshua Chamberlain, though growing in prominence among Civil War buffs, failed to excite the American imagination or figure prominently in popular culture. Strangely, it was in the immediate aftermath of the Vietnam War that the most crucial pillar of the legend appeared, and this particular piece of the story reached deep into the American mind.

In the early 1970s, an instructor of English literature with a deep love of Shakespeare found in Joshua Chamberlain an iconic hero whose story fit his desires perfectly. Michael Shaara was a veteran of the 82nd Airborne Division and a proud American whose family had roots in Italy. On occasional trips back to his ancestral homeland, his Italian relatives often took great pains to tease him about America's lack of real history, heroes, or hallowed ground. When asked to identify something in America as old as, say, the Colosseum in Rome, Shaara could only explain that his country was too young for such monuments to the past. His American pride wounded at the lack of a hero on the level of Julius Caesar or an empire the equal of ancient Rome, Shaara could only endure the teasing, knowing that America's historical past paled in comparison to that of Europe. On one of his trips back from Italy, however, Shaara decided to do something about his predicament. If he could write something to prove to his Italian relatives that his country did have great heroes, even Shakespearean-style heroes, it might make his next trip a bit easier. He only needed to find a place and a story that fit his needs.[24]

Landing at a Washington, D.C., airport, he rented a car and drove to Gettysburg, a place certain to have the kind of hallowed ground and colossal heroes he sought. Sitting alone under a tree where the battle's tumultuous final charge met its immortal demise, the idea formed in his head. In 1974, that idea, in the form of his novel *The Killer Angels*, first appeared in print and later won the Pulitzer Prize for fiction. In writing the series of vignettes that made up his novel, Shaara needed characters and stories that would be as compelling to readers as the Shakespearean literature that he had taught his students. He soon found that his choice of Gettysburg fit the bill nicely.

Described correctly, Pickett's Charge could stand comparison to the Charge of the Light Brigade. The poignant friendship of opposing generals Lewis Armistead and Winfield Hancock, torn asunder by the tragedy of war and wounded just yards apart as one led an attack on the other, might well have found its way into one of his plays, had Shakespeare written after Gettysburg. To Shaara, Gettysburg might just as well have been *Henry V*.

Determined to prove his Italian relatives wrong, and in so doing to give himself and other Americans the kind of heroes that Europe celebrated, Shaara found another heroic character to fit his model. In Joshua Chamberlain he found the story of a man trained to be a minister who led men in war. He was an eloquent, studious man, who achieved great accomplishments at Gettysburg in the horror of combat. In short, he was a "killer angel." Anointing Chamberlain as his central Shakespearean hero, Shaara's novel reveals its title through a conversation between the Maine professor's character and his father. The younger Chamberlain refers to *Hamlet* (2.2), comparing man to an angel. Amused at his son's lofty ideas, the stoic, more grounded father allowed that man might be an angel, but if so he is a "murderin' angel." The fictionalized conversation led the son's character to write an oration in college entitled "Man: The Killer Angel." This passage in the novel is a remarkable blending of heroic legend, Shakespearean tale, and Shaara's ideal image of Chamberlain. The three appear as inseparable elements.[25]

Shakespeare's gift, like Shaara's, was the ability to take a small, seemingly insignificant event and create epic drama from it. Romeo and Juliet, after all, were just a couple of love-struck teenagers until Shakespeare got hold of the story. When he was finished with it, however, it had become the most romantic story ever told. In writing his novel, Shaara meant to expose a wonderful, glorious, and tragic past to a generation of Americans still soured on the idea of war as a just and honorable entity. He sought perhaps also to reinstill a sense that America and Americans had once been something more noble and honorable than the legacy of Vietnam made them seem. For this, the Chamberlain story was a wonderful model.

With all of this in mind, it is no wonder that Shaara's novelized version of Chamberlain's day at Gettysburg exceeds by any measure the historical fact of the event. Novels are not bound by fact. They have an emotive quality that only fiction can provide and often must provide in order to succeed. When one examines, however, the material available to a Florida State University English instructor in the 1970s, it is a wonder that a reader would recognize the Chamberlain story at all. Basing his fictionalized account of the fighting at Little Round Top on readily available sources meant that Shaara's narrative passed along the elements of the Chamberlain legend established in the writings of Oates, Gerrish, and an editor at *Hearsts* magazine. Had he gathered more clear facts at the start and then added a novelist's license, the result would have been faulty enough. But to begin from these flawed sources and then embellish meant that the story he depicted was far more legend than history. By the time Shaara was finished, Chamberlain's story was exactly the kind of tale that even skeptical Italian relatives had to respect.

Though it failed, at first, to reach into the public imagination still seared by Vietnam, *The Killer Angels* won the Pulitzer Prize for fiction in 1974. As years passed and post-Vietnam antiwar attitudes eased, the novel found a growing audience, selling millions of copies. Though it is difficult to determine exactly why, there seems to be a public acceptance of much of this novel as fact. While readers of Civil War literature recognize the fictionalized characters and stories in classic novels such as *The Red Badge of Courage* or *Gone with the Wind*, something in *The Killer Angels* elicits a belief in the reality of it. Perhaps the real characters described in the novel or the lack of gratuitous romantic scenes foster such a notion. Perhaps it is the compelling way in which the author told the story, touching on that same element that draws so many to Shakespeare year after year. Perhaps Shaara simply gave people what they felt they needed: heroes and heroic stories.

Fifteen years after Shaara's novel, in 1990, the Chamberlain story found its second Lord Tennyson—or perhaps it is more accurate to say that the telling of the story created a Lord Tennyson. Filmmaker Ken Burns has said that he wrote and produced his award-winning series, *The Civil War*, because of the Chamberlain legend. It is difficult to determine, however, whether the Chamberlain legend helped bring about the Burns film, or the film helped shape the legend. While Burns reintroduced the nation to a somewhat forgotten Civil War hero, it was also the hero who reintroduced Burns to the Civil War.

"For all intents and purposes," pondered Burns a year after the series aired, "it was the life of Chamberlain which convinced me to embark on the most difficult and satisfying experience of my life, to tell the whole story of the Civil War." In a sense, Burns and Chamberlain helped create each other. The legendary character drove the literature (or film), and the film elevated the legend.[26]

If films are to succeed, they need something to enliven them. In the Chamberlain legend, Burns not only had a seldom heard story of a remarkable American but also a figure to represent what he found to be good in his own sense of American. When he speaks of Chamberlain he conjures a somewhat Shakespearean story himself. Burns's Chamberlain is the quintessential hero "especially at Gettysburg where on Little Round Top he executes an obscure textbook maneuver that saves the Union army and quite possibly the Union itself." In support of his point, the Gettysburg section of Burns's film prominently quotes Theodore Gerrish, applies Oates's mistaken figures, and repeatedly uses the Hearst article "Through Blood and Fire at Gettysburg" to paint his heroic portrait.[27]

The story of a college professor trained as a minister who becomes a great war hero follows an archetypal pattern. Burns was looking for the kind of American history that could make him proud, the kind of hero to hold up as America at its best. He found near perfection in the Chamberlain of legend. To Burns, and many who saw his film, Chamberlain's is the great modern American tale. The story of a trained minister who is not a lover of war but a defender of freedom. A professor, not a brutish warrior; an ingenious thinker who uses his finely honed wits to defeat the enemy. Never mind that there is no textbook or that there was no "maneuver" in the sense Burns describes, or even that in his lifetime Chamberlain repeatedly denied ordering a charge. He is as heroically American as a modern legend can be—or needs to be.

In images such as this, Burns asks his viewers to ignore the facts. Historians point out that there was no military maneuver in any textbook. Also, to say that Chamberlain saved the Union Army at Gettysburg is to ignore the 15,000 or more men held in reserve in close proximity to Little Round Top when the 20th Maine made the charge. The Alabamians who attacked Chamberlain never had a real chance to take the hill or doom the Union Army, but the story without such hyperbole lacks the needed weight. If the hero's actions were not crucially important to the fate of a nation, the story would not elicit the desired reaction. So Burns simply applied to the Chamberlain story his own sense of how great it was or how great he wanted it to be.

Admiring the professor in Chamberlain, Burns creates "an unlikely textbook maneuver" where there was none. He did so because professors use textbooks and the story of the "humble professor succeeding gloriously in combat" needs such elements in order for it to work, to reach people. Americans developed the myth of Lincoln writing the Gettysburg Address on the back of an envelope while en route to the event in order to embellish his intellect. In the same way, Burns credited Chamberlain with the skill to draw on his scholarly background to fashion a scholarly solution to his problem. To make it more compelling, as filmmakers are inclined to do, he created in this small event something so critical that it threatened the future of the nation.

Flush with the success of Burns's film in reigniting a passion among Americans for their Civil War past, Hollywood rediscovered *The Killer Angels* just two years later. Filmmaker Ronald Maxwell had spent more than a decade trying to convince studios and networks of the potential for success in a film version of the novel. In 1992, with financial backing from Ted Turner's film production assets, Maxwell put the story on film nearly twenty years after the novel's first printing. The following September, retitled simply as *Gettysburg* (focus groups said the original title sounded like a biker movie), the film reached theaters. The story of Chamberlain at Gettysburg, which makes up the lion's share of the film's first two hours, reached its largest audience ever. More than a year after its release to theaters, Turner Network Television aired the four-hour film to 40 million viewers—the largest television audience ever to watch a cable drama.

As a result of the film, Chamberlain's stock grew to epic proportions. Annual visitation at the Gettysburg battlefield tripled and the 20th Maine monument became the central focus of the field for millions of tourists. Close behind the film's release, marketers and gift shop owners quickly capitalized on the Chamberlain mania sweeping the small tourist town. Admiring tourists eagerly gathered up T-shirts, pillows, clocks, key chains, anything bearing Chamberlain's image. Schoolchildren from Ohio left poems to Chamberlain on the 20th Maine monument, despite the admirable record of their own state's regiments at Gettysburg. Another school group left a small shrine to their new hero at the place where Pickett's Charge ebbed on the third day—a place Chamberlain likely never set foot during the battle except in the movie. Hundreds of reenactors in full period dress paused for a photo of themselves at the famous monument, though many did so while portraying Confederates. Hundreds of visitors made inquiries at the National Park Visitor Center about the location of the grave of Buster Kilrain, a fictional character in the novel and film. One man, from the very city in Pennsylvania where Chamberlain's mortally wounded commander Strong Vincent had come, focused not on his hometown hero but on a man from five states away. He made this admission about a vacation in Maine in 1999. "Before the trip I vowed to myself when no one was looking to kiss the ground of Maine in honor of what these men did July 2, 1863."[28]

Nearly a century and a quarter after William Oates used the wrong muster roll data to inadvertently set in motion this chain of events, Joshua Chamberlain is quite likely the most popular figure in Civil War circles. As Homer was to Troy and Longfellow to Paul Revere, so must we recognize both Shaara and Burns for creating a hero befitting our time. To be sure, this is not a conspiracy of people intentionally building a legend for their own ends—though there is ample evidence of that among other heroic stories. Oates's mistake seems genuine and Gerrish simply wrote the best account he could given his absence from the fight. While Hearst's people surely had motive in elevating the details of the story to legendary status, it is reasonable to assume that Chamberlain did the best he could from his notes and memory in reproducing the Gettysburg report. Shaara wrote a novel and, as such, had more than ample license to distort or embellish without being thought to mislead his readers or the historical record. Setting aside the normal limitations of human memory that alone can greatly affect the "facts" as they are reported, these flaws greatly compound our inability to see the past with any clarity.

The human revelation in this story may not lie in the motivation of the sources, but rather in the reasons that tourists, buffs, and even professional historians accept the flawed sources as fact today. As Joseph Campbell so often explained, people reinvent their legends and myths in order to meet some need or fill some void in their present. This is not necessarily a conscious behavior but is more often a slow, subtle, subconscious process. At a time when Americans find it increasingly hard to find untarnished heroes, it is possible that they find comfort in the past instead. Perhaps they accept the flawed historical sources without deeper research because they find in them a story that places their present in a more palatable context. A story that makes them feel more satisfied with who they are and where they came from. A story that gives them a noble, honorable American hero.

To acknowledge a more factual version of Chamberlain at Gettysburg is to accept that he was stricken by malarial fever and likely even diarrhea, a common affliction in the army at that time. Having received his promotion to colonel the day before the battle, he was the least senior colonel in the entire Union Army. Despite this and other challenges, he conducted himself with great composure, providing a model of military leadership for his men. The "true" story of Chamberlain on Little Round Top is that of a man overcoming great difficulty to follow his orders and hold his position, but not in the most physically attractive manner.

Soon after Ronald Maxwell cast Jeff Daniels in the role of Chamberlain for the movie *Gettysburg*, the actor went to Maine to learn more about the man. At an early lunch meeting, one historian teased him by revealing that the actor was "about a foot too tall." Chamberlain, the historian explained, was of average height for his day—about five feet seven inches. Daniels thought only a moment before replying. "Well," he said, "he's going to be six-three. Some things even Hollywood can't change."

As Ken Burns pointed out, in Chamberlain we find "a different kind of heroism there that we need so desperately to be aware of today." True enough. But to do so, that hero must meet a certain set of ideas that we, as a society, collectively hold in our present. If he does not, then he will likely succeed as a heroic persona only if we reshape him in the image we wish to see.[29]

With this in mind, Daniels's statement and the one made by Maxwell in casting him make an interesting point. When Hollywood went looking for someone to play Shaara's heroic version of Chamberlain, they cast an actor with blond hair and blue eyes, who was six foot three—the kind of character moviegoers would rather see. To be faithful to historic truth, Maxwell would have had to cast a short Chamberlain, fever-stricken and hampered by diarrhea—and what audience would warm to a hero such as that?

CHAPTER 8

THE WORLD'S LARGEST COLLECTION OF OUTDOOR SCULPTURE

Standing by these numerous monumental dedications, it is simply amazing to hear the most preposterous and absurd claims. Each regiment seems to have the impression that it had the conspicuous honor of saving the day. I account for this general tendency, partly because the members of each command saw only what transpired in its immediate front, and then again, the recollections of what did occur are frequently colored by camp-fire stories, until fact and fancy become intermingled.

DAVID A. BUEHLER[1]

Visitors to the Gettysburg battlefield over the past century or so have often marveled at the elaborate system of more than thirteen hundred monuments, memorials, and markers spread out over the landscape. These structures of granite, bronze, stone, and iron seem to tell the story of the battle as the visitor travels from one point to the next. Many pilgrims to this hallowed ground are fascinated by the various tales, as if they were placed in their natural position under the guidance of some overriding plan. The fact of the matter is, however, that they were placed at different times by different organizations all trying to tell different stories. Unaware that these sentinels of the past were not systematically arranged according to some grand scheme, passersby are often overheard asking questions such as, How did they get the bullet holes out of them after the battle? Few are prompted to dig deeper into the story and the process of placing Gettysburg's memorials, which locals call "monumentation."

The first monument placed on the field, outside of the Soldiers National Cemetery, was the small stone erected in 1878 by Pennsylvania veterans to mark the spot—or one of them—where their comrade Colonel Strong Vincent was mortally wounded on Little Round Top. The 3rd Massachusetts placed the first regimental monument in 1879, and friends of General Gouverneur Warren erected the first statue on the field in 1888 when they depicted in bronze the moment when Warren discovered—or did not discover—the Confederate approach to the Round Tops.

During the period in which most of the monuments now on the field made their appearance, the battlefield was under the control of the Gettysburg Battlefield Memorial Association. As caretaker of the field, this group confronted a number of issues at its meetings so that the monumentation of the field crept up on it. First one, then another veterans organization sought to commemorate their actions or memorialize their dead at Gettysburg by placing a marker that would tell their story in perpetuity. In time, the GBMA began to establish norms, if not rules, to govern the process. Minutes of a meeting in 1887 reveal the struggle to achieve some sense of organization despite the lack of an overall road map. "The Association, desire that chaste, artistic structures, be erected, and to prevent the use of cheap monuments, which by their size should over-top others of better material, and real merit, have spread upon their records a resolution to that effect that, 'hereafter monuments erected on this field must be constructed of granite or real bronze.'"[2]

As the movement to place monuments on the battlefield surged in the 1880s, the GBMA found itself serving as referee and judge. In 1887 John

Bachelder was the superintendent of tablets and legends, a position that gave him tremendous control over not only what monuments would go on the field but also what the inscriptions on each would say. In an effort to rein in some of the more outrageous ideas coming from veterans groups, he drafted a circular that read in part, "We are not unmindful of the fact that Gettysburg is now classed among the great battles of the world, or that this field is already the best marked battlefield in the world, or that it is our desire that the artistic character of the monuments shall be of the same high order."[3]

One of the harsher tests of the association's resolve on this matter came in 1889 when a representative of the 1st Minnesota shared his regiment's intentions regarding its monument when he wrote, "Of course we want something that will attract attention therefore *odd* in design—as well as appropriate."[4] If a unique design was not enough, he contrived, then it should also be the most expensive. "We will not have a monument," he added, "costing less than $12,000 or inferior to any on the Battlefield which marks a *single regiment*."[5] What the Minnesotans had in mind was a gaudy statue of a Union soldier bayoneting a giant serpent to death. With this design, they hoped to show, symbolically of course, how Minnesota helped kill the serpent Secession. Rejected by Bachelder and the association as not in keeping with their idea of "artistic character" and "high order," the Minnesotans settled for the statue of a soldier running to meet the enemy; not to be completely outdone, they placed it on an enormous pedestal.

In the last half of the 1880s as the push to place monuments on the field reached its zenith, veterans offered the GBMA varying and conflicting opinions on what, if any, overriding principles or guidelines should govern the process. Some expressed a desire to severely limit their placement. As one veteran wrote to John Bachelder, "Haphazard erection of monuments on the battlefield would be of little use to the future historian and would simply be a waste of money and it would be better that they were off the field than on it. They would confuse and not instruct, or aid investigation."[6] Another veteran, this one the Union general whose men fought off Pickett's famous charge, weighed in on the subject while demonstrating how other controversies eventually spilled over into monument placing. "I would stop bogus monuments at once," he suggested to Bachelder. "Just [as] I would stop the bogus claims of Sickles, Butterfield and such."[7] In response to the disorganized way in which veteran groups were placing monuments on the field, the GBMA began to establish rules to govern their design, construction, placement, and foundations.

One example of the need for guidelines came about after the invention of a new metal called "white bronze," an inexpensive soft zinc alloy that faded to a light blue patina in time. Use of this new alloy led to problems on the field when the soft, hollow structures failed to stand up over time. The most noticeable of these was the tall monument on Cemetery Hill placed by veterans of the 4th Ohio Infantry Regiment. Originally more than thirty-two feet tall, it is now just a twelve-foot-high pedestal on which a tall pillar was originally topped by the statue of a soldier. On its looks alone the GBMA rejected any further use of this new metallic concoction. Four weeks after the Ohioans dedicated the monument, the GBMA voted that in the future, all new monuments would have to be made of real bronze or granite.[8]

Faced with the apparent need for an overriding set of guidelines, the GBMA turned to John Bachelder. In May 1887, he first decided that "a committee be appointed to consider the advisability of removing the monuments which have been erected out of line to their correct position on the line of battle, and to report a plan to carry this resolution into operation, and further that hereafter regiments erecting monuments on the grounds of this Association be required to locate and place them on the line of battle."[9]

This "line of battle" rule acquired great significance in the years to follow. Essentially, it required that veterans place monuments on the spot where they "entered the fight," the definition of this to be ultimately determined by the GBMA. One benefit of this policy was that it squelched efforts by Confederate units to place monuments on parts of the field where key action occurred. Since the Union forces fought a largely defensive battle and allowed the Confederate forces to do the attacking, Southern battle lines were a great distance away from the ground on which they eventually met the Union forces and fought. Thus the Confederate units entered the fight as much as a half mile away from the areas of the battlefield where most of the fighting took place. Their monuments, in reflecting this, would not be located in the areas most sought after by those who would visit the fields in the decades to follow.

Two months after dealing with monument locations, Bachelder sought to control the monuments themselves, when the GBMA directed "that the Superintendent of Tablets and Legends be requested to prepare detailed specifications covering the foundations, cementing and lettering of monuments, to be hereafter erected, and said specifications when approved by Executive committee to become by virtue thereof rules of the Association."[10] Having established these new rules, Bachelder and the GBMA would have their hands full fighting with veterans to enforce them. Perhaps by necessity, adherence to these rules became extremely rigid, the best example of this being the 84th Pennsylvania Regiment.

At the same meeting in which Bachelder sought to control the placement of monuments on the field, he also convinced the GBMA to add, "That hereafter regiments and commands which shall erect monuments or memorials on the battlefield, shall be required at the same time to mark the flanks of their position."[11] Two years later, the 84th Pennsylvania received permission to place a monument on the field in an area set aside for units that had not been present on the field during the battle but made a significant contribution to the Union victory in the campaign. The 84th spent the battle guarding supply trains in the area around Westminster, Maryland, about twenty miles south of Gettysburg. In 1889 they placed their monument in the position assigned to them by the GBMA but were obliged to follow the rule that required flank markers. Thus the inscription on their monument points out that they were not on the field, while two smaller stones, placed equidistant from the main structure, designate the exact location where their left and right flanks never rested.

Another confusing monument on the field sits a few yards away from the climactic scene of Pickett's Charge and within view of the famous copse of trees. On it sits the statue of an older veteran, seated with a cane in his right hand. This is the monument to the Grand Army of the Republic, the most influential of all postwar veteran organizations. Given its location just outside the building that houses the Cyclorama painting, it receives a healthy share of attention. Cast in bronze atop this monument sits the "heroic size (over life size)" likeness of Albert Woolson, the last surviving Union soldier who reportedly died at the age of 109 in 1956. This would be a more fitting tribute, however, had he been at Gettysburg. Woolson did not even enlist in the Union Army until October 1864—and as a drummer boy at that. Not only was he not at Gettysburg, but he was not even in a regiment that served in the eastern theater of the war. The closest Albert came to Gettysburg during the Civil War, was Chattanooga, Tennessee, and his regiment never engaged in battle. On Woolson's birthday in 1953, a national newspaper wire story claimed that the "youthful drummer boy stood with Union forces at the tide-turning battle of Gettysburg," and that "he was in the line at Gettysburg and recalls desperate Confederate cavalry charges during that crucial engagement."[12]

Despite Woolson's absence from Gettysburg, his statue is honored each November, when the annual parade in Gettysburg on Remembrance Day, the anniversary of Lincoln's famous speech, ends with a commemoration paying tribute at the monument with dignitaries and reenactors alike laying wreaths.

Among the many monument myths that circulate around Gettysburg visitors is the belief that the equestrian statues on the battlefield share a design pattern that indicates the fate of the general on the horse. As the story goes, a standing requirement governed the sculpting of the horse-and-rider monuments on the field to the effect that the horses' hooves revealed how well the rider came out of the battle. One hoof raised off the ground meant that the rider was wounded; two hooves up meant he was killed at Gettysburg. Three hooves up, of course, meant that it was one talented horse. While this pattern was, until the 1990s, an accurate indicator of the rider's fate, it was a pure coincidence. No such rule governed the creation of memorials, and the Gettysburg equestrians were sponsored by different groups and sculpted by varying artists who had no contact with one another or awareness of a traditional pattern.

Defenders of this so-called tradition created something of a controversy when modern-day supporters of General James Longstreet commissioned an equestrian statue of the much maligned Confederate commander in 1998. As designed and sculpted, the Longstreet equestrian depicted horse and rider in action rather than the stoic, statuesque equestrians that had been placed on the field a hundred or more years prior. Longstreet's new memorial is a reproduction of the general reining in his hurrying horse—an active general in the midst of battle. What most caught the eye of critics, however, was that two of the hooves were in motion, one completely off the ground and another resting on a small cloud of dust. Since Longstreet was neither killed nor wounded at Gettysburg—though one could argue that his reputation suffered a mortal blow there—the new monument violated the venerable equestrian tradition.

In addition, the style was not what visitors to battlefields were used to. Most battlefield statues are dominating structures that depict the heroic subject in a serious, upright stance and not a realistic pose. Longstreet's equestrian followed a new paradigm, a realistic depiction that is as nonintrusive to its battlefield surroundings as possible. Unlike the Virginia state memorial, which portrays Robert E. Lee literally raised up on a pedestal some thirty feet in the air, Longstreet sits atop a horse whose hooves—most of them, anyway—were on the ground rather than on an elaborate base. Criticism of this latest equestrian on the battlefield is an enlighten-

ing revelation about how people see the battle story and its main characters. When a depiction in bronze or granite is lifelike, with realistic
dimensions and a modest design, it somehow does not meet the expecta-
tions of those who encounter it on the field. They have come to see those
who have been immortalized by Gettysburg myths and legends as literally
larger than life and thus expect the memorials that portray these heroes
to do the same.

At times the desire to commemorate a beloved commander led to
monument issues that bordered on the laughable. This was especially true
when the veterans of the 83rd Pennsylvania designed the monument that
would mark their regimental position on the second day of the battle.
Placed on the south slope of Little Round Top, it needed to be elaborate
and noticeable so as to fit into the growing importance of the hill in veterans' reminiscences, but the veterans wanted to accomplish something
else with their memorial. The commander of the brigade that by the
1880s was considered to have saved Little Round Top for the Union was
Colonel Strong Vincent of Erie. Prior to rising to brigade command, Vincent had served as the commander of the 83rd Pennsylvania, and veterans
of that regiment held a special fondness for him. When the time came to
place their regimental monument at Gettysburg, they naturally sought to
commemorate the actions of their fallen colonel. At that time, however,
the Pennsylvania State Monuments Commission supervised the design
and placement of all of its state memorials and, wishing to commemorate
the common deeds of the Pennsylvania soldier, prohibited any personal
statements, inscriptions, or depictions.[13]

The design plan for the monument, then, included a life-size statue of
a "Union officer" or a "model Pennsylvania soldier" which, by something
less than pure coincidence, bore a striking resemblance to Colonel Strong
Vincent—including his unique and substantial sideburns. Years afterward,
members of the veterans association continued to sarcastically uphold the
ruse, insisting, with tongue firmly in cheek, that the statue was not
Colonel Vincent.

On July 3, 1887, at a Gettysburg reunion of the Philadelphia Brigade, the 69th and 71st Pennsylvania regiments dedicated their monuments along the stone wall at The Angle. Following this lead, the regiment that fought between them, the 72nd Pennsylvania, made plans for its own monument and a group of them began digging a hole for the foundation along the same stone wall the following December. The GBMA responded by saying that "the act of the representatives of the 72d was regarded as a trespass, and they were arrested and enjoined from proceeding further."[14] This act set in motion the most controversial monument issue ever raised at Gettysburg. At first glance, it might seem perfectly appropriate to place monuments to the three regiments in line along the area where they fought, but the circumstances of the fighting at the very apex of The Angle are far too complicated for easy solutions. When the men of the 72nd chose the site for their monument, even their comrades in the 69th Pennsylvania raised a howl.

When the final assault on the Union center began on July 3, General Alexander Webb commanded the Philadelphia Brigade and placed them along the stone wall that made The Angle. The 69th Pennsylvania occupied the wall closest to the enemy with a few companies of the 71st Pennsylvania. The remainder of the 71st was back at the rearward stone wall while the perpendicular wall that connected them remained unoccupied. At the crest of the ridge behind the men of the 69th, Webb had placed the 72nd regiment as his reserve to be sent in to fill any gaps that might open in his line. As the Confederate attackers crested the first stone wall, the companies of the 71st Pennsylvania fell back to the rest of their regiment and left a gaping hole right at the apex of The Angle. Seeing this, Webb reacted quickly, but the story of what occurred next is the subject of one of those classic Gettysburg controversies.

The colonel of the nearby 19th Massachusetts had a clear view of the situation and wrote years later of the moment when Webb sought to lead the 72nd into the widening gap. "Gen. Webb," he wrote, "had rushed back to his second line with the evident purpose of hurrying them forward to meet Pickett's men now swarming over the stone wall. They were immovable not withstanding Webb's protests and appeals."[15] Webb failed to ignite a charge in the men of the 72nd "though he may throw himself with reckless courage in front to face the storm and beg, threaten, and command."[16]

Years later, Webb recalled how he tried to get the regiment's color bearer to instigate a charge. "I ordered him forward, he moved in place but did not carry the colors out of the regimental line."[17] Not only would the color bearer not go himself, but he would not let Webb lead the charge with his flag either. "[He] pulled back and did not go to the front. I could not drag him forward. So let it be. Rather him be forgotten."[18] Frustrated and angered by the situation, Webb moved back toward the wall alone, hoping to do what he could there with the men of the 69th Pennsylvania.

Seeing that the Philadelphia Brigade was failing, Colonel Norman Hall, commander of the brigade to Webb's left, ordered his men to charge into the swarm of gray-clad soldiers within the walls of The Angle. At about this time the leader of these Confederates, General Lewis Armistead, was hit by at least two bullets and fell beside a cannon, just inside the wall. Lacking any leadership or supporting reinforcements, Southerners who were not killed or wounded simply threw down their guns in surrender. Back at the top of the ridge, the 72nd was still holding its line when Hall's brigade entered the fray. After some cajoling from a staff officer, the 72nd Pennsylvania finally moved forward toward The Angle, but by this point, remembered Webb, "men pressed to the fence after the Rebels laid down their arms, and lots of warriors developed like sand flies when the bullets stopped 'bee-ing' all around our ears."[19]

Thus it was with boldness and defiance that the men of the 72nd Pennsylvania sought to place their monument along the wall that, in Webb's eyes at least, they had refused to defend. When veterans of the unit came to the field and began to dig a hole for the foundation, the GBMA called an immediate halt, telling them they were digging in the wrong place. By virtue of the rules set in place by the association, the rightful position of the 72nd Pennsylvania was in their brigade line at the top of the crest. If they chose to, the 72nd would be allowed to place a smaller advance marker at the wall, but their main monument would be back where they had been in line when the shooting started.[20]

So determined were the veterans of the 72nd to gain a place of honor at the wall that they filed suit against the GBMA in Adams County court. When the county judge dismissed their case, they appealed, eventually carrying the case all the way to the state supreme court. In the meantime, the veterans purchased a small plot of privately owned land on the Confederate side of the wall so that if they lost the case, they could place their monument just over the wall without the GBMA's consent.[21] After three years in the court system, however, the state supreme court ruled in favor of the veterans of the 72nd Pennsylvania, and they dedicated their monument at the wall on July 4, 1891. The GBMA noted in the minutes of its next meeting that both the court master who oversaw the case and the presiding judge attended the dedication ceremonies as guests of the 72nd.[22]

The controversy regarding the actions of the 72nd Pennsylvania at The Angle lingered. In 1908 the Massachusetts commander of the Military Order of the Loyal Legion of the United States (MOLLUS) published a ninety-four-page book entitled *The Battle of Gettysburg by Frank Aretas Haskell, First Lieutenant, 6th Wisconsin Infantry, Aide to General Gibbon, Colonel, 36th Wisconsin Infantry, U.S. V.*[23] This document was actually a letter written by Lieutenant Haskell to his brother on July 16, 1863, and Haskell's service at Gettysburg seems above reproach. In his official report of the battle, General Winfield S. Hancock, who commanded the corps of Union soldiers who bore the brunt of Pickett's Charge, singled Haskell out.

I desire particularly to refer to the services of a gallant young officer, First Lieutenant F. A. Haskell, Aide-de-Camp to General Gibbon, who at the critical point of the Battle, when the contending forces were not fifty yards apart, believing that an example was necessary, and ready to sacrifice his life, rode between the contending lines with the view of giving encouragement to our and leading it forward, he being at the moment the only mounted officer in a similar position. He was slightly wounded and his horse was shot in several places.[24]

What Haskell had to say to his brother less than two weeks after the battle was damning to the 72nd Pennsylvania and its hard-won monument location. He recounted a confrontation with the major commanding the 72nd while it was still standing firmly in its rearward position. "Major," he shouted, "lead, lead your men over the crest,—they will follow!" When the Pennsylvanian refused, claiming the book of tactics dictated that a major's place was behind the line of his men, Haskell implied he was a coward. "I see *your* place is in rear of the men. I thought you were fit to lead."

Next Haskell tried to urge a captain to lead the men forward but to no avail. Finally he rode up to the color-bearer who moments before had wrestled the flag back from the clutches of General Webb. Calling on his honor, Haskell shouted, "Sergeant, forward with your color. Let the rebels see it close to their eyes once more before they die." When this appeal finally got the color sergeant moving, Haskell turned back to the rest of the regiment shouting, "Will you see your color storm the wall alone?" Still, by Haskell's memory, only one man in the 72nd lurched forward. Finally the color sergeant went down, the flag following with him, and the sight of their colors dropping to the ground finally lit the spark that sent the 72nd Pennsylvania into the breach.

Though it confirmed the events as painted by both Webb and Colonel Devereaux—or perhaps because it did—the surviving veterans of the 72nd could not let Haskell's account stand unchallenged. In 1910, under the auspices of the Philadelphia Brigade Association, they published a forty-two-page pamphlet sarcastically entitled *The Battle of Gettysburg:*

How General Meade Turned the Army of the Potomac Over to Lieutenant Haskell, See Page 10.[25] As if the formal title—printed on the cover complete with the reference to the juicy page—was not enough, the association added an additional subtitle on the inside page. "Reply of the Philadelphia Brigade Association to the Foolish and Absurd Narrative of Lieutenant Frank A. Haskell Which Appears to be endorsed by the Military Order of the Loyal Legion, Commandery of Massachusetts and the Wisconsin History Commission."[26]

Speaking at the dedication of the monument to the 42nd New York Regiment, the regiment that had been just to the left of the 72nd's rearward position, controversial General Dan Sickles could not help but fire a rhetorical shot at the Supreme Court for its decision to allow the 72nd Pennsylvania a forward position for its memorial.

> I cannot perform this duty without giving expression to the surprise and indignation felt by the veterans of this famous battalion when they see their monument standing in a rear line, from which they advanced and repulsed the approaching enemy, whilst troops that refused to advance in obedience to the repeated orders of their brigade commander, are permitted to place their monument on a line much further to the front than they ventured to march, until after the victory was won. I know that the trustees of the Battle-field are in no sense responsible for this outrage upon history.[27]

Issues such as this led Sickles to run for Congress for the first time since he committed murder while serving in the office decades earlier. In 1892, at the age of seventy-four, the one-legged general campaigned on a single platform plank—to have the Gettysburg battlefield turned over to the control of the federal government. He not only won election but also succeeded in getting the field purchased by and brought under control of the U.S. War Department in 1895, causing the GBMA to disband and removing decisions on monuments from the state level.

While serving as chairman of the New York State Monuments Commission, Sickles was part of an ongoing rivalry between New York and Pennsylvania regarding which state had done more to win the battle and which should receive the most credit by way of memorials. For Pennsylvanians, the culmination of this debate was the construction of the largest monument on the entire field, literally a cathedral to the men of Pennsylvania who fought at Gettysburg. Costing $182,000, this enormous structure is seventy feet tall and includes seven life-size bronze statues and plaques listing the names of more than 34,000 Pennsylvania soldiers who served at Gettysburg. Though no one ever admitted it in writing, this monument is clearly as much a reaction to the New York monuments as it is a memorial to the soldiers of Pennsylvania.

By the last decade of the nineteenth century, New Yorkers had placed monuments to every regiment and battery that had been present at Gettysburg as well as a number of statues to the state's generals. In the ongoing struggle to place New York's recognition higher than that of any other state—Pennsylvania included—the monument commission chaired and driven by Dan Sickles proposed yet another memorial, this one larger than any previous structure. Never one to do things in a small or inconspicuous way, Sickles decided that New York needed a monument to commemorate the sacrifice of the state's Gettysburg dead, and the commission first proposed a building on the grounds of the Soldiers National Cemetery. This met with immediate resistance from veterans of the units who had served on that ground during the battle. Among them was James Hall, the commander of the 2nd Maine Battery. Getting word of the proposal, he fired off a letter to John Bachelder in which he made his feelings clear.

As to the spot where my battery was on Cemetery Hill July 2d and 3d, if New York or any other state or party comes up on said spot, with a building, from that day, I will d——n the association as vandals in every newspaper that I can get to publish my articles. There ought not to be any cause for me to fight for justice in this matter.[28]

Eventually Sickles and the New Yorkers "settled" for a monument a few dozen yards outside of the soldiers' burial area. This was a fifty-foot tall structure topped with a statue of the female figure depicted on the left side of the state seal. She is holding a laurel wreath in the direction of the burial plot for New York's Gettysburg dead. The statue alone is thirteen feet high. The elaborate monument includes reliefs depicting the wounding of Sickles and Hancock, the death of Reynolds (a Pennsylvanian), and a council of war held by General Slocum. It also includes depictions of other New York generals and the names of every New York officer killed at Gettysburg. In all, it cost nearly $60,000.

Neither this crowning achievement in monumentation nor Dan Sickles's death completely satisfied the New York Monument Commission's thirst for recognition. In 1925 it placed one of the strangest monuments on the field when it dedicated what it called the New York Auxiliary Monument. Since the state could claim nineteen of its citizens as generals at Gettysburg, but only eight were honored with statues at that time, this new memorial, spanning forty-two by twenty-four feet, listed the names of these additional New Yorkers and twenty-one others with the inscription, "The State of New York in recognition of the services rendered by those corps, division, and brigade commanders at Gettysburg not elsewhere honored on this field." Locals occasionally refer to this as the monument to "the guys we forgot to name somewhere else."

In the midst of all of this monument making for the Union side, an unusual set of circumstances surrounded the placement of the first memorial to a Confederate officer at Gettysburg, one that is today known as the Armistead marker. As the fame and perceived importance of the High Water Mark and the Bloody Angle area of the battlefield grew, so did the relationship between the two groups of men who fought there. The Confederate veterans of Pickett's Division and their former Union counterparts of the Philadelphia Brigade met at the scene of their former conflict in July 1887. Flush with a newfound feeling of national reunion, the members of Pickett's Division proposed that a monument to their regiments be placed at the point of their furthest penetration into the Union lines.

This idea had a romantic basis in that it was the moment depicted in the paintings by Rothermel, *Battle of Gettysburg,* and Bachelder/Walker, *Repulse of Longstreet's Assault,* and Philippoteaux's Cyclorama—an instant in time now immortalized by Bachelder's promotional skills. But a quarter century was not long enough to quell strong feelings against the Confederate cause, and placing a large monument to a Rebel division was still out of the question. When the GBMA denied their request, the Virginians instead placed their monument on Pickett's grave in Richmond.

Though the division's monument never made it inside The Angle, a marker to commemorate its furthest penetration did come about. The minutes of the GBMA ten days after the reunion read: "Resolved, That the Committee on Location and Col. Bachelder be authorized to mark with a suitable tablet, the spot where Gen. L. A. Armistead, of the Confederate army, fell mortally wounded July 3d 1863, in accordance with the action of this Association adopted Oct. 1884, and that said committee be requested to attend to this duty promptly."[29] As depicted in popular paintings, the spot where Armistead fell became synonymous with the apex of the assault.

Five months later a four-and-a-half-foot-tall monument carved in the shape of a scroll was placed approximately eighty-five feet inside the stone wall that marked the Union line along The Angle. On its face, it bears a simple inscription: "Brigadier General Lewis A. Armistead C.S.A. fell here July 3, 1863." The controversy surrounding this marker is not based on its design or inscription, but rather its placement. No account has the general falling that far inside the wall and most accounts state that he fell much closer to it—no more than five to twenty-five feet inside.[30]

During the trial over placement of the 72nd Pennsylvania years afterward, veteran Rene Boerner of that unit gave one explanation of how John Bachelder determined the site where Armistead fell. "Our monument that we have up there now, we got it photographed, and after the photograph was over he asked us if any of us men knew the position where General Armistead fell, and I told him I could give him a little information as long as I recollect the field, and I come in between four and five feet and he marked it—about two feet (from) where I had marked it—he drove the stake in."[31] During the same court case, however, various witnesses from the same regiment claimed that Armistead fell a significant distance from where the marker indicates. One said it was "about fifteen feet" from the stone wall, while another testified, "where he fell I don't think it was not more than twenty or twenty-five feet from the wall." Recalling the marker specifically, "I have seen the marker to show where Armistead fell. I don't think that marker is correct, not to my notion. I think he was shot nearer the wall than where the marker is."[32]

Two groups were most able to remember the location—the men of Pickett's Division and the Philadelphia Brigade—and both Pickett's men and the veterans of the 72nd Pennsylvania had a vested interest in establishing it as far into Union lines as possible. The further the Virginians got, the closer they came to success and the more remarkable was their accomplishment. On the other hand, the 72nd Pennsylvania had an interest in showing that Armistead had been mortally wounded in front of their line, making their position the one of greatest danger. In addition, since the 72nd had charged forward from a point in the rear, every step that Armistead and his men took after they crossed over the wall made it more likely that the charge of the 72nd saved the collapsing regiments to their front. In short, the further they could show Armistead penetrating the Union line, the more it appeared that the 72nd Pennsylvania saved the day at Gettysburg. Although records show that "Friends of the Family of General Armistead" sponsored the monument, it was actually paid for by survivors of the 72nd Pennsylvania.

Though it is designed to say more about a Pennsylvania infantry regiment than the place where a Southern general fell, the Armistead marker has become, in legend and lore, the actual high water mark. Those who visit the field perceive it as the spot where the last Confederate feet stopped—a critical piece of four-foot-square real estate—and it is in this role that it led to yet another Southern monument and a controversy that reminds us of William Faulkner's axiom, "History isn't dead, it isn't even past."

In a 1905 history of his artillery battery, Thomas Aldrich recalled the final moments when Pickett's Charge came to an ebb just in front of his cannons.

> . . . as a regiment of Pettigrew's brigade was charging the position held by the battery and the 14th Connecticut and 1st Delaware regiments of infantry, and had almost reached the wall just in front of us, Sergt. Amos M. C. Olney cried out: "Barker, why the d– don't you fire that gun! pull! pull!" [Barker] obeyed orders and the gap made in that North Carolina regiment was simply terrible. Armistead had just fallen, and Pickett's charge had failed. This was the last shot fired from our battery when the rebels broke in retreat, and Gettysburg was won.[33]

This poignant story of firing a double load of small iron balls directly into the faces of "that North Carolina regiment" has become one of the iconic moments of Gettysburg legends. Artists have recreated it on canvas, books and articles have referenced it, and the makers of the movie *Gettysburg* recreated a version of it on film. But a key question seemingly never asked of this story is, How did Aldrich know the men he had just slaughtered with his cannon shot were North Carolinians? Aldrich does not explain whether this piece of information came from prisoners captured or bodies buried. In the mass of soldiers that the Confederate assault melted into by the time it reached The Angle, it was probably impossible to distinguish one regiment from another. Even if he did obtain this information accurately, there is some question as to whether his memory of the unit's designation was accurate forty-two years afterward.

Nevertheless, it was this single account that North Carolinians used as evidence when choosing the location for an advance marker for the 26th North Carolina in October 1986. A few feet over the wall, just in front of the cannons that represent the location of Aldrich's battery, they placed a granite marker to designate the furthest point reached by the men attacking the wall. As with Armistead's marker, this newer memorial provides visitors to Gettysburg a place to pause and note the exact location that the last pair of Confederate legs reached before turning back in defeat. At the same time, as with the Armistead marker, there is some question about the accuracy of the account and the motives of those who placed the marker.

These particular monument issues go back to the days immediately following the battle, when the earliest newspaper reports began to reach Southerners back home. Newspapers based in Richmond, the Confederate capital and the most media-rich city in the South, dominated reports of the battle. Newspapers in other Southern cities "clipped" or copied the Richmond news stories in their own columns. As a direct result, the earliest forms of the Gettysburg story in Dixie focused on Virginia soldiers. As Carol Reardon points out in her book *Pickett's Charge in History and Memory*, this created a disproportionate share of credit for the Virginians under General Pickett's command and even led to the name now given to the charge. In fact, however, Pickett's division made up only half of the attacking force, and the Virginian general was not in command of the other half—a group of men under the command of General Johnson Pettigrew. Most of Pettigrew's men, including the general himself, were North Carolina soldiers.

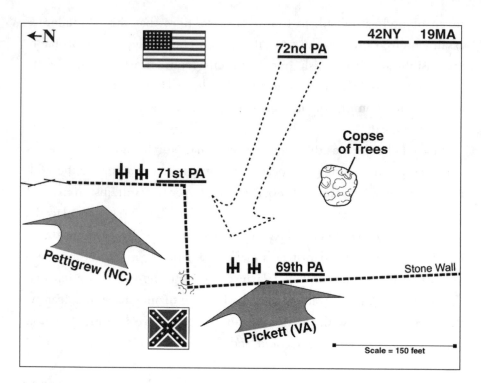

MAP 8.1 *Attack at The Angle*

At the apex of what became known as "Pickett's Charge" the Virginia side of the assault, under General Pickett, breached the Union line at the stone wall. General Pettigrew's North Carolinians, though they did not cross over the wall in great numbers, reached a point farther along than the Virginians. The angle of the old farm wall thus created a situation where each side could claim it had "gone further" in attacking the Federal position, making possible the long-debated question. One side got farther but did not cross the wall, while the other did not get as far but did breach the wall.

Since the beginning of the Republic in 1776—or perhaps even earlier—a cultural rivalry has existed between Virginia and North Carolina over relative importance and regional dominance. At Gettysburg, North Carolina provided more troops and suffered more casualties than did Virginia, or any other Southern state, yet Virginia's control of the Southern media system meant that the Tarheels regularly received second billing to their Virginia rivals. Perhaps no other instance has more inflamed this squabble than the results of what some historians now call the Pickett-Pettigrew Charge.

Six thousand Virginians lined up on the right side of the assault, separated by a field and small tree line from an equal number of mostly North Carolinians. Across the field they each marched under withering artillery fire. Shortly into the movement toward the Yankee center a group on the North Carolina end wavered and turned back, yet history has largely forgotten that these were Virginia soldiers. As the two groups neared their destination, they met a stone wall with an angle in it so that the Virginia portion of the force reached the closer portion of the wall, while the North Carolina wing had to march further to reach the portion of The Angle set farther back. From the moment both sides returned from the failed assault, the squabbling began over who was to blame for the failure. Virginians blamed the Tarheels for being less resolute and lacking the requisite bravery. Since Armistead and his men breached the wall and penetrated the Union works, they could claim they had gone further. But on the other hand, the North Carolinians could claim supremacy for having reached a point farther on since the angle in the wall placed the enemy further back.

Those who doubt that these feelings of animosity still thrive in the region need only visit The Angle today and glance at the position of that 26th North Carolina advance marker. It is several full paces forward of the Armistead marker, the symbol of Virginia's greatest penetration. As late as 1986 North Carolinians still seethed at the thought that Virginia claimed the lion's share of honor from the charge. The placement of their monument was clearly designed to finally get the better of their rivals while setting the new story in stone. When the location of the 1986 marker became pubic, the "which state was better at Gettysburg" controversy flared anew in magazines and newspapers across the country.

No regiment can stake a greater claim to making the greater sacrifice at Gettysburg than the 26th North Carolina. In the fighting on both the first and third days of the battle, the regiment lost 687 officers and men, a casualty rate exceeding 81 percent.[34] But in the placement of their monument at that particular location, the claim is suspect at best.

The only account of the battle that places any North Carolina regiment in front of Aldrich's battery at The Angle is that written by Aldrich himself nearly a half century afterward. No Southern account describes the horrible carnage of his final double canister shot. In fact, the historical evidence seems to strongly indicate that the 26th was a hundred yards or more down the line. This conclusion is confirmed by the fact that soldiers of the 12th New Jersey, a unit positioned about one hundred yards further away from The Angle, captured the flag of the 26th North Carolina.[35] As one historian who studied the issue contends, "The 26th simply was not in front of Olney's gun. On the contrary, the North Carolina regiment was hundreds of feet north of the monument placed in 1986."[36] Nevertheless, based on the single account of a Union artillery veteran and despite evidence to the contrary, the North Carolina monument committee placed a marker that satisfied their rivalry toward the Armistead marker—which, by the way, was actually placed by Philadelphians. All of these are within an area made famous by a New Hampshire watercolor painter who promoted it as the nucleus of the Civil War.

Visitors to Gettysburg spend a disproportionate share of their battlefield touring time wandering among the monuments, markers, stone walls, and trees that make up the area now generally known as the High Water Mark. National Park rangers offer daily walking programs of the site, bus tours stop to allow visitors to disembark, and crowds meander from marker to marker exploring the physical memorials to what

175

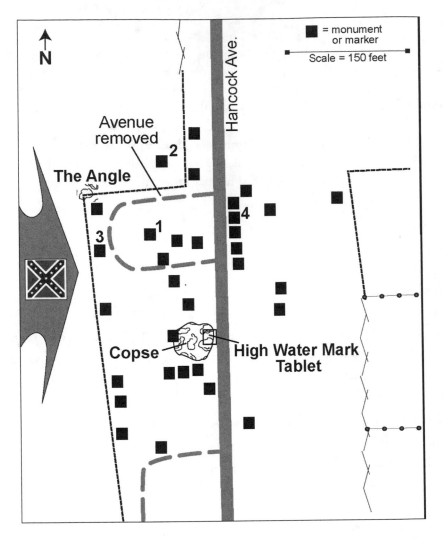

MAP 8.2 *The High Water Mark*

In 1888, members of the Philadelphia Brigade solicited members of General Lewis A. Armistead's family to place a monument (1) that incorrectly marks the spot where Armistead fell mortally wounded during the charge. This is often looked upon as the furthest point that any Confederate soldier reached. In 1986, the State of North Carolina placed an advance position marker for its troops (2) several paces forward of the Armistead marker, much to the consternation of many Virginians. After a protracted legal battle in the State Supreme Court,

(Continues)

(Continued)

the 72nd Pennsylvania succeeded in getting its monument (3) placed at the wall in 1892, while the statue of General Webb (4) placed in 1915 is back at the 72nd's original battle position. All of this monumentation was the direct result of John Bachelder's work to isolate this area, highlighted by the Copse of Trees and his High Water Mark Tablet, as the most important site of the Civil War. There are also several cannons and interpretive markers in the area. In the early 1960s, the National Park Service built a modern structure to house the Cyclorama painting just north of this site.

occurred there. What few if any realize as they read the inscriptions and walk from one to another is that there is a deep and enlightening story behind the placement of each monument. Beginning with John Bachelder's efforts to sculpt it into the central focus of the entire Civil War and progressing through the discussions, arguments, and court battles that led to one monument after another, the place is now a constructed view of a certain version of the past, rather than a factual depiction of some historical truth.

At the height of the monument-placing frenzy of the late 1880s and early 1890s, one veteran wrote a letter to another veteran in which he aptly explained all of this fuss. "One great monument would have sufficiently commemorated the battle as a whole. But that would not have satisfied the American idea of individualism. That idea led to the commemorating [of] the part taken by each regiment and organization. No other battlefield was ever so marked, and no other will be so marked. This is our one memorial battlefield."[37]

WHERE'S BUSTER KILRAIN BURIED?

Colonel darling. Rise up, me bucko. Oh, I'm sorry darling but we got a bit of a problem here, Colonel. Would you like to hear about it?
BUSTER KILRAIN IN THE MOVIE *GETTYSBURG*

If someone took a poll, most Americans could confirm that George Washington once crossed the Delaware River. Few of them could explain what he did when he got across, but most know that he made the crossing standing in a boat with a flag behind him. The explanation for this phenomenon is not the result of an incredibly popular but incomplete book or article on the subject. Rather, it is a painting titled *Washington Crossing the Delaware,* created in 1851 by the artist Emanuel Leutze. Though rife with inaccuracies—Washington could not have safely *stood* in the boat, and the flag depicted was not then in use—the painting is the primary, if not singular, source of knowledge of this event for millions of Americans. The patriotic image it elicits is so powerful that numerous groups and corporations have imitated it. One can now find true or corrupted reproductions of Leutze's image in a print by Currier & Ives, beer steins sold by Miller Brewing Company, collector plates in pewter, ceramic, and fine china, even the name of a town in Pennsylvania. So deeply set is this image in our culture that most Americans can and probably do carry a copy of it in their pocket. In 2000 the U.S. Mint issued the New Jersey commemorative state quarter with a rendering of Leutze's painting on the back. This painting and its powerful image, now more than 150 years old, has misinformed several generations of Americans about their past. Beyond the brush, when it comes to the memory of the past, the old saying "the pen is mightier than the sword" holds true.

More than eighty-five years after the revolutionary battles of Lexington and Concord, a Boston silversmith named Paul Revere was a minor regional legend in New England. As the nation plunged into uncertainty in 1861, Maine poet Henry Wadsworth Longfellow used the Revere legend to help rally patriotic fervor to the Union cause. Longfellow wrote his poem *Paul Revere's Ride* to motivate the people of his time rather than to inform them of their history, but it is the historical aspect of his work that achieved much greater impact. Elevating the silversmith to mythic legend, Longfellow's work left in obscurity William Dawes and Dr. Samuel Prescott, who also rode along and might have replaced Revere in the work had their names been more rhythmically useful. If not for Longfellow and his attempt to inspire his brethren to sustain the Union in 1861, the nation today would hardly remember the Paul Revere of 1775.[1]

If literature, art, and now film have distorted our view of the Revolutionary War, they have certainly misinformed and misguided our understanding of the Civil War, particularly the Battle of Gettysburg, the most written about event of the war. This is demonstrated by people who visit the battlefield today.

One of the Union soldiers who appears in the movie *Gettysburg* and the novel *Killer Angels* on which it is based is a telling example. The character Buster Kilrain was a figment of the late Michael Shaara's literary imagination. Shaara even hinted that "Buster" was actually the author's way of writing himself into the story. Buster is a confidante of one of the heroes of the story, Maine Colonel Joshua Chamberlain. At the climax of the

20th Maine's fight on Little Round Top, Buster takes two Confederate bullets in the right armpit—then comically exclaims that he was hit "in the *bloody* armpit," as if wounds in other places did not bleed—and the wounds shortly prove to be mortal.

Shaara's character is depicted as Irish, though the name Kilrain is English in origin, making it an insulting moniker for any true Irishman of the 1860s. Further, it is unlikely that there could have been a "Buster" Kilrain in the 20th Maine, for the unavoidable reason that "Buster" did not become a popular name until Buster Keaton became a famous movie actor fifty years after the Civil War. Nevertheless, in the years following the movie's release, thousands of visitors to the Gettysburg battlefield made impassioned inquiries into the whereabouts of Buster's grave in the Soldiers National Cemetery. Still more expressed their dismay at not finding his name among the list of the fallen on the monument to the 20th Maine dead on Little Round Top.

Strangely, it does not seem to bother people that the character is a middle-aged, overweight private who follows his commanding officer around telling him what to do while calling him "darling." Nor does it seem to register that the Kilrain to whom they refer is a Hollywood version of a character from a novel. The little Irish soldier is so endearing, they simply wish he were real and follow that instinct despite all of the evidence to the contrary. This phenomenon is but one of many examples of the power of a single novel and its adaptation to film to influence popular beliefs.

Michael Shaara wrote his now famous novel as a Shakespearean-style epic about the men of both sides in the battle. Numerous publishers turned it down before a small press finally published it in 1975. It received the Pulitzer Prize for fiction that year but failed to achieve popular success or garner the author any career advancement because it was a story about war heroes in a country that had just passed through an intensely unpopular war. The last thing most Americans wanted to read about after the conflict in Vietnam was a novel that seemed to romanticize warfare. In time, however, the book's popularity grew and by 1990 it had sold millions of copies.

Two years later, after more than a decade of trying, director Ron Maxwell convinced media mogul Ted Turner to finance a film version of the novel. Because focus groups expected a film called "Killer Angels" to be about biker gangs, producers decided on the more recognizable *Gettysburg*. The result was the second longest feature film of all time and a considerable box office flop, grossing less than $11 million dollars in theaters.

Where Gettysburg failed on the silver screen, however, it succeeded impressively on cable television. A year after its release, Turner aired the epic on his television network TNT to the largest audience ever to watch a drama on cable television. Forty million viewers tuned in to watch Hollywood's version of Shaara's now classic novel.

In an epilogue to the airing of the movie, Turner filmed a brief piece expressing his thoughts on the epic conflict while woefully misstating the facts numerically. More men died at Gettysburg, he told the viewing audience, than in the entire Vietnam War. In fact, only about one-sixth as many men died at Gettysburg, and the total of killed, wounded, and missing does not equal, much less surpass, the number of Americans killed in Vietnam. Despite the thousands of scholarly works on the subject, popular voices such as Turner's have done more to shape people's understanding of the Gettysburg story than the army of professional historians who produced these works.

In the film *Remember the Titans*, Denzel Washington plays a Virginia high school coach struggling to unite his multiracial football team while he himself suffers under the racial tensions of the 1950s. In an important moment of the film, he forces his players to take a late-night jog around the Gettysburg battlefield. While passing the Soldiers National Cemetery, he stops to give his panting squad a motivational lesson in history.

"This is where they fought the Battle of Gettysburg," he tells them. "Fifty thousand men died right here on this field fighting the same fight that we're still fighting amongst ourselves today . . . You listen and take a lesson from the dead."[2]

Ironically, it is not the dead from whom this fictional lesson came, but from those who have sought to attach meaning to their death, often exaggerating it. It is not clear whether the screenwriter of *Remember the Titans* saw Ted Turner's comments or included this scene based on a loose understanding of one of Gettysburg's many myths, but the impression left by both of these instances demonstrates how strongly films can affect our view of the past.

There are many other elements of the film that have affected the popular perception of the battle, despite obvious flaws. One scene, for example, depicts the two Chamberlain brothers, Tom and Joshua, having survived the brunt of Pickett's Charge at the critical center hugging each other in relief as the sun sets slowly behind them . . . in the *east*. Setting aside the fact that nineteenth-century Puritan men simply did not hug, particularly in front of their army comrades, neither Chamberlain brother was anywhere near the fighting during the real Pickett's Charge. Nevertheless, when General Armistead leads his men over the wall at the apex of the charge and is mortally wounded, there is the character Tom Chamberlain—whose unit was actually more than half a mile away during the battle—kneeling at his side to comfort him. Many decades after the battle, but only a few years after the film's release, a group of schoolchildren were among those who left tributes to the Chamberlains at the Bloody Angle, where Pickett's Charge ebbed. Naively believing they were standing at the spot where the brothers hugged, these children left a ceremonial shrine, complete with a small flag, candles, and words of thanks to men who were nowhere near that spot in 1863.

Borrowing from Shaara's work, the film contains many elements and arguments from the Lost Cause. General Ewell failed to attack despite the fact that "a blind man should have seen it." General Stuart left the army blind by reaching the field too late to provide important intelligence information: "It is the opinion of some excellent officers that you have let us all down." Perhaps its most significant contribution to the mythology of Gettysburg is the somewhat successful attempt to rehabilitate the reputation of James Longstreet. Since the fallen general first set himself at odds with Jubal Early and his ilk in the literary wars of the Lost Cause, Longstreet's reputation was largely one of failure and blame. Painting a sympathetic picture of Lee's most active corps commander at Gettysburg, Shaara's book and then Maxwell's movie created a groundswell of support and interest that eventually enabled a private group to raise enough money to place a life-size statue of the general on the battlefield, making it the only Southern equestrian statue on the field other than the Virginia state memorial on which sits Robert E. Lee and his beloved Traveler.

In an effort to pay tribute to the general while observing the more modern trend toward preserving the battlefield undisturbed, the group chose to have Longstreet portrayed in a modest size sitting in the saddle, reining in his horse. This action pose is distinctly different from the statuesque poses in which other horseback generals were depicted on the battlefield. Lacking a grand pedestal, it seemed incongruous to many who were used to larger, more dominating structures. Not long after its initial design was revealed, locals and Civil War aficionados began calling it the "troll on a pony."

One other distinct feature of the statue bears in bronze a testimony to the effect of the movie *Gettysburg* on the story and the battlefield. Despite the work of historians that shows Longstreet was wearing an officer's "Kepi" style hat during the battle, and wartime photos that show his long, narrow beard, the solid metal image that future generations will see at Gettysburg is the image of . . . well . . . Tom Berenger, the actor who played Longstreet in the movie with a horribly false, wide beard and a hat reminiscent of a western cowboy.

Another strange feature of the film not attributable to Shaara was the puzzling habit of filmmakers who would hold up a well-known painting of the Civil War and inform the actors and extras that they were going to recreate this image as closely as possible on film. The most obvious is the scene where Tom Chamberlain and three Confederate prisoners awkwardly recreate a living version of the famous Winslow Homer painting *Prisoners from the Front*. This is even more confusing to viewers, since Homer's work had nothing to do with either Tom Chamberlain or the Battle of Gettysburg.

While motion pictures have played a powerful role in shaping public perception of history, the still image has also had a lasting effect. Gettysburg in art began in earnest in 1870, when John Bachelder hired out the work that had set him on the path to Gettysburg in the first place, resulting in James Walker's painting *The Repulse of Longstreet's Assault*, which toured the country until 1901. Just one year after the Walker/Bachelder work, the Pennsylvania legislature commissioned the state's well-known artist Peter Rothermel to paint his strangely similar *Battle of Gettysburg* on a canvas measuring thirty-two feet wide and sixteen feet high.

If viewers were impressed by Rothermel's colossus as it toured the nation, then they must have been deliriously wide-eyed at the sight of Paul Philippoteaux's Gettysburg Cyclorama in 1883. A popular painting genre of the time, the idea was to paint a huge circular image so that the viewer could stand inside the arc and see the view in any direction. Philippoteaux's rendition—reproduced in several copies—was thirty feet high and three hundred sixty feet around. Influenced by the popular perception of the time that focused on the culminating moments of Pickett's Charge as the quintessential Gettysburg scene, Philippoteaux followed the same path as Walker and Rothermel before him, depicting the anxious moment when a handful of Confederates crested the wall at the now famous Bloody Angle.

Philippoteaux's knowledge of the scene was based almost entirely on a series of ten photographs made the previous spring by Gettysburg native and photographer William Tipton, showing the field as it existed in 1882. At the artist's request, Tipton had a platform erected at the center of the scene where Pickett's Charge met its fate and photographed the view in every direction, giving the artist a 360-degree visual model of the landscape. As a result, writes photographic historian William Frassanito, "the painting's climactic focal point portraying a stand of trees—Bachelder's 'High Water Mark'—[appears as] more than twenty years old, when in fact the clump was a rambling patch of adolescent scrub at the time of the battle."[3]

Careful examination of the copy still on display at Gettysburg reveals the influence of the artist's homeland. Farm fields contain large French-style hay bales, while Union soldiers run from place to place wearing the white-legged uniforms of the French army, and the wounded are carried from the field via a two-seated mule-borne apparatus used by the French in the Crimean War but never by any American army. Taking his entitled license, the artist even painted himself and Abraham Lincoln into the action; his own image in a Union officer's uniform and a gaunt Lincoln being borne to a hospital on a stretcher. For many around the nation whose only knowledge of Gettysburg had come from reading, the chance to view Pickett's Charge surrounding them was an entertaining opportunity as the painting traveled from city to city. Never mind that it misinformed a bit on the facts.

Interest in the Civil War surged following Ken Burns's film series in 1990, and a thriving industry has grown up around the artists who paint scenes from the war, capturing in vivid color and action a moment from another time and selling framed prints of the image for hundreds of dollars. The Gettysburg end of this industry fairly exploded in late 1993, when Maxwell released his film. These paintings, whose subjects often resemble the movie actors more than the real people they portrayed, often borrow from famous—and therefore marketable—scenes depicted in a popular book. In turn, subsequent books often use these images as cover art or illustrations, art imitating art while it imitates art.

One of the most illustrative examples of how strongly one of these paintings can influence popular perception of the battle involves the story of how Joshua Chamberlain lost his hat on Little Round Top. In 1988 Civil War artist Don Troiani set out to create the first modern painting of the famous charge of Joshua Chamberlain and the 20th Maine on Little Round Top. While creating the work he later called *Bayonet!* Troiani, a meticulous researcher obsessed with historical accuracy, found himself unable to determine exactly what kind of hat Colonel Chamberlain wore on that eventful day. Rather than guess, Troiani decided to paint the regiment's leader without a hat. Better, he thought, to assume it had fallen off in the confusion of battle than to make a mistake by guessing and perhaps painting the wrong style of hat.

The story might have ended here as the tale of an artist's dedication to the historical nature of his work had not Troiani's struggle for authenticity created a ripple effect. In time other paintings began to appear with a hatless Chamberlain, and even the makers of the movie *Gettysburg* followed his lead when the character Chamberlain inexplicably yanks off his cap moments before he leaps down the hill in the midst of his men. Thus, when the climactic charge occurs, viewers see the image of the hatless Chamberlain created not at Gettysburg in 1863, but in an artist's work in the 1980s.[4]

This example of Gettysburg art imitating art has yet another level, however. As a marketing tie-in to the film, producers contracted with a different historical artist to paint scene snapshots as they occurred in the film. The resulting visual images proliferated and now appear on everything from coffee mugs to pillows and even credit cards: all of them with the hatless Joshua Chamberlain charging down Little Round Top. The ironic ending to this particular story is that the stickler Troiani eventually learned what kind of hat the Maine colonel wore on Little Round Top, and he created a different painting of the same scene, only this time the prime subject is no longer hatless.

Though various issues may arise in an artist's rendition of a historical event, it might seem hard to find large disagreements on straight photographic evidence, which leaves out the painter's interpretation of facts. As with nearly every Gettysburg issue, however, finding varying opinions on any subject is never a weighty chore. Probably the best example of how photography has affected the story of Gettysburg lies in its two most famous images. One is the often misunderstood view of three Confederate prisoners—or deserters—taken three days after the battle, while the other is the often reprinted image of a Confederate "sharpshooter" in Devil's Den. This image, coupled with the high mortality of Union officers hundreds of yards away on Little Round Top, led to the widespread notion that special Confederate snipers had fired remarkably accurate shots over long distances through the smoke and haze of battle, finding their mark among the Federal command structure on the famous hill.

In 1974 William Frassanito published the first of several groundbreaking studies on Civil War photography. His *Gettysburg: A Journey in Time* was a remarkable look at how images created within days of the battle helped shape the story of Gettysburg. This work, along with his later *Early Photography at Gettysburg,* demonstrated a unique ability for analyzing photographs, a skill he honed as a U.S. military intelligence analyst in Vietnam. One of the more fascinating revelations in his first book came from his analysis of the photographs taken by Alexander Gardner and his crew on July 6, 1863, in the area in and around Devil's Den. Comparing the group of images taken of the famous "Sharpshooter's Last Sleep" with those of another death scene nearby, Frassanito determined that the body pictured in these two separate groups was the same dead soldier, meaning that Gardner and his crew had moved the body and posed it at the more famous location. Frassanito pointed out that not only was there no particular "sharpshooter quality" to the soldier, but that one of the most famous of Civil War photographs was actually staged by the photographers.

In 1988 Richard Pougher analyzed the same two sets of photographs as part of his graduate study on the battlefield uniforms and equipment of Confederate soldiers. Recognized as a leading expert in Confederate material culture, Pougher's study helped debunk the myth that Southern soldiers were a ragtag lot sadly lacking in proper clothing and equipment.

In the Devil's Den photos Pougher, analyzing the dead soldier's clothing where Frassanito had focused with a photographer's eye, noticed important differences in the bodies depicted in the two sets of images.

"Initially," he wrote, "the viewer is struck with the similarities between the man in the first four views and the one in the second two with the result that it appears that they are the same person."[5] These similarities, Pougher explains, are not surprising since, contrary to popular perception, Confederate soldiers from the same unit tended to wear very similar uniforms. Since the two sets of views were taken in close proximity, the two soldiers may well have come from the same unit and thus were clothed in a similar or even nearly identical manner.[6]

Training his expert eye on the clothing worn in each set of photos, Pougher points out that one soldier wears leggings but the other does not. Although the same type of coat is worn in both views, the depth of the breast pocket of each varies, as does the spacing of the button holes. Further evidence of his two-body theory is revealed in the pants. In each of the images in the first set, the pants and coat are of a matching material and tone, while in the second set of views there is a "marked contrast" between the two.[7]

More convincing, argues Pougher, are the differing physical features of the two subjects. "The man in the first set has a short, extremely dished, turned up nose. The man in the second has a long, narrow nose which borders on being Roman in profile."[8]

For more than a century after the battle the famous sharpshooter image led those who studied Gettysburg to erroneously assert that specially trained riflemen operated in and around Devil's Den. When that idea was challenged by detailed photographic analysis, popular opinion shifted to a recognition that at least one Civil War photographer had fraudulently created a battlefield image. Still later, another qualified in a different field argued that, while the sharpshooter legend is likely false, the soldier in each set of photos is not the same man, implying that Gardner had not falsified the scene after all.

It is likely that we will never know exactly what these two groups of images really tell us about the Battle of Gettysburg, but the interest that they have generated and the debate that continues about them tell us a great deal about the ever changing story that our popular culture has created and continues to rework regarding the conflict.

One unusual issue that has helped confuse society's knowledge of Gettysburg is its attractiveness to writers who recognize a good story when they see it. In the same manner in which John Bachelder made the High Water Mark the center of attention for millions who followed him, journalists and novelists, with no particular training in the field of history, seem drawn to Gettysburg's stories, while their gift for communicating these stories in a compelling way—whether factual or not—has helped perpetuate many of the legends and myths surrounding it. It may not be far from the truth to say that the work of a few novelists and journalists has had a more profound effect on society's understanding of Gettysburg than the total product of all trained historians combined. This has helped make Gettysburg a famous and popular story although not always accurate or factual.

No novelist has more profoundly affected the popular image of Gettysburg than Michael Shaara, whose long fascination with Shakespeare led him to novelize the Gettysburg story, raising it to the level of Shakespearean drama. While his *Killer Angels* sold millions of copies and the movie version reached tens of millions more, other writers have also found great stories in Gettysburg mythology.

Like Shaara, Shelby Foote had little or no formal education in judging sources and evaluating historical data, yet millions of Americans have learned about the Civil War from his work. From 1954 to 1974 he wrote his trilogy *The Civil War: A Narrative*, choosing in the end not to include any footnotes on which others might build or follow up his research. As a result, his work tends to perpetuate myths. On several occasions, for example, Foote has written and spoken on what he considers the true cause of the Battle of Gettysburg. It happened, he states, because the

Confederate Army went into Gettysburg to raid a well-known shoe factory there. Despite the fact that county records show that there was no shoe factory, warehouse, or other substantial supply of footwear in Gettysburg at any time in the 1800s, this myth has persisted among Civil War enthusiasts.

In 1994 Foote released the Gettysburg chapter of his original three-volume work as a separate book entitled *Stars in Their Courses*. It spread his version of the battle, including the fictitious shoe factory, extending its influence to an even wider audience. Foote was heavily influenced by fellow Mississippi writers William Faulkner, Eudora Welty, and his close friend Walker Percy, each of them known for the dark tragedy and failure of their Southern characters, much of it coming out of personal and familial experiences. In this genre the romantic drama of the Old South and the Lost Cause were naturally intertwined, an understandable attraction to Foote.

For several decades, including the surge of interest surrounding the one hundredth anniversary of the Civil War in the 1960s, Bruce Catton held sway as the most prominent and influential of Civil War writers. A journalist by training and experience, this Cleveland newspaperman became the first editor of *American Heritage* magazine, a position that gave him a wide audience and an influential voice in shaping popular notions of the American past. One of the phrases for which he was famous revealed a lot about his motives and style. "Whatever else it is, history ought to be a good yarn."[9] Critics of Catton's historical quality might retort that what he should have said was, Whatever else it is, history ought to be accurate. Catton's knack for knowing a good story when he saw one did not always extend to recognizing a story too good to be true. Nevertheless, his work is responsible for turning millions of Americans into Civil War enthusiasts even if he added greatly to the legends and myths that still surround the era.

Catton was not alone among journalists whose keen eye for drama focused on the story of Gettysburg. Glenn Tucker was an Indiana writer transplanted to North Carolina after a notable career as an advertising executive and a newspaper writer. His books *High Tide at Gettysburg* and *Lee and Longstreet at Gettysburg*, among others, demonstrate a notable Southern slant.[10]

Not all of the Civil War authors who migrated from journalism, however, lacked credentials. Douglas Southall Freeman was editor of the *Richmond News-Leader* from 1915 to 1949, when he retired to write what is often called the definitive biography of Robert E. Lee. It is sometimes argued among historians that Freeman is almost singularly responsible for the modern image of Robert E. Lee, an image complicatedly intertwined with the story of Gettysburg. Unlike other newspaper writers turned historians, Freeman had earned his Ph.D. in history before turning to journalism. His biography of Robert E. Lee stretched through four volumes and won the Pulitzer Prize for biography in 1935. His three-volume *Lee's Lieutenants* also added to his influence over popular perception of the Civil War. Clearly the story of Gettysburg was constructed from many different sources from many different backgrounds. The fact that so many seekers of the "great story" gravitated toward that particular battle and became recognized as leading authorities on it, is at the heart of an ongoing debate.

The debate revolves around the idea that modern academia either ignores the Civil War as a politically incorrect subject or approaches it in heavy, stolid prose. Allan Nevins once caricatured the average academic historian as "Professor Dryasdust." In 1979 Lawrence Stone helped reignite the debate when he argued that the majority of the American population is interested in history "but cannot stomach indigestible statistical tables, dry analytical argument, and jargon-ridden prose."[11] When historians do write in an engaging style, the argument goes, they avoid the battles and details of military history in favor of broader themes and social issues.

If professional historians are thus partly to blame for the public's misshapen views of the Civil War, then so-called amateur historians have left their mark as well. In an interview with the editor of the *Journal of American History*, filmmaker Ken Burns boldly stated to the academic historical community, "I believe you have failed and lost touch absolutely in the communication of history to the public and that it has fallen to the amateur historians, if you will, to try to rescue that history."[12] As it concerns Gettysburg, however, Burns's idea of rescuing history includes the creation and perpetuation of myths. Thus rescued, his audience believes that Shelby Foote's fictitious shoe factory was the cause of the battle or that Burns's invention of a "textbook military maneuver" attributed to Joshua Chamberlain saved the Union from certain defeat.

Regardless of where on this spectrum of argument we may see ourselves—with the boring academics, the mythmaking amateurs, or somewhere in between—the debate itself exposes an ongoing recognition that our knowledge of the Civil War is seriously flawed.

CHAPTER 10

AMERICAN VALHALLA

It always seems to me that legends and yarns and folk tales are as much
a part of the real history of a country as proclamations, provisos, and
constitutional amendments.
STEPHEN VINCENT BENET

At the conclusion of all great battles, according to Norse mythology, winged female creatures hover over the slain in search of the warriors who fought the most valiantly. When they find the bravest of combatants, these winged Valkyries spirit them away to the mythical banquet hall at Valhalla. Here Odin, the greatest of Norse gods, entertains the slain heroes with a sumptuous feast. When the morning dawns, the warriors again take to the field of battle, this time in Odin's kingdom. After a day spent demonstrating their courage and martial skill against one another, these heroes, including those killed in the fighting who now rise, return to the banquet hall to begin the same cycle again. The highest of honors in Norse culture was to prove oneself worthy enough on the field of battle to be selected by the Valkyries and taken to Valhalla to spend eternity in combat and fellowship among the greatest warriors.

In the relatively short history of the United States, the national culture has developed its own unique myths. Although they may not measure up to the elaborate religion of ancient Greece, they are still a powerful source of knowledge and culture. The story of Gettysburg is America's Valhalla, and though George Meade and Robert E. Lee may not measure up to the likes of Odin or Zeus or Apollo in the minds of many, the sociological process is the same, and many of those who immerse themselves in the story of the battle are, in their own way, waiting for the Valkyries.

Dan Sickles spent his life trying to lift himself up to greatness, though he seemed to thwart his own designs. Whether by murdering his wife's lover, making some political misstep, or creating a scandal, he managed to help illustrious fame escape him—until Gettysburg. Failing to achieve unquestionable greatness on the battlefield, he successfully engaged in mythmaking. Within hours after he was carried from the battlefield on a stretcher, he began telling his story to President Lincoln and anyone else of authority or prominence he could find. Though he had to bend the facts to his whim—or ignore them altogether—his lifelong campaign for the lion's share of credit for the great victory there enabled him to write, near the end of his life, "I won the great and decisive battle of Gettysburg."[1]

Though this statement was a bit bolder than time has judged it, in the years following 1863, he saw to the design and placement of most of the New York monuments on the field. He shaped Gettysburg history by creating one of its greatest sources of debate and controversy, significantly affecting what veterans wrote and how they wrote it. And he was almost single-handedly responsible for the establishment of Gettysburg National Military Park as a federal entity.

In 1913, six months after avoiding arrest and prison for embezzling the balance of the New York Monuments Commission's treasury, the ninety-three-year-old Sickles made his final visit to Gettysburg to take part in the fiftieth anniversary ceremonies and reunion. During this visit, he was asked whether he was disappointed that there was no monument to him on the battlefield. Advancing age had not robbed him of his ability to turn an issue on its head. "Hell," he replied. "The whole damned battlefield is my memorial!"[2]

As a matter of history, it is not possible to determine whether Sickles was right or wrong at Gettysburg—this is a question of opinion with no absolute answer. It is, however, possible to assess how the one-legged old politician managed to shape the story of Gettysburg in the popular mind. In that sense, what he did after July 2, 1863, may be a far more useful subject of historical inquiry than are his actions on the field.

John Bachelder tried to paint the greatness he felt for the Battle of Bunker Hill. Unable to capture it in the way he hoped, he set out in search of another great moment in history. When he decided Gettysburg would serve his purposes, he spent decades trying to make the world see it as the pivotal battle of the war. By doing so, he elevated his own stature as the central Gettysburg historian of his time and served as an important gatekeeper for those who wished to shape the story or the battlefield in a particular way. Gettysburg gave Bachelder's life a greater meaning and purpose, and made him something of a celebrity among those who had fought there or sought to understand the fighting. What is most revealing about Bachelder's relationship with Gettysburg is that despite all of the data he amassed, all of the veterans he personally walked the field with, three decades of intense study, and more than enough money to accomplish the task, he found he simply could not tell the factual story of Gettysburg either on canvas or in print. In the end, he came to see that truth is a malleable force and history has few absolute conclusions.

Unlike many of his comrades and foes at Gettysburg, Jubal Early's postwar quest was less interested in the martial glory of Valhalla than a larger theme. That the Valkyries had passed him by seemed not to matter at all. In his efforts to shape the history of the war and of Gettysburg, Early focused not so much on his own stature as on his desire to promote a way of life that had passed. A vehement defender of antebellum Southern culture, Early used his influence over the story of Gettysburg to promote certain ideals, elevating some men to near sainthood while vigorously working to destroy others. That he moved beyond exaggeration and into the realm of fabrication—as with the "sunrise attack order"—seemed not to matter as much as the way people would someday come to view the cultural norms of his past.[3]

Contrary to what most visitors to Gettysburg perceive, the life of Joshua Chamberlain after Gettysburg was one of misery and pain. Nearly a year after leading his regiment in its now famous defense of Little Round Top, the former professor personally led an assault on the Confederate works at Petersburg. As he turned to encourage his men, a bullet pierced his right hip, tore a hole through him that nearly killed him and caused permanent leakage in his bladder. He survived the wound that doctors were certain was mortal, only to be shot again the following April. At Appomattox, he was chosen by General Grant to preside over the surrender of the Confederate infantry before returning home to life in Maine. He served four one-year terms as governor of his home state, then thirteen more as president of Bowdoin College, his alma mater.

In the half century that made up his postwar years, his life was dominated by almost constant pain from repeated bladder infections caused by the Petersburg wound along with recurring bouts of malaria, among other ailments. The second factor, which dominated his writings and his reputation after the Civil War, was Gettysburg. Though he could claim far greater credit and fame for his courageous actions at Petersburg and on the road to Appomattox, Chamberlain's thoughts of war seemed fixed on Gettysburg. As the fame and importance of the battle grew, so did its prominence in his memories. When one of his former students recommended him to the U.S. Army's Record and Pension Office for a Medal of Honor, he cited his entire military career. The law governing the medal, however, required that a single event be the basis of the citation and, since Gettysburg was the most famous battle in which he was engaged, the citation lists his "courage and tenacity" at Gettysburg.[4]

Like the foot doctors who found a connection between their profession and the battle through a mythical shoe factory, people from all walks of life gravitate to the story of Gettysburg and find some aspect of it that is connected to them. Their involvement with the story and the place seems to touch many of them deeply as they pursue the record of a relative, someone from their hometown, or any other relationship to this heroic past. Artists visit the field to study the changing styles of sculpture through the years, evident in the Confederate state monuments placed in varying decades. Geologists have studied the ground in search of some connection to their work and the battle's outcome, and musicians compose and perform many styles of music about the events of 1863.

All of them seek some connection with the heroism, chivalry, and importance that they associate with the Gettysburg story. They are, in a sense, waiting for the Valkyries to lift them up to Valhalla by association.

The sight of wool-clad reenactors and women in elaborate Southern dress walking up and down the sidewalk would startle the residents of most towns, but in Gettysburg, it is a daily occurrence. Even when men dressed as soldiers carry their muskets, swords, and side arms into stores and restaurants, few take notice. This small Pennsylvania hamlet has become a place to commune with those who already dine at Valhalla. On summer evenings it is not at all unusual to find someone dressed in full 1863 military regalia standing by a monument greeting passersby, often "in character" as if the battle had occurred the day before. This is not something that happens regularly anywhere else. The people who wander the grounds of Philadelphia's Independence Hall dressed as Ben Franklin or Thomas Jefferson are paid employees of the National Park Service. Most of those who spend time in period dress regaling the public with their tales at Gettysburg do it as a regular Saturday evening out, without any sanction or endorsement from the Park Service or any other historically minded association. Though some have researched their roles in depth, for many their knowledge of the events they describe is often cursory at best.

The search for a spiritual connection to times past has even sought to overcome the barriers of life and death. All of the men who fought at

Gettysburg have long since passed on but thousands of visitors to Gettysburg spend summer nights strolling the town on one of the many ghost tours in which tour guides dressed in period clothing tell tales of soldiers whose spirits have yet to completely leave the battlefield for whatever lies beyond. Advertising Gettysburg as "the most haunted place in America," ghost books, T-shirts, videos, tours, and conventions have become a thriving part of a Gettysburg industry that measures the search for Valkyries in dollars—lots of them. A 1990s study sponsored by the Friends of the National Parks at Gettysburg determined that the economic impact of the battlefield on Adams County, Pennsylvania, is estimated at $250 million annually.

WHEN THE FIGHTING ENDED AT GETTYSBURG, few people in the nation perceived it as the great crucible—the great turning point—of the conflict. In fact, a year after the battle there was a widespread feeling that the Union was losing the war. Things were so bad by August 1864 that even President Lincoln's supporters doubted he could win reelection in the coming fall. In a letter to Lincoln, *New York Tribune* editor Horace Greeley begged the president to give in. "Our bleeding, bankrupt, almost dying country," he wrote, "longs for peace—shudders at the prospect of fresh conscriptions, of further wholesale devastations, and of new rivers of human blood. I entreat you to submit overtures for pacification to the Southern insurgents."[5] A month later, Greeley made his feelings public. In an editorial in the *Tribune* he declared, "Mr. Lincoln is already beaten. He cannot be elected. And we must have another ticket to save us from utter overthrow."[6] Lincoln himself was no more optimistic when he confided to a friend, "You think that I don't know I am going to be beaten, but I do and unless some great change takes place badly beaten."[7]

As it happened, a great change did take place when Union forces in the field won significant and decisive victories in two different theaters and the nation gave Lincoln a vote of confidence to continue the struggle. Clearly, the nation in 1864 did not see Gettysburg as the pivotal event on which the entire war swung. Instead, this perception grew and developed into a common belief after the war ended. Today the idea is so firmly entrenched in the popular belief that it is only rarely even considered, much less debated.

It is interesting, then, that Lincoln and Gettysburg have become so deeply intertwined. Four and a half months after the Confederate Army turned for home, on November 19, 1863, Lincoln spoke at the dedication of the Soldiers National Cemetery. Though he spoke for less than three minutes, his words further elevated the story of Gettysburg. As with the importance of Gettysburg, however, Lincoln's speech was not considered by everyone to be as profound then as it is today. The immediate reaction of the crowd left even Lincoln with the impression that it had been a failure. To his friend Ward Lamon he remarked, "It is a flat failure and the people are disappointed." Many newspaper reporters in attendance at Lincoln's address panned the speech. A Harrisburg newspaper editorial wrote, "We pass over the silly remarks of the President; for the credit of the Nation we are willing that the veil of oblivion shall be dropped over them and that they shall no more be repeated or thought of."[8] That same day, the *Chicago Times* opined that "the cheeks of every American must tingle with shame as he reads the silly, flat, and dishwatery utterances." The editor of the *Chicago Tribune* offered a different perspective: "The dedicatory remarks by President Lincoln will live among the annals of man."[9]

Today Lincoln's Gettysburg Address is revered as one of the greatest public speeches ever and has its own monument in the National Cemetery, though it was placed a hundred yards or more from where Lincoln actually stood. Entwined with its greatness, however, is the idea that Lincoln gave little or no effort to writing the speech. As Garry Wills describes it in his *Lincoln at Gettysburg*, "the silly but persistent myth is that he jotted it on the back of an envelope." Lincoln had in fact written the speech weeks before the event and had asked several people to read it over for him before he traveled to Pennsylvania.

This Lincoln and Gettysburg myth began with the prominent men who had been with the president prior to the speech. As Wills points out, they crafted various stories about how the president rather cavalierly scribbled down the words almost without thought. "They wanted to be intimate with the gestation of the extraordinary speech," Wills writes, "watching the pen or pencil move under the inspiration of the moment."

Once the story was in place, and in print, the perpetuation of the idea stemmed from a perceived correlation between Lincoln and the nation he represented. The symbolism is of the rough backwoods youth emerging from the frontier and rising to international prominence with such inherent brilliance that he is able to scratch immortal phrases on a handy scrap of paper with little effort. This is a powerful metaphor for the American nation as a whole. A rough-and-tumble collection of states carved out of the wilderness possessed such natural power and intellect that, with little effort, it summoned greatness in words and deeds formerly the exclusive ability of royalty. Historian Goldwin Smith touched on this when he wrote that "not a sovereign in Europe, however trained from the cradle for state pomps, and however prompted by statesmen and courtiers, could have uttered himself more regally than did Lincoln at Gettysburg."[10]

It is a formula repeated often in human history—a handful of people present at a critical moment embellish or fabricate a story that gains them some personal importance and the story, fulfilling a cultural need or perception, is accepted through the generations as the truth of the matter. This is the essence of mythology, and the Gettysburg story is fertile ground for this type of cultural behavior.

Among the often discussed and misunderstood elements of the Gettysburg story is the number of casualties, specifically the number killed, during the fighting. Veterans discussed casualties in Civil War battles in terms of killed, wounded, and missing. The last category tended to distort the numerical judgment of a battle. A list of missing was usually created soon after the battle by unit commanders who simply took a head count and deducted the new number from the most recent roll call. Thus any soldier who was not with the unit when this occurred might be included. This figure included men whom the enemy had captured, but it also counted those who fled in fear, became lost in the confusion of battle, or helped a wounded comrade to the rear. The missing figures were often overstated as many of the men soon returned to the regiment. In addition, wounded who went to the rear occasionally found themselves better off than they had first thought and returned the regimental line within a few hours.

Another category that is difficult to clearly define is the number of soldiers killed at Gettysburg. Most historians estimate that between eight and twelve thousand men lost their lives, but the number included in this category depends on varying definitions of the word "killed." Approximately 8,000 dead bodies lay on or under the battlefield as the fighting ended, with many more to come in the days and weeks that followed. It is these later deaths that are sometimes hard to categorize. For example, Lieutenant Arad Linscott of the 20th Maine Regiment found himself in a field hospital on July 3 with a bullet wound in his thigh. Linscott's commander originally listed him as wounded, and he slowly gained strength under the care of Union medical personnel. By mid-July Linscott was well enough that doctors decided he should return home and finish his recuperation under the care of his family. He safely reached home on furlough but contracted a virus or infection and died at home on July 27. Technically, Linscott died of an illness and not the trauma of a gunshot wound. It is possible that the wound somehow contributed to his death, but this is far from a certainty. As a result, there is some question as to whether Linscott should be listed as killed or wounded at Gettysburg, or whether the overall war record should count him as "killed in battle" or "died of disease." On learning of his death, members of his unit thought of him as "mortally wounded," but his death is now among those counted on his regiment's monument as killed in battle. It is not unusual to see such a case like Linscott's accidentally listed numerically in both the wounded and the killed categories—first listed as "wounded" and then moved to "killed" without correcting the wounded number.

Adding to the confusion—or flexibility—of Gettysburg casualty numbers is the fact that no central governmental body kept track of the figures beyond initial battlefield reports. The Federal government had no office of casualty calculation that followed the condition and recorded the final disposition of each man initially listed as wounded. The numbers used in historical accounts, then, can come from several sources, and someone writing an article or script about the battle can choose the means of calculation that best suits his or her purposes. It is no wonder that the public is confused by so many different sets of numbers.

Another issue that confronts those trying to numerically gauge the impact of the battle is the fact that both armies were made up of people considered Americans. While many were recent immigrants or even foreign nationals fighting for the Union or Confederacy, the nature of a civil war is that the two sides make up a part of a former whole, and since the U.S. Civil War resulted in the reunification of the two sides, the number of men lost is, in a way, double that of wars in which the United States fought a foreign power. Unlike all other wars, the Civil War casualties on both sides are now listed as American.

In the midst of the confusion and misunderstanding it is easy to imagine how those without a deep knowledge of the events can take the most commonly used number of Gettysburg casualties—52,000 killed, wounded, and missing—make a small slip of the tongue and conclude that more than 50,000 Americans died at Gettysburg, obviously a gross overstatement. Add just one more miscalculation and a true myth is born. In an epilogue to the airing of the movie *Gettysburg* on his network in 1994, Ted Turner expressed his thoughts on the epic conflict while woefully misstating the numerical facts. More men died at Gettysburg, he told an audience of 40 million viewers, than died in the entire Vietnam War. In fact, only one-sixth as many men died at Gettysburg, and the total of killed, wounded, and missing does not equal, much less surpass, the number killed in Vietnam. Nevertheless, the back of the packaging for the home video version of the film reads: "When it was all over, 50,000 men had paid the ultimate price."

Equally confusing results stem from issues that are largely a matter of opinion. Was Lee a better general than Meade? Was Sickles to blame for nearly losing the battle? Which regiment fought hardest? The answers to these questions have no basis in fact. They are issues open to interpretation and misunderstanding, and as such they can be distorted and shaped in a certain way for a certain purpose. When veterans such as Dan Sickles or Jubal Early work actively, even relentlessly, to shape popular knowledge of past events, they literally make history, building a belief in a particular version of the story even if it is partly fabricated.

This mythmaking process is not unique to the story of Gettysburg. Napoleon was not short, Vikings did not wear horns, and the Pilgrims did not land on Plymouth Rock, though these misconceptions remain firmly entrenched in the popular mind. Particularly (though not exclusively) in a military sense Gettysburg has gained a special place in American mythology, and its many meanings are summoned repeatedly in the context of other significant events. In light of the effort spent elevating Gettysburg to mythical status, those who have constructed the story can reflect on a lasting success.

In many ways, Gettysburg has become a bellwether of U.S. history, and American culture will continue to measure the great events of years to come against the importance attributed to the conflict of 1863. In the same way that veterans of the battle measured their experience against the great historical epics that came before them such as Waterloo, Balaclava, and Thermopylae, Americans have regularly looked back at Gettysburg to find a comparison for events that occur in the present.

Speaking at the dedication ceremonies for the Oklahoma City National Memorial in 2000, President Bill Clinton reached back to Gettysburg as he sought to comfort those who survived the bombing of the Murrah

Federal Building. "America will never forget," Clinton said. "There are places in our national landscape so scarred by freedom's sacrifice that they shape forever the soul of America—Valley Forge, Gettysburg, Selma. This place is such sacred ground."[11]

In trying to find a historical context for the destruction of the World Trade Center in New York, a Milwaukee newspaper reporter recalled the Oklahoma parallel along with two other iconic stories. "The site of the Murrah Office Building," he wrote, "is no longer just a piece of down-town real estate; Gettysburg is no longer just a quiet rural area in Penn-sylvania; and Pearl Harbor is no longer just a Navy base."[12]

It has been many decades since Americans used the story of Gettysburg in a public way to the extent that politicians and journalists have sum-moned its meanings in the wake of the tragedies of September 11, 2001. At a memorial service marking the first anniversary of this event, organizers asked New York Governor George Pataki to offer words of consolation and inspiration. Rather than craft words of his own to help give some meaning to this current tragedy, he instead stepped to the podium and read from Abraham Lincoln's Gettysburg Address. As with Eisenhower, Roosevelt, Wilson, and Carter before him, Gettysburg was good context for a politician in difficult yet auspicious circumstances.[13]

During the year after the World Trade Center attacks, those who sought to define the scope of the event continually compared it to Gettysburg. Perhaps not so much the Gettysburg that veterans may have remembered on July 4, 1863—no one got up in Manhattan and spoke of Longstreet's tactics or Meade's strategy—but rather a generalized idea that has come to mean something greater than just another historical event. A visitor to New York's Ground Zero told a Denver newspaper reporter, "In my mind, it's the same thing as visiting Gettysburg. It's a battleground of freedom."[14] A group known as the World Trade Center Living History Project seeks to memorialize the attacks of September 11, 2001, by recording the memories of the people who worked at Ground Zero in the aftermath. The group's literature introduces its concept and mission by explaining that "scholars have weighed the position of the WTC attack in American History as only rivaled by Civil War Gettysburg in importance and scale of losses."[15]

The discovery of mythology where once there seemed to be fact might produce disillusionment with the study of history. If pure truth can only seldom—if ever—be ascertained, then what is the point of the pursuit? The answer is that there is a deep and highly useful knowledge that can be gained by studying the past and observing its processes, especially those that involve story building. While we may never know exactly which regiment was at a given point at a certain hour, the pursuit of this type of detailed information leads to an understanding of not only the events of the battle but also the process through which human beings create a record of the past. This knowledge, this awareness of the process and how it happens, is an invaluable tool in understanding nearly everything that humans have ever recorded.

While the details of how people constructed the Gettysburg story may vary from the history of the American Revolution, the Roman Empire, or the Cold War, the basic processes are remarkably similar and are still operating today. From the Clinton scandals of the 1990s, the Florida election of 2000, the events of September 11, 2001, to the invasion of Iraq, all of these tend to follow the same basic formula through which the collective human psyche envisions and understands its past. Each of these historical events has its Dan Sickles and Jubal Early, engaged in an almost daily struggle to see that the record left behind today is seen by the people of tomorrow in a particular light. Each of these has its budding mythology of sorts, framed in what media experts now call "talking points" and "spin."

Was George Bush fairly elected U.S. president in 2000, or was the election stolen from Al Gore? There is no factual, unassailable answer to questions such as these, and consequently a constant battle rages among supporters of both sides who seek to sway the popular opinion—and the history books—to one point of view or another. Whether Al Gore or

George Bush was "right" is no easier to decipher than whether George Meade or Robert E. Lee was the better general—Meade won the "decisive" battle, yet Lee is considered the better commander—and our perceptions of these issues are largely the product of the same kind of struggle between people to shape our view of the past. Today this struggle is greatly intensified by technological advances in communication. While it took John Bachelder nearly half a lifetime to create the idea of the High Water Mark of the Rebellion, today a handful of e-mails and a website can create powerful urban legends in a matter of weeks.

Gettysburg has become as much a laboratory as it is a national historic landmark. Here one can study the ways in which people learn about the past and how they pass it along to others in an endless chain that is more often flawed than accurate. Here veterans carefully, persistently, and sometimes inadvertently shaped the "factual" record so that following generations would see the picture that they wanted them to see. Succeeding generations of people see the flawed record and shape it into something else before passing the story—now mythology—on to the next. There is still much to learn from Gettysburg. But instead of teaching us every detail about an event that is largely unknowable, what the place and its story can tell us is that we have a distinct and observable way of making our history. Learning more about that process, we can understand an immeasurable amount about our past, our present, and even our future.

NOTES

INTRODUCTION

1. *USA Today Weekend Magazine,* March 2001.
2. Burns, quoted in *Bowdoin*, Spring-Summer 1991, p. 6.

CHAPTER ONE:
THE MANY MEANINGS OF GETTYSBURG

1. Garry Wills, *Lincoln at Gettysburg:Words That Remade America* (New York: Simon & Schuster, 1992), p. 20.

2. Glenn LaFantasie, "Monty and Ike at Gettysburg," *Quarterly Journal of Military History*, August 1995, p. 68. The author is deeply indebted to Glenn LaFantasie for his help in any number of ways, and here for his work on the Ike and Monty controversy.

3. LaFantasie, "Monty and Ike," p. 70.

4. LaFantasie, "Monty and Ike," p. 71.

5. LaFantasie, "Monty and Ike," p. 71.

6. LaFantasie, "Monty and Ike," p. 72.

7. LaFantasie, "Monty and Ike," p. 72.

8. "Jimmy Carter's Big Breakthrough," *Time*, May 10, 1976.

9. Carter's national security adviser, Zbigniew Brzezinski, quoted in the documentary film *Jimmy Carter,* an episode of the PBS series *American Experience.* Also in Brzezinski, *Power and Principle* (New York: Farrar, Straus, Giroux, 1985).

10. Patrick Horvath, "Jimmy Carter's Mediation in Camp David." Strategies and Results: Seminar in International Politics 2000, University of Vienna.

11. Gary Wills, *Lincoln at Gettysburg*, p. 20.

12. Among the many Gettysburg titles are two that emphasize this point: *Death of Nation* by Clifford Dowdey and *Last Chance for Victory* by Scott Bowden.

CHAPTER TWO:
INFIRM FOUNDATIONS

1. Frank Aretas Haskell, *Battle of Gettysburg* (Madison: Wisconsin History Commission, 1908), pp. 181–182. This was a letter he wrote to his brother in July 1863.

2. Haskell, *Battle of Gettysburg*, p. 182. The phrase "*the battle as it was*" is emphasized in the original.

3. Haskell, *Battle of Gettysburg*, p. 182.

4. Livermore to "Brother Charles," July 6, 1863, Maine Historical Society Collection.

5. Millett served as captain of Company E, 27th Infantry Regiment. His bayonet charge occurred in the vicinity of Soam-Ni, Korea, on February 1, 1951. He was awarded the Medal of Honor on August 2, 1951.

6. From the personal recollections of a number of those present with Millett that day, subsequently interviewed by author.

7. George G. Meade to John Bachelder, December 4, 1869, in David Ladd and Audrey Ladd, eds., *The Bachelder Papers* (Dayton, Ohio: Morningside, 1995), 1:380.

8. John M. Stone to Joseph R. Davis, March 1868, in Ladd and Ladd, *Bachelder Papers*, 1:328.

9. Gerald Linderman, *Embattled Courage: The Experience of Combat in the American Civil War* (New York: Free Press, 1987), p. 267.

10. Linderman, *Embattled Courage*, p. 268.

11. William C. Oates, *The War Between the Union and the Confederacy and Its Lost Opportunities* (New York: Neale, 1905), p. 216.

12. William C. Oates to William Robbins, April 1, 1902 (GNMP, Oates correspondence file).

13. William R. Bond, *Pickett or Pettigrew? An Historical Essay* (Weldon, N.C.: Hall & Sledge, 1888), p. 6.

14. A. F. Sweetland, "First Day at Gettysburg: Some Criticisms of Comrade McConnell's Account," *National Tribune*, November 2, 1916.

15. Thomas W. Bradley, "At Gettysburg," *National Tribune*, February 4, 1886.

16. W. S. Hancock, in *Galaxy*, December 1876. Copy in G. K. Warren Papers, SC10668, New York State Archives.

17. Sweetland, "First Day at Gettysburg."

18. G. K. Warren to Porter Farley, July 24, 1872, G. K. Warren Papers, SC10668, New York State Archives.

19. For a good version of the fable, see John Godfrey Saxe, *The Blind Men and the Elephant; John Godfrey Saxe's Version of the Famous Indian Legend, Pictures by Paul Galdone* (New York: Whittlesey House, 1963).

20. O. W. Norton to John Nicholson, October 18, 1910, GNMP monument files.

21. John Nicholson to O. W. Norton, October 31, 1910, GNMP monument files.

22. Oliver W. Norton, *The Attack and Defense of Little Round Top* (New York: Neale, 1913).

23. This signed copy of the book *Attack and Defense of Little Round Top*, inscribed to Ellis Spear, is in the possession of the author.

24. "Address of Lieutenant O. W. Norton," in Pennsylvania State Monuments Commission, *Pennsylvania at Gettysburg: Ceremonies at the Dedication of the Monuments* (Harrisburg, Pa.: William Stanley Ray, 1914), 2:464.

25. G. K. Warren Papers, SC10668, New York State Archives.

26. G. K. Warren to John Bachelder, October 26, 1876, in Ladd and Ladd, *Bachelder Papers*, 3:1928.

27. Porter Farley to G. K. Warren, November 8, 1877, G. K. Warren Papers, SC10668, New York State Archives.

28. Porter Farley to Compte de Paris, October 21, 1877, G. K. Warren Papers, SC10668, New York State Archives.

29. Porter Farley to John Bachelder, May 8, 1878, in Ladd and Ladd, *Bachelder Papers*, 1:548.

30. Norton, *Attack and Defense*, p. 124.

31. Norton, *Attack and Defense*, p. 140.

32. G. K. Warren to Porter Farley, July 13, 1872, G. K. Warren Papers, SC10668, New York State Archives.

33. G. K. Warren to Porter Farley, July 24, 1872, G. K. Warren Papers, SC10668, New York State Archives.

34. Willard Brown, *Signal Corps, U.S.A. in the War of the Rebellion* (New York: Arno, 1974).

35. Brown, *Signal Corps.*

36. Warren to Farley, August 14, 1872, G. K. Warren Correspondence, New York State Archives.

37. In 1996 the author, with the help of another National Park employee, tested the glistening theory with a mirror and two-way radios. The conclusion was that no reflection or glistening whatsoever could be directed toward Little Round Top from the area where the Confederates are known to have assembled. Presumably, the even duller finish of Civil War bayonets would also have been unable to provide the key element to Warren's discovery of the Rebels.

38. *Official Records*, ser. 1, vol. 27/3 [S#45], p. 487.

39. *Official Records*, ser. 1, vol. 27/3 [S#45], p. 489.

40. Porter Farley, "Bloody Round Top," *National Tribune*, May 3, 1883.

41. Benjamin F. Rittenhouse, "The Battle of Gettysburg As Seen from Little Round Top," in Military Order of the Loyal Legion of the United States, District of Columbia Commandery, *War Papers*, 1:784.

42. Thomas Scott, "On Little Round Top." *National Tribune*, August 2, 1894.

43. O. W. Damon, diary entry for July 2, 1863.

CHAPTER THREE: THE STRUGGLE OVER MEMORY

1. Gary Gallagher, in *Gettysburg: 135th Anniversary Historians Round Table*, in *The Unknown Civil War* home video series (Greystone Communications, 1999).

2. Gallagher, in *Gettysburg.*

3. Gallagher, in *Gettysburg.*

4. Charles Minor Blackford in Susan Leigh Blackford, *Letters from Lee's Army* (New York: Barnes, 1947), p. 153.

5. Carol Reardon, *Pickett's Charge in History and Memory* (Chapel Hill: University of North Carolina Press, 1997).

6. Champ Clark et al., *Gettysburg: The Confederate High Tide* (Alexandria, Va.: Time-Life Books, 1985), p. 155.

7. John B. Gordon, "An Incident of Gettysburg," *Southern Historical Society Papers*, 21:337–339.

8. John B. Gordon, *Reminiscences of the Civil War* (New York: Scribner's, 1903), p. 153.

9. William Hannah, "The Barlow-Gordon Incident? The Yank Never Met the Reb: A Gettysburg Myth Exploded," *Civil War Times Illustrated*, May 1985.

10. Francis Barlow to his mother, July 7, 1863, GNMP Files.

11. Gallagher in *Gettysburg: 135th Anniversary*.

12. Letter from Henry Hunt to John Bachelder, May 15, 1882, *Bachelder Papers*.

13. Henry Hunt to Senate Military Committee, listed by Hunt as being Senate Document Report 555, pt. 2, 45th Congress, 3rd sess., pp. 458–459. Hunt describes this letter in correspondence with John Bachelder in Ladd and Ladd, *Bachelder Papers*, 1:647; 1:674–676.

14. Henry Hunt to John Bachelder in Ladd and Ladd, *Bachelder Papers*, 2:790–829.

15. Henry Hunt to John Bachelder, May 16, 1882, in Ladd and Ladd, *Bachelder Papers*, 2:865–666.

16. Testimony of Anthony McDermott, 69th Pennsylvania Infantry, "Appeal of the Gettysburg Battlefield Memorial Association (GBMA) from the decree of the Court of Common Pleas of Adams County," Paper Book of Appellants, Supreme Court of Pennsylvania, Middle District, May Term 1891, nos. 20, 30, p. 383.

17. *New York Times*, July 4, 1863.

18. Edwin B. Coddington, *The Gettysburg Campaign: A Study in Command* (Norwalk, Conn.: Easton, 1989), p. 686 n. 52.

19. *Lancaster Intelligencer,* November 7, 1902.

20. Clipping in GNMP monument files on the Pennsylvania state monument.

21. Story related in Henry Steele Commager, ed., *The Blue and the Gray: The Story of the Civil War As Told by the Participants* (Indianapolis: Bobbs-Merrill, 1950), 2:601–602.

22. Journal of William J. Robbins, Southern Historical Collection, University of North Carolina, typescript at GNMP.

23. Heth's report in *Official Records*, ser. I, vol. 27, pt. 2, p. 637.

24. *OR*, ser. I, vol. 27, pt. 2, p. 637.

25. "Executive Insights," *APMA News*, March 1997, p. 16.

26. "Battle for Boots," *In Step*, Summer 1997, 13. Newsletter of the Scholl College of Podiatric Medicine.

27. Even this comparison is overstated, since the combatants on both sides at Gettysburg were Americans. The total number of dead in Vietnam was closer to 60,000.

28. The myth is still prevalent. During the 2000 presidential campaign reporter Fred Francis (MSNBC), following George W. Bush, reported from Gettysburg as one of his stops, telling his viewing audience that the importance of Gettysburg was, in part, the fact that "50,000 men died here."

CHAPTER FOUR: RASCALITY AND STUPIDITY

1. Charles S. Wainwright, diary entry for March 6, 1864. In Allan Nevins, ed., *A Diary of Battle: The Personal Journals of Colonel Charles S. Wainwright, 1861–1865* (New York: Harcourt, Brace & World, 1962).

2. Allan Nevins, ed., *Diary of George Templeton Strong* (New York: Macmillan, 1952), 2:77–78.

3. The best description of Sickles's character, as well as his attack and acquittal, is W. A. Swanberg, *Sickles the Incredible* (New York: Scribner's, 1956).

4. William F. Fox, *Regimental Losses in the American Civil War, 1861–1865* (Albany: Albany Publishing, 1889), p. 71.

5. James F. Rusling, *Men and Things I Saw in Civil War Days* (New York: Eaton & Mains, 1899), pp. 12–14.

6. Benedict, "Meade's Letter on Gettysburg," *Philadelphia Weekly Press*, August 11, 1886. Meade's Report in *OR*, ser. I, vol. 27, pt. 1, p. 116.

7. *New York Tribune*, October 19, 1863. *CCW*, 1865, 1:304.

8. Welles, *Diary of Gideon Welles* (New York: Houghton, Mifflin, 1911), 1:472.

9. *OR*, ser. I, vol. 27, pt. 1, p. 16.

10. Diary of Marsena Rudolph Patrick, entry for December 16, 1863. Published in Marsena L. Patrick and David S. Sparks, eds., *Inside Lincoln's Army: The Diary of Marsena Rudolph Patrick* (New York: Yoseloff, 1964). New York Colonel George H. Sharpe was a friend of Sickles whom Hooker had made chief of the army's Bureau of Military Intelligence.

11. Hans Louis Trefousse, *Benjamin Franklin Wade: Radical Republican from Ohio* (New York: Twayne, 1963).

12. Testimony of General Daniel Sickles Before the Joint Committee on the Conduct of the War, *CCW* 1:295–304; 1:297–298.

13. *CCW,* 1:297–298.

14. *CCW,* 1:311.

15. Abner Doubleday, "Meade at Gettysburg. His Proposed Retreat on the Night of the 2nd of July, Gen. Doubleday's Defense of His Statement That Meade Was Overruled By the Action of a Council of War," *New York Times*, April 1, 1883.

16. *OR*, ser. 27, 1:366. Hancock's dispatch is recorded as 5:25 P.M., July 1, 1863.

17. Abner Doubleday, "Meade at Gettysburg. His Proposed Retreat on the Night of the 2nd of July, Gen. Doubleday's Defense of His Statement That Meade Was Overruled By the Action of a Council of War," *New York Times*, April 1, 1883.

18. Testimony of Albion P. Howe Before the Joint Committee on the Conduct of the War, *CCW* 1:325–329.

19. *CCW*, 1:XIX.

20. *CCW*, 1:XIX.

21. Meade to Margaret Meade, March 6, 1864, in George G. Meade, ed., *The Life and Letters of George G. Meade* (New York: Scribner's, 1913), 2:169.

22. Meade, *Life and Letters*, 2:169.

23. Charles S. Wainwright, diary entry for March 6, 1864. In Nevins, *Diary of Battle,* pp. 347–358.

24. Historicus, "The Battle of Gettysburg—Important Communication From an Eye-Witness—How the Victory Was Won and How Its Advantages Were Lost—Generals Halleck's and Meade's Official Reports Refuted, etc.," *New York Herald*, March 12, 1864.

25. George G. Meade to Colonel E. D. Townsend, March 15, 1864, *OR*, ser. I, vol. 27, pt. 1, Reports, no. 43, pp. 128–143.

26. Henry W. Halleck to George G. Meade, March 20, 1864, *OR*, ser. I, vol. 27, pt. 1, Reports, no. 43, pp. 128–143.

27. Abraham Lincoln to George G. Meade, March 29, 1864, *OR*, ser. I, vol. 27, pt. 1, Reports, no. 43, pp. 128–143.

28. George G. Meade to Henry W. Halleck, March 22, 1864, *OR*, ser. I, vol. 27, pt. 1, Reports, no. 43, pp. 128–143.

29. Another Eye-Witness, "The Battle of Gettysburg," *New York Herald*, March 16, 1864; Staff Officer of V Corps, "The Battle of Gettysburg: The Truth of History, Etc.," *New York Herald*, March 18, 1864; James Barnes, "The Battle of Gettysburg," *New York Herald*, March 21, 1864.

30. Historicus, "Battle of Gettysburg."

31. James Barnes, "The Battle of Gettysburg," *New York Herald*, March 21, 1864.

32. Barnes, "Battle of Gettysburg."

33. William S. Tilton to James Barnes, March 14, 1864, James Barnes Papers, New York Historical Society. Reprinted in *New York Herald* as "Letter from Colonel Tilton," March 22, 1864.

34. Historicus, "The Battle of Gettysburg—Historicus in Reply to General Barnes and the Staff Officers of the Second and Fifth Corps. The Evidence Before the Committee on the Conduct of the War, &c.," *New York Herald*, April 4, 1864.

35. Daniel E. Sickles to Zachariah Chandler, February 30, 1864, Zachariah Chandler Papers, Library of Congress. Reprinted in Swanberg, *Sickles the Incredible*, p. 253.

36. Swanberg, *Sickles the Incredible*, pp. 233–234.

37. Testimony of General Daniel Butterfield Before the Joint Committee on the Conduct of the War, *CCW*, 1:417–435.

38. *CCW*, 1:435–439. Report of the Committee, *CCW*, lv–lxxvii.

39. *CCW*, 1:436.

40. *Round Table* (New York), March 12, 1864.

41. A Staff Officer of V Corps, "Battle of Gettysburg"; Swanberg, *Sickles the Incredible*, p. 257.

42. Robert G. Carter, "My Dear Colonel Graham," April 23, 1925. Printed in W. A. Graham, *The Custer Myth: A Source Book of Custeriana* (Harrisburg, Pa.: Stackpole, 1953), p. 318.

43. Graham, *The Custer Myth*. There is little evidence that Bachelder was or could have been behind the Historicus letters. In 1864 he clearly had other issues in mind and was committing great energy in other areas. His whereabouts at the time of the committee's work and his lack of knowledge of the details contained in the letters make it virtually impossible that he was a driving force.

44. Swanberg, *Sickles the Incredible*, p. 258.

45. Coddington, "The Strange Reputation of George G. Meade: A Lesson in Historiography," *Historian* 23 (1962): 147.

46. Abner Doubleday, "Meade at Gettysburg. His Proposed Retreat on the Night of the 2nd of July, Gen. Doubleday's Defense of His Statement That Meade Was Overruled By the Action of a Council of War," *New York Times*, April 1, 1883.

47. For a good summary of Sickles's postwar career, see Swanberg, *Sickles the Incredible*.

48. *New York Times*, January 28, 1913, quoted in Swanberg, *Sickles the Incredible*, p. 387.

49. Richard D. Sauers, *A Caspian Sea of Ink* (Baltimore: Butternut & Blue, 1989), p. 149.

50. Swanberg, *Sickles the Incredible*, p. 234.

CHAPTER FIVE: THE SELF-FULFILLING PROPHECY OF JOHN BADGER BACHELDER

1. John Bachelder to G. K. Warren, November 23, 1877, G. K. Warren Papers.

2. Bachelder was commissioned a lieutenant colonel in the Pennsylvania militia in 1851. See the commission in Ladd and Ladd, *Bachelder Papers,* 3:1914–1915.

3. John B. Bachelder, *Descriptive Key to the Painting of the Repulse of Longstreet's Assault at the Battle of Gettysburg* (Boston: John B. Bachelder, 1870), p. 49. The story of J. B. Bachelder is available to historians due to the work of Richard Sauers. Bachelder is the subject of Sauers's own research as well as a few other of his published pieces, and Sauers's work on him has allowed later historians to more easily understand Bachelder's effect on the story of Gettysburg. For a brief biographical synopsis on Bachelder, see Sauers, "John B. Bachelder: Government Historian of the Battle of Gettysburg," *Gettysburg Magazine* 3 (1990): 115–127.

4. It is not clear what date he actually arrived on the battlefield. At various times he remembered it as July 5 or 7. Testifying in an 1891 court case, he said, "I am not able to tell you exactly, but it was before all of the dead were buried." See Bachelder testimony in "Appeal of the Gettysburg Battlefield Memorial Association (GBMA) from the decree of the Court of Com-

mon Pleas of Adams County," Paper Book of Appellants, Supreme Court of Pennsylvania, Middle District, May Term 1891, nos. 20, 30.

5. Bachelder testimony, "Appeal of the GBMA," p. 247.

6. "Appeal of the GBMA," p. 248.

7. "Appeal of the GBMA," pp. 247–249.

8. John Bachelder to U. S. Grant, November 14, 1867, in Ladd and Ladd, *Bachelder Papers*, 1:317.

9. Joseph B. Kershaw to John Bachelder, April 1, 1876, in Ladd and Ladd, *Bachelder Papers*, 1:483.

10. Joseph Carr to John Bachelder, May 15, 1882, in Ladd and Ladd, *Bachelder Papers*, 2:864.

11. Wheelock Veazey to John Bachelder, August 21, 1866, in Ladd and Ladd, *Bachelder Papers*, 1:280.

12. William H. Morgan to John Bachelder, April 1886, in Ladd and Ladd, *Bachelder Papers*, 2:1273–1283.

13. Bachelder's collection of letters, recollections, maps, and other information is today held in the Bachelder Papers at the New Hampshire Historical Society in Concord. Much of it is also available in David Ladd and Audrey Ladd, eds., *The Bachelder Papers*, 3 vols. (Dayton, Ohio: Morningside, 1995).

14. Morris Schaff, in Archibald Gracie, *The Truth About Chickamauga* (Boston: Houghton Mifflin, 1911), p. 440.

15. John Bassler to J. B. Bachelder, 1882, Bachelder Papers.

16. George G. Briggs to John Bachelder, March 26, 1888, in Ladd and Ladd, *Bachelder Papers*, 3:1531.

17. Abner Doubleday to John Bachelder, January 22, 1885, in Ladd and Ladd, *Bachelder Papers*, 2:1096.

18. Gulian V. Weir to Winfield S. Hancock, December 7, 1885, in Ladd and Ladd, *Bachelder Papers*, 2:1160.

19. Alpheus Williams to John Bachelder, October 1, 1864, in Ladd and Ladd, *Bachelder Papers*, 1:183.

20. Frederick Hecker to John Bachelder, March 10, 1878, in Ladd and Ladd, *Bachelder Papers*, 1:528.

21. John Geary to John Bachelder, October 14, 1865, in Ladd and Ladd, *Bachelder Papers*, 1:200.

22. Samuel W. Crawford to John Bachelder, August 30, 1886, in Ladd and Ladd, *Bachelder Papers*, 3:1451.

23. Levi E. Pond to John Bachelder, March 13, 1888, in Ladd and Ladd, *Bachelder Papers*, 3:1530.

24. Samuel W. Crawford to John Bachelder, August 30, 1886, in Ladd and Ladd, *Bachelder Papers*, 3:1451.

25. Vincent A. Witcher to Secretary of War, March 27, 1884, in Ladd and Ladd, *Bachelder Papers*, 3:1480–1482.

26. Robert G. Carter, from a 1925 letter quoted in Graham, *Custer Myth*, 318.

27. Ladd and Ladd, *Bachelder Papers*, 1:11.

28. Winfield S. Hancock to John Bachelder, December 20, 1885, in Ladd and Ladd, *Bachelder Papers*, 3:1949.

29. Lafayette McLaws to John Bachelder, February 2, 1865, in Ladd and Ladd, *Bachelder Papers*, 1:185.

30. James L. Kemper to L. Stevenson, November 12, 1865, in Ladd and Ladd, *Bachelder Papers*, 1:224.

31. Robert Todd Lincoln to John Bachelder, July 29, 1868, in Ladd and Ladd, *Bachelder Papers*, 1:346.

32. Thanks to photographic historian William A. Frassanito and his highly enlightening book, *Early Photography at Gettysburg*, which pointed out the varying interests of early visitors to Gettysburg.

33. Frassanito, *Early Photography at Gettysburg*, pp. 238–239.

34. John B. Bachelder, "Report to Col. C.H. Buehler, GBMA, February 1, 1894," Bachelder Papers.

35. Bachelder, "Report."

36. John B. Bachelder, *Descriptive Key to the Painting of the Repulse of Longstreet's Assault at the Battle of Gettysburg* (Boston: John B. Bachelder, 1870), p. 9.

37. John B. Bachelder, "Report."

38. Minute Book of the GBMA, July 1887.

39. John Bachelder in "Report on Construction of the High Water Mark Tablet," in Ladd and Ladd, *Bachelder Papers,* 3:1859.

40. Ladd and Ladd, *Bachelder Papers,* 3:1859.

41. Ladd and Ladd, *Bachelder Papers,* 3:1855.

42. Ladd and Ladd, *Bachelder Papers,* 3:1856.

43. Ladd and Ladd, *Bachelder Papers,* 3:1857.

44. Ladd and Ladd, *Bachelder Papers,* 3:1857.

45. Joseph H. Sinex to John Bachelder, May 1878, in Ladd and Ladd, *Bachelder Papers*, 1:531.

46. Charles E. Foster to John Bachelder, March 5, 1886, in Ladd and Ladd, *Bachelder Papers*, 3:1952.

47. Earl J. Hess, *Pickett's Charge: The Last Attack at Gettysburg* (Chapel Hill: University of North Carolina Press, 2001), p. 399.

48. Troy D. Harman, *Cemetery Hill: The General Plan Was Unchanged* (Baltimore: Butternut & Blue, 2001). My numerous conversations with Ranger Harman on this and other subjects have been infinitely helpful in getting at the core of Gettysburg mythology. Hess, *Pickett's Charge*, p. 387.

49. Minutes of the Gettysburg Battlefield Memorial Association, GNMP.

50. See correspondence on the matter in the Bachelder Papers.

51. James A. Beaver to John Bachelder, May 6, 1890, in Ladd and Ladd, *Bachelder Papers*, 3:1722.

52. Bryon M. Cutcheon to John Bachelder, June 25, 1890, in Ladd and Ladd, *Bachelder Papers*, 3:1741–1742.

53. Daniel S. Lamont to John Bachelder, May 25, 1893, in Ladd and Ladd, *Bachelder Papers*, 3:1851.

54. Joseph B. Kershaw to John Bachelder, August 7, 1882, in Ladd and Ladd, *Bachelder Papers*, 2:901.

55. Russell A. Alger to John Bachelder, January 4, 1886, in Ladd and Ladd, *Bachelder Papers*, 2:1176.

56. George G. Briggs to John Bachelder, February 8, 1888, in Ladd and Ladd, *Bachelder Papers*, 3:1523.

CHAPTER SIX: LOST IN THE LOST CAUSE

1. Mosby to Aristides Monteiro, June 9, 1894; Mosby to Judge Reuben Page, June 11, 1902, both in the John S. Mosby Collection, Eleanor S. Brockenbrough Library, Museum of the Confederacy. Both reprinted in Adele H. Mitchell, ed., *The Letters of John S. Mosby* (Richmond, Va.: Stuart-Mosby Historical Society, 1986), pp. 68–69, 113.

2. Harman, "The Great Revival of 1863," in *The American Civil War in 1863: Programs of the Eighth Gettysburg National Military Park Seminar* (Gettysburg: Gettysburg National Military Park, 2001), p. 113.

3. *Richmond Christian Advocate,* quoted in Harman, "Great Revival," p. 115.

4. Harman, "Great Revival," p. 113.

5. John H. Worsham, quoted in Bell I. Wiley, ed., *One of Jackson's Foot Cavalry: His Experience and What He Saw During the War, 1861–1865* (Wilmington, N.C: Broadfoot, 1991).

6. Wiley, *One of Jackson's Foot Cavalry*.

7. Harman, "Great Revival," pp. 119–120.

8. Edward A. Pollard, *The Lost Cause: A New Southern History of the War* (New York: E. B. Treat, 1866).

9. David W. Blight, *Race and Reunion: The Civil War in American Memory* (Cambridge: Harvard University Press, 2001), p. 262.

10. United Daughters of the Confederacy statement on its history in its own published literature.

11. Gaines Foster, *Ghosts of the Confederacy* (New York: Oxford University Press, 1987), p. 4.

12. George H. Reese, ed., *Proceedings of the Virginia Secession Convention of 1861* (Richmond: Virginia State Library, 1865), 4:58–59.

13. Gallagher, "From Antebellum Unionist to Lost Cause Warrior," in John Y. Simon and Michael E. Stevens, eds., *New Perspectives on the Civil War: Myths and Realities of the National Conflict* (Madison, Wis.: Madison House, 1998), p. 113.

14. Edward P. Alexander to John Bachelder, May 3, 1876, in Ladd and Ladd, *Bachelder Papers*, 1:483.

15. Fanny Downing, "Perfect Through Suffering," *The Land We Love*, January 4, 1868, 193–205.

16. J. Williams Jones, *The Army of Northern Virginia Memorial Volume* (Richmond: Randolph & English, 1880), p. 122.

17. Longstreet to J. M. G. Parker, June 3, 1867, published in the New Orleans *Picayune*.

18. Longstreet, *From Manassas to Appomattox*, chap. 44.

19. Longstreet, *From Manassas to Appomattox*.

20. Foster, *Ghosts of the Confederacy*, p. 57.

21. Early, *The Campaigns of Robert E. Lee: An Address Delivered By Lieutenant General Jubal A. Early, Before Washington and Lee University, January 19th, 1872* (Baltimore: J. Murphy, 1872).

22. Pendleton, "Personal Recollections of Robert E. Lee," *Southern Magazine* 15 (1874): 623–628.

23. Tucker, *Lee and Longstreet*, p. 13.

24. Nolan, in Simon and Stevens, *New Perspectives*, p. 26.

25. Burns, *The Civil War*, "Episode Five: The Universe of Battle."

26. Richard D. Pougher, *The Confederate Enlisted Man in the Army of Northern Virginia: A Reevaluation of His Material Culture*, 2 vols. (Williamsburg, Va.: William and Mary College, 1988), p. xiv.

27. Pougher, *Confederate Enlisted Man*, p. 3.

28. Douglas Southall Freeman, *Lee's Lieutenants: A Study in Command* (New York: Scribner's, 1944), 3:162.

29. Nolan, "Considering Lee Considered," in Simon and Stevens, *New Perspectives*, p. 39.

30. Gallagher, *Lee and His Army*, p. 163.

31. Gallagher, *Lee and His Army*, p. 170.

32. Hess, *Pickett's Charge*, p. 391.

33. This is perhaps yet another myth of Gettysburg. Though widely repeated as a quote from Pickett, finding a reliable source for it is difficult. One source is the widely disparaged writing of his widow, LaSalle Corbell Pickett, in an article titled "My Soldier," *McClure's*, 1908, p. 569.

34. William Faulkner, *Intruder in the Dust* (New York: Random House, 1948), pp. 194–195.

35. Andrew Curry, "The Better Angels: Why Americans Are Still Fighting Over Who Was Right and Who Was Wrong in the Civil War," *US News and World Report*, September 30, 2002.

CHAPTER SEVEN: CONSTRUCTING THE CONSUMMATE GETTYSBURG HERO

1. Mark Bloch, *Feudal Society*, p. 92.

2. James Longstreet, "Letter to Augustus Baldwin Longstreet," *SHSP*, 5:54–55; William C. Oates, "Gettysburg: The Battle on the Right," *SHSP*, 6:172–182.

3. Oates, "Gettysburg," 6:172–182.

4. Oates, "Gettysburg," 6:178.

5. William C. Oates, *The War Between the Union and the Confederacy and Its Lost Opportunities* (New York: Neale, 1905), p. 222.

6. Oates, *War*, p. 222.

7. Oates, *War*, pp. 215–216.

8. Statistical profile of Gerrish from the 20th Maine Regimental Records, National Archives, and the 20th Maine Muster Rolls at the Maine State

Archives. Theodore Gerrish, *Army Life: A Private's Reminiscences of the Civil War* (Portland, Me.: Hoyt, Fogg, and Donham, 1882); John J. Pullen, *Joshua L. Chamberlain: A Hero's Life and Legacy* (Camp Hill, Pa.: Stackpole, 1999), pp. i–ii.

9. Gerrish, *Army Life*. Gettysburg is described in chapter 6, pp. 100–119.

10. Gerrish, *Army Life,* pp. 107–108.

11. Both Gerrish's service record and the 20th Maine regimental books at the National Archives concur on his absence from the regiment from April or May through September.

12. Gerrish, *Army Life,* pp. 107–108.

13. For a complete accounting of the casualties of the 15th Alabama at Gettysburg, see Desjardin, *Stand Firm Ye Boys from Maine*, pp. 195–202.

14. Chamberlain's official report of the Battle of Gettysburg is printed in *War of the Rebellion: Official Records of the Union and Confederate Armies, OR,* ser. I, vol. 27, pt. 2, pp. 222–226.

15. Chamberlain to Governor Coburn, August 7, 1863, Records of the Adjutant General of Maine, Civil War, Maine State Archives.

16. Chamberlain to Governor Coburn, August 7, 1863.

17. Chamberlain Official Report Correspondence, National Archives, RG 94, Entry 729, "Union Battle Reports," no. 196. My appreciation goes out to Tim Smith, Jim Clouse, and a handful of other licensed battlefield guides at Gettysburg for helping discover and unravel this part of the mystery.

18. Records of the Adjutant General's Office, March 3, 1884.

19. Chamberlain to Adjutant General Hodsdon, November 4, 1863, Records of the Adjutant General of Maine, Maine State Archives, Augusta, Maine.

20. Chamberlain to "Mrs. Eckstrom," May 28, 1913, in Chamberlain Family Papers, Fogler Library Special Collections, University of Maine, Orono, Maine. Elliot Dill to Chamberlain and his reply, June 11 and 12, 1913, Records of the Adjutant General of Maine, Maine State Archives.

21. Chamberlain, "Through Blood and Fire at Gettysburg," *Hearsts,* June 1913.

22. Kenneth Roberts information from Pullen, personal conversation with author, 1996.

23. John J. Pullen, *The Twentieth Maine* (New York: Lippincott, 1957).

24. This appears to have been a stock story of Shaara's, as he related it almost verbatim to a number of people, including Gabor Borritt of Gettysburg College and James McPherson of Princeton University, among others. These people and others have, in turn, related it to the author on a number of occasions.

25. Michael Shaara, *The Killer Angels* (New York: McKay, 1974), p. 126.

26. Burns, quoted in "The Best Kind of History, the Best Kind of American," *Bowdoin*, Spring-Summer 1991, p. 6.

27. Burns, quoted in *Bowdoin*, p. 6.

28. Personal correspondence to the author, August 1999.

29. Burns, quoted in *Bowdoin*, Spring-Summer 1991, p. 6.

CHAPTER EIGHT: THE WORLD'S LARGEST COLLECTION OF OUTDOOR SCULPTURE

1. David A. Buehler to John Bachelder, December 13, 1886, in Ladd and Ladd, *Bachelder Papers*, 3:1460–1461.

2. Minute Book of the Gettysburg Battlefield Memorial Association, February 25, 1887.

3. John Bachelder in circular letter, July 6, 1887, in Ladd and Ladd, *Bachelder Papers*, 3:1498.

4. Orville D. Thatcher to John Bachelder, July 2, 1889, in Ladd and Ladd, *Bachelder Papers*, 3:1605.

5. Orville D. Thatcher to John Bachelder, July 2, 1889.

6. Thomas J. Grier to John Bachelder, June 1, 1888, in Ladd and Ladd, *Bachelder Papers*, 3:1552–1554.

7. Alexander S. Webb to John Bachelder, July 13, 1887, in Ladd and Ladd, *Bachelder Papers*, 3:1504.

8. Minutes of the Gettysburg Memorial Association, February 27, 1887, GNMP.

9. Minutes of the Gettysburg Memorial Association, May 5, 1887, GNMP.

10. Minutes of the Gettysburg Memorial Association, July 12, 1887, GNMP.

11. Minutes of the Gettysburg Memorial Association, May 5, 1887.

12. *Gettysburg Times*, February 12, 1953.

13. Pennsylvania State Monuments Commission, *Pennsylvania at Gettysburg: Ceremonies at the Dedication of the Monuments* (Harrisburg, Pa.: William Stanley Ray, 1914), 1:464.

14. Minutes of the GBMA, August 25, 1891.

15. Arthur Devereaux to John Bachelder, July 2, 1889, in Ladd and Ladd, *Bachelder Papers*, 3:1609.

16. Arthur Devereaux in Ladd and Ladd, *Bachelder Papers*, 3:1878.

17. Webb testimony, "Appeal of the Gettysburg Battlefield Memorial Association (GBMA) from the decree of the Court of Common Pleas of Adams County," Paper Book of Appellants, Supreme Court of Pennsylvania, Middle District, May Term 1891, nos. 20, 30.

18. Letter from Alexander S. Webb to Peter F. Rothermel, Webb File, Participant Accounts files, GNMP Library.

19. Alexander S. Webb to John Bachelder, June 16, 1887, in Ladd and Ladd, *Bachelder Papers*, 3:1554.

20. Minutes of the GBMA, July 12, 1889, GNMP.

21. *Pennsylvania at Gettysburg*, 1:464.

22. Minutes of the GBMA, August 25, 1891. Modern legal scholars who have examined the court transcript have found no legitimate legal justification for either the ruling of the court or the position of the 72nd.

23. Haskell, *Battle of Gettysburg.*

24. Haskell, *Battle of Gettysburg*, p. vi.

25. Philadelphia Brigade Association, *The Battle of Gettysburg: How General Meade Turned the Army of the Potomac Over to Lieutenant Haskell* (Philadelphia: Bowers, 1910).

26. Philadelphia Brigade Association, *Battle of Gettysburg.*

27. Swanberg, *Sickles the Incredible*, p. 365.

28. James A. Hall to John Bachelder, April 11, 1889, in Ladd and Ladd, *Bachelder Papers*, 3:1580.

29. Minutes of the GBMA, July 12, 1887, GNMP.

30. The author wishes to thank historian Wayne Motts for his research and aid regarding the Armistead marker, among many other subjects.

31. Testimony of Rene Boerner, 72nd Pennsylvania Infantry, "Appeal of the Gettysburg Battlefield Memorial Association (GBMA)," p. 190.

32. Testimony of Rene Boerner and Robert McBride, 72nd Pennsylvania Infantry, "Appeal of the Gettysburg Battlefield Memorial Association (GBMA)," pp. 190, 217.

33. Thomas M. Aldrich, *The History of Battery A, First Regiment Rhode Island Light Artillery, in the War to Preserve the Union, 1861–1865* (Providence: Snow & Farnham, 1904), p. 26.

34. John W. Busey and David G. Martin, *Regimental Strengths and Losses at Gettysburg* (Highstown, N.J.: Longstreet House, 1994), p. 290.

35. For a good survey of the potential location of the 26th North Carolina during Pickett's Charge, see Bruce A. Trinque, "The Gap Made in That . . . Regiment Was Simply Terrible": Arnold's Battery and the 26th North Carolina," *Gettysburg,* January 1995.

36. Trinque, "Gap."

37. Bryon M. Cutcheon to J. C. Johnson, June 25, 1889, in Ladd and Ladd, *Bachelder Papers*, 3:1601–1602.

CHAPTER NINE:
WHERE'S BUSTER KILRAIN BURIED?

1. For a thorough look at the memory of Paul Revere and his ride, see David Fischer, *Paul Revere's Ride* (New York: Oxford University Press, 1994).

2. *Remember the Titans*, chap. 10, "Lesson from the Dead," Walt Disney Pictures, 2002.

3. Frassanito, *Early Photography*, p. 18.

4. The story of the hatless Chamberlain was related by Don Troiani to the author in a personal conversation.

5. Pougher, *Confederate Enlisted Man,* p. 495.

6. Pougher, *Confederate Enlisted Man,* p. 502.

7. Pougher, *Confederate Enlisted Man,* pp. 503–504.

8. Pougher, *Confederate Enlisted Man,* p. 505.

9. Catton wrote for the *Cleveland Plain Dealer, Cleveland News,* and the *Boston American* before becoming the first editor of *American Heritage* magazine.

10. Tucker wrote for newspapers in Illinois, Wisconsin, Indiana, and New Jersey before becoming White House reporter for the *New York News* and Washington correspondent for the *Indianapolis News.* He lived in Flat Rock, North Carolina, and was an active member of the North Carolina Writers Conference.

11. James McPherson, *Drawn with the Sword: Reflections on the American Civil War* (New York: Oxford University Press, 1994), pp. 232–235.

12. McPherson, *Drawn with the Sword*, p. 238.

CHAPTER TEN:
AMERICAN VALHALLA

1. *New York Times*, January 28, 1913.

2. Swanberg, *Sickles the Incredible*, p. 390.

3. Gallagher, "From Antebellum Unionist to Lost Cause Warrior," in Simon and Stevens, *New Perspectives*.

4. According to letters in his service record at the National Archives, Thomas M. Hubbard, Bowdoin College class of 1857, petitioned the War Department for Chamberlain's Medal of Honor.

5. Horace Greeley to Abraham Lincoln, July 7, 1864, Abraham Lincoln Papers, Library of Congress.

6. *New York Tribune*, August 5, 1864.

7. William Frank Zornow, *Lincoln and the Party Divided* (Norman: University of Oklahoma Press, 1954), p. 112.

8. *Harrisburg Patriot and Union*, November 20, 1863.

9. *Chicago Tribune*, November 20, 1863; "The President at Gettysburg," *Chicago Times*, November 23, 1863.

10. John Mason Potter, "The Gettysburg Address," *Cornell Library Journal*, Winter 1966.

11. "Remarks by the President at the Dedication of the Oklahoma City National Memorial Dedication, April 19, 2000," Clinton Presidential Materials Project, NARA.

12. Edward Linenthal, "Ground Zero Belongs to All of Us," *Milwaukee Journal Sentinel*, March 10, 2002.

13. Timothy Williams, "Names of 2,801 Victims Read Aloud in Somber Ground Zero Ceremony," Associated Press, September 11, 2002.

14. Kris Hudson, "Prime View of New York City's Revival," *Denver Post*, September 11, 2002.

15. The World Trade Center Living History Project can be found online at www.wtclivinghistory.org.

BIBLIOGRAPHY

MANUSCRIPT COLLECTIONS

Gettysburg National Military Park Library,
Gettysburg, Pennsylvania

Battlefield Monuments Files
Gettysburg Newspaper Clippings Files
Regimental Files
Minute Book of the Gettysburg Battlefield Memorial Association,
   1872–1895

Gilder-Lehrman Collection, Pierpont Morgan Library,
New York

John B. Bachelder Papers
Hawthorne-Longfellow Library, Special Collections, Bowdoin College,
   Brunswick, Maine
Joshua L. Chamberlain Papers

Library of Congress, Washington, D.C.

Abraham Lincoln Papers
Diary of Marsena Rudolph Patrick
Zachariah Chandler Papers

Museum of the Confederacy, Eleanor S. Brockenbrough Library,
Richmond, Virginia

John S. Mosby Collection

National Archives and Records Administration,
Washington, D.C.

Clinton Presidential Materials Project
Records of the Adjutant General's Office, Records of the War Records
　　Office, Union Battle Reports." Record Group 94.

New Hampshire State Historical Society,
Concord, New Hampshire

John B. Bachelder Papers
New York State Archives, Albany, New York
Gouverneur K. Warren Papers

Pejepscot Historical Society, Brunswick, Maine

Joshua L. Chamberlain Papers

COURT CASES

"Appeal of the Gettysburg Battlefield Memorial Association (GBMA) from
　　the decree of the Court of Common Pleas of Adams County." Paper
　　Book of Appellants, Supreme Court of Pennsylvania, Middle District,
　　May term 1891, nos. 20, 30.

PAMPHLETS

Bachelder, John B. *Descriptive Key to the Painting of the Repulse of Longstreet's*
　　Assault at the Battle of Gettysburg. Boston: John B. Bachelder, 1870.
Meade, George, Jr. *Did General Meade Desire to Retreat at the Battle of Gettys-*
　　burg? Philadelphia: Porter & Oates, 1883.

BOOKS

Aldrich, Thomas M. *The History of Battery A, First Regiment Rhode Island Light*
　　Artillery, in the War to Preserve the Union, 1861–1865. Providence: Snow &
　　Farnham, 1904.
The American Civil War in 1863: Programs of the Eighth Gettysburg National Mili-
　　tary Park Seminar. Gettysburg: Gettysburg National Military Park, 2001.
Blight, David W. *Race and Reunion: The Civil War in American Memory.* Cam-
　　bridge: Harvard University Press, 2001.

Bloch, Marc. *Feudal Society: The Growth of Ties of Dependence*. Chicago: University of Chicago Press, 1988.

Brown, Willard. *Signal Corps, U.S.A. in the War of the Rebellion*. New York: Arno, 1974.

Busey, John W., and David G. Martin. *Regimental Strengths and Losses at Gettysburg*. Highstown, N.J.: Longstreet House, 1994.

Clark, Champ, et al. *Gettysburg: The Confederate High Tide*. Alexandria, Va.: Time-Life Books, 1985.

Cleaves, Freeman. *Meade of Gettysburg*. Norman: University of Oklahoma Press, 1960.

Commager, Henry Steele, ed. *The Blue and the Gray: The Story of the Civil War As Told by the Participants*. 2 vols. Indianapolis: Bobbs-Merrill, 1950.

Desjardin, Thomas A. *Stand Firm Ye Boys from Maine: The 20th Maine and the Gettysburg Campaign*. New York: Oxford University Press, 2000.

Doubleday, Abner. *Chancellorsville and Gettysburg*. New York: Scribner's, 1882.

Faulkner, William. *Intruder in the Dust*. New York: Random House, 1948.

Foster, Gaines. *Ghosts of the Confederacy*. New York: Oxford University Press, 1987.

Fox, William F. *Regimental Losses in the American Civil War, 1861–1865*. Albany: Albany Publishing, 1889.

Frassanito, William. *Early Photography at Gettysburg*. Gettysburg: Thomas, 1995.

Freeman, Douglas Southall. *Gettysburg: A Journey in Time*. New York: Scribner's, 1974.

————. *Lee's Lieutenants: A Study in Command*. 4 vols. New York: Scribner's, 1944.

Gallagher, Gary W. *Lee and His Army in Confederate History*. Chapel Hill: University of North Carolina Press, 2001.

Gerrish, Theodore. *Army Life: A Private's Reminiscences of the Civil War*. Portland, Me.: Hoyt, Fogg, and Donham, 1882.

Gracie, Archibald, *The Truth About Chickamauga*. Boston: Houghton Mifflin, 1911.

Graham, W. A. *The Custer Myth: A Source Book of Custeriana*. Harrisburg, Pa.: Stackpole, 1953.

Harman, Troy D. *Cemetery Hill: The General Plan Was Unchanged*. Baltimore: Butternut & Blue, 2001.

Haskell, Frank. *The Battle of Gettysburg.* Boston: Massachusetts Commandery, Military Order of the Loyal Legion of the United States, 1908.

Hess, Earl J. *Pickett's Charge: The Last Attack at Gettysburg.* Chapel Hill: University of North Carolina Press, 2001.

Holmes, Richard. *Acts of War: The Behavior of Men in Battle.* New York: Free Press, 1985.

Jones, J. Williams. *The Army of Northern Virginia Memorial Volume.* Richmond: Randolph & English, 1880.

Kammen, Michael. *Mystic Chords of Memory: The Transformation of Tradition in American Culture.* New York: Knopf, 1991.

Ladd, David, and Audrey Ladd, eds. *The Bachelder Papers.* 3 vols. Dayton, Ohio: Morningside, 1995.

Linderman, Gerald. *Embattled Courage: The Experience of Combat in the American Civil War.* New York: Free Press, 1987.

Longacre, Edward G. *Joshua L. Chamberlain: The Soldier and the Man.* Conshohocken, Pa.: Combined Books, 1999.

Meade, George, G., ed. *The Life and Letters of George G. Meade.* 2 vols. New York: Scribner's, 1913.

Mitchell, Adele H., ed. *The Letters of John S. Mosby.* Richmond, Va.: Stuart-Mosby Historical Society, 1986.

Nevins, Allan, ed. *A Diary of Battle: The Personal Journals of Colonel Charles S. Wainwright, 1861–1865.* New York: Harcourt, Brace & World, 1962.

————. *Diary of George Templeton Strong.* 4 vols. New York: Macmillan, 1952.

Norton, Oliver W. *The Attack and Defense of Little Round Top.* New York: Neale, 1913.

Oates, William C. *The War Between the Union and the Confederacy and Its Lost Opportunities.* New York: Neale, 1905.

Patrick, Marsena L., and David S. Sparks, eds. *Inside Lincoln's Army: The Diary of Marsena Rudolph Patrick.* New York: Yoseloff, 1964.

Pennsylvania State Monuments Commission. *Pennsylvania at Gettysburg: Ceremonies at the Dedication of the Monuments.* 3 vols. Harrisburg, Pa.: William Stanley Ray, 1914.

Perry, Mark. *Conceived in Liberty: William Oates and the American Civil War.* New York: Viking, 1997.

Philadelphia Brigade Association. *The Battle of Gettysburg: How General Meade Turned the Army of the Potomac Over to Lieutenant Haskell.* Philadelphia: Bowers, 1910.

Pollard, Edward A. *The Lost Cause: A New Southern History of the War*. New York: E. B. Treat, 1866.

————. *The Twentieth Maine: A Volunteer Regiment in the Civil War*. Philadelphia: Lippincott, 1957.

Pougher, Richard D. *The Confederate Enlisted Man in the Army of Northern Virginia: A Reevaluation of His Material Culture*. 2 vols. Williamsburg: William and Mary College, 1988.

Pullen, John J. *Joshua L. Chamberlain: A Hero's Life and Legacy*. Camp Hill, Pa.: Stackpole, 1999.

Reardon, Carol. *Pickett's Charge in History and Memory*. Chapel Hill: University of North Carolina Press, 1997.

Reese, George H., ed. *Proceedings of the Virginia Secession Convention of 1861*. 4 vols. Richmond: Virginia State Library, 1865.

Rusling, James F. *Men and Things I Saw in Civil War Days*. New York: Eaton & Mains, 1899.

Sauers, Richard D. *A Caspian Sea of Ink*. Baltimore: Butternut & Blue, 1989.

Scott, Robert N., ed. *The War of the Rebellion: A Compilation of the Official Records of the Union and Confederate Armies*. 128 vols. Washington, D.C.: Government Printing Office, 1880–1901.

Shaara, Michael. *The Killer Angels*. New York: McKay, 1974.

Simon John Y., and Michael E. Stevens, eds. *New Perspectives on the Civil War: Myths and Realities of the National Conflict*. Madison, Wis.: Madison House, 1998.

Smith, Diane Monroe. *Fanny and Joshua: The Enigmatic Lives of Frances Caroline Adams and Joshua Chamberlain*. Gettysburg: Thomas, 1999.

Swanberg, W. A. *Sickles the Incredible*. New York: Scribner's, 1956.

Trefousse, Hans Louis. *Benjamin Franklin Wade: Radical Republican from Ohio*. New York: Twayne, 1963.

Trulock, Alice. *In the Hands of Providence: Joshua L. Chamberlain and the American Civil War*. Chapel Hill: University of North Carolina Press, 1992.

United States Congress. Joint Committee on the Conduct of the War. *Report of the Joint Committee on the Conduct of the War, at the Second Session Thirty-eighth Congress*. 2 vols. Washington, D.C.: GPO, 1865.

Weiner, Jonathan. *Time, Love, Memory: A Great Biologist and His Quest for the Origins of Behavior*. New York: Knopf, 1999.

Welles, Gideon. *Diary of Gideon Welles*. 2 vols. New York: Houghton, Mifflin, 1911.

Wiley, Bell. *The Life of Johnny Reb: The Common Soldier of the Confederacy*. Baton Rouge: LSU Press, 1943.

Wiley, Bell I., ed. *One of Jackson's Foot Cavalry: His Experience and What He Saw During the War, 1861-1865*. Wilmington, N.C: Broadfoot, 1991.

Wills, Garry. *Lincoln at Gettysburg: Words That Remade America*. New York: Simon & Schuster, 1992.

Zornow, William Frank. *Lincoln and the Party Divided*. Norman: University of Oklahoma Press, 1954.

ARTICLES

Burns, Ken. "The Best Kind of History, the Best Kind of American." *Bowdoin*, Spring-Summer 1991, p. 1.

Chamberlain, Joshua L. "My Story of Fredericksburg." *Cosmopolitan*, January 1913.

_____. "Through Blood and Fire at Gettysburg." *Hearsts*, June 1913.

Coddington, Edwin. "The Strange Reputation of George G. Meade: A Lesson in Historiography." *Historian* 23 (1962): 147.

Longstreet, James. "Letter to Augustus Baldwin Longstreet." *Southern Historical Society Papers* 5 (1878): 54–55.

Oates, William C. "Gettysburg: The Battle on the Right." *Southern Historical Society Papers* 6 (1878): 172–182.

Sanders, Richard. "Enduring Tales of Gettysburg: The Death of Reynolds." *Gettysburg*, January 1996.

Sauers, Richard. "Gettysburg Controversies." *Gettysburg*, January 1991.

Trinque, Bruce A. "The Gap Made in That . . . Regiment Was Simply Terrible": Arnold's Battery and the 26th North Carolina." *Gettysburg,* January 1995.

INDEX

PHOTO CREDITS

John Bachelder and Wife   *Gettysburg National Military Park (Tipton Collection)*
Woodrow Wilson at Reunion, 1913   *Gettysburg National Military Park*
Three Eisenhower Photos   *Eisenhower National Historic Site*
Group at High Water Mark, 1902   *Author's Collection*
Daniel Sickles   *Gettysburg National Military Park*
Abner Doubleday   *Battles and Leaders*
Daniel Butterfield   *Battles and Leaders*
Albion Howe   *Battles and Leaders*
Ku Klux Klan on Battlefield, 1926   *Author's Collection*
Confederate Prisoners   *Library of Congress*
Sharpshooter in Devil's Den   *Library of Congress*
Sharpshooter near Devil's Den   *Library of Congress*
Winslow Homer   *Library of Congress*
Bayonet!   *Historical Art Prints*
1st Minnesota Original Design   *Gettysburg National Military Park*
1st Minnesota Monument   *Gettysburg National Military Park*
    (Tipton Collection)
4th Ohio Monument   *Gettysburg National Military Park (Tipton Collection)*
Excelsior Brigade Monument   *Gettysburg National Military Park*
    (Tipton Collection)
Franklin Roosevelt, 1938   *Gettysburg National Military Park*
Crowd at Peace Light Dedication, 1938   *Gettysburg National Military Park*

Grand Army of the Republic Monument   *Author's Collection*
New York Auxiliary Monument   *Author's Collection*
Monuments at the Bloody Angle   *Author's Collection*
Summit of Little Round Top   *Gettysburg National Military Park*
     (Tipton Collection)
Longstreet Monument   *Author's Collection*